Nuclear Materials and Disaster Research

Reactor Safety Recommendations

Insights from the Fukushima Dai-Ichi Accident

NUCLEAR MATERIALS AND DISASTER RESEARCH

Additional books in this series can be found on Nova's website under the Series tab.

Additional E-books in this series can be found on Nova's website under the E-book tab.

SAFETY AND RISK IN SOCIETY

Additional books in this series can be found on Nova's website under the Series tab.

Additional E-books in this series can be found on Nova's website under the E-book tab.

NUCLEAR MATERIALS AND DISASTER RESEARCH

REACTOR SAFETY RECOMMENDATIONS

INSIGHTS FROM THE FUKUSHIMA DAI-ICHI ACCIDENT

KENTON I. VINSON
AND
RUPERT E. GILLIAM
EDITORS

Nova Science Publishers, Inc.
New York

Copyright © 2012 by Nova Science Publishers, Inc.

All rights reserved. No part of this book may be reproduced, stored in a retrieval system or transmitted in any form or by any means: electronic, electrostatic, magnetic, tape, mechanical photocopying, recording or otherwise without the written permission of the Publisher.

For permission to use material from this book please contact us:
Telephone 631-231-7269; Fax 631-231-8175
Web Site: http://www.novapublishers.com

NOTICE TO THE READER

The Publisher has taken reasonable care in the preparation of this book, but makes no expressed or implied warranty of any kind and assumes no responsibility for any errors or omissions. No liability is assumed for incidental or consequential damages in connection with or arising out of information contained in this book. The Publisher shall not be liable for any special, consequential, or exemplary damages resulting, in whole or in part, from the readers' use of, or reliance upon, this material. Any parts of this book based on government reports are so indicated and copyright is claimed for those parts to the extent applicable to compilations of such works.

Independent verification should be sought for any data, advice or recommendations contained in this book. In addition, no responsibility is assumed by the publisher for any injury and/or damage to persons or property arising from any methods, products, instructions, ideas or otherwise contained in this publication.

This publication is designed to provide accurate and authoritative information with regard to the subject matter covered herein. It is sold with the clear understanding that the Publisher is not engaged in rendering legal or any other professional services. If legal or any other expert assistance is required, the services of a competent person should be sought. FROM A DECLARATION OF PARTICIPANTS JOINTLY ADOPTED BY A COMMITTEE OF THE AMERICAN BAR ASSOCIATION AND A COMMITTEE OF PUBLISHERS.

Additional color graphics may be available in the e-book version of this book.

Library of Congress Cataloging-in-Publication Data

ISBN 978-1-61942-645-0

Published by Nova Science Publishers, Inc. † New York

CONTENTS

Preface		**vii**
Chapter 1	Recommendations for Enhancing Reactor Safety in the 21st Century: The Near-Term Task Force Review of Insights from the Fukushima Dai-Ichi Accident *U.S. Nuclear Regulatory Commission*	1
Chapter 2	Statement of Gregory B. Jaczko, Chairman, United States Nuclear Regulatory Commission. Hearing on "Review of the NRC's Near-Term Task Force Recommendations for Enhancing Reactor Safety in the 21st Century	81
Chapter 3	Recommended Actions to be Taken without Delay from the Near-Term Task Force Report *R. W. Borchardt*	
Chapter 4	Prioritization of Recommended Actions to be Taken in Response to Fukushima Lessons Learned *R. W. Borchardt*	105
Index		**153**

PREFACE

This book examines the Near-Term Task Force, which was established in response to Commission direction to conduct a systematic and methodical review of the U.S. Nuclear Regulatory Commission processes and regulations to determine whether the agency should make additional improvements to its regulatory system and to make recommendations to the Commission for its policy direction, in light of the accident at the Fukushima Dai-Ichi Nuclear Power Plant. The Task Force recognizes that there likely will be more than 100 nuclear power plants operating throughout the United States for decades to come. In examining the Fukushima Dai-Ichi accident for insights for reactors in the United States, the Task Force addressed protecting against accidents resulting from natural phenomena, mitigating the consequences of such accidents, and ensuring emergency preparedness.

Chapter 1 - The Near-Term Task Force was established in response to Commission direction to conduct a systematic and methodical review of U.S. Nuclear Regulatory Commission processes and regulations to determine whether the agency should make additional improvements to its regulatory system and to make recommendations to the Commission for its policy direction, in light of the accident at the Fukushima Dai-ichi Nuclear Power Plant. The Task Force appreciates that an accident involving core damage and uncontrolled release of radioactive material to the environment, even one without significant health consequences, is inherently unacceptable. The Task Force also recognizes that there likely will be more than 100 nuclear power plants operating throughout the United States for decades to come. The Task Force developed its recommendations in full recognition of this environment. In examining the Fukushima Dai-ichi accident for insights for reactors in the United States, the Task Force addressed protecting against accidents resulting from natural phenomena, mitigating the consequences of such accidents, and ensuring emergency preparedness. The accident in Japan was caused by a natural event (i.e., tsunami) which was far more severe than the design basis for the Fukushima Dai-ichi Nuclear Power Plant. As part of its undertaking, the Task Force studied the manner in which the NRC has historically required protection from natural phenomena and how the NRC has addressed events that exceed the current design basis for plants in the United States.

Chapter 2 – The author first wants to thank, on behalf of the Commission, Dr. Charles Miller and the other members of the Task Force for all of their work in conducting the 90-day review. Also wants to acknowledge the numerous other NRC staff who were available to the Task Force as a resource in conducting its review, as well as the Federal Emergency Management Agency, which engaged the Task Force in discussions of offsite emergency preparedness and provided insights on the U.S. National Response Framework, the Institute of Nuclear Power Operations – which shared information on the industry's post-Fukushima actions, and other groups and individuals who shared their views with the Task Force. In his testimony, the author would like to provide with a summary of the Task Force findings and recommendations.

Chapter 3 - The purpose of this paper is to provide, for Commission consideration, the recommendations of the U. S. Nuclear Regulatory Commission (NRC) staff, regarding those Near-Term Task Force (NTTF) recommendations that can and, in the staff's judgment, should be initiated, in part or in whole, without delay. In the Commission notation vote paper due on October 3, 2011, the staff plans to provide the prioritization of the NTTF recommendations to (1) reflect regulatory actions to be taken by the staff in response to the Fukushima lessons learned; (2) identify implementation challenges; (3) include technical and regulatory bases for the prioritization; (4) identify additional recommendations, if any; and (5) include a schedule and milestones with recommendations for appropriate stakeholder engagement and involvement of the Advisory Committee for Reactor Safeguards (ACRS).

Chapter 4 - The purpose of this paper is to provide, for Commission consideration, the staff's proposed prioritization of the Fukushima Near-Term Task Force (NTTF) recommendations to (1) reflect regulatory actions to be taken by the staff in response to the Fukushima lessons learned; (2) identify implementation challenges; (3) include the technical and regulatory bases for the prioritization; (4) identify additional recommendations, if any; and (5) include a schedule and milestones with recommendations for appropriate stakeholder engagement and involvement of the Advisory Committee on Reactor Safeguards (ACRS). The enclosure provides detailed information to address these points.

In: Reactor Safety Recommendations
Editors: Kenton I. Vinson and Rupert E. Gilliam
ISBN: 978-1-61942-645-0
© 2012 Nova Science Publishers, Inc.

Chapter 1

RECOMMENDATIONS FOR ENHANCING REACTOR SAFETY IN THE 21ST CENTURY: THE NEAR-TERM TASK FORCE REVIEW OF INSIGHTS FROM THE FUKUSHIMA DAI-ICHI ACCIDENT[*]

U.S. Nuclear Regulatory Commission

July 12, 2011.

DEDICATION

This report is dedicated to the people of Japan and especially to those who have responded heroically to the nuclear accident at Fukushima. It is the fervent hope of the Near-Term Task Force that their hardships and losses may never be repeated.

Throughout its tenure, the Near-Term Task Force has been inspired by the strength and resilience of the Japanese people in the face of the inconceivable losses of family and property inflicted by the Great East Japan Earthquake and tsunami of 2011 and exacerbated by the ongoing radioactive releases from the Fukushima Dai-ichi Nuclear Power Plant. The heroes of Fukushima shouldered the emotional impacts of the devastation around them and labored on in the dark, through the rubble, with increasing levels of radiation and contamination. They undertook great efforts to obtain power and cooling to prevent the unthinkable from occurring. The outcome—no fatalities and the expectation of no significant radiological health effects—is a tribute to their efforts, their valor, and their resolve. It is our strong desire and our goal to take the necessary steps to assure that the result of our labors will help prevent the need for a repetition of theirs.

---

[*] This is an edited, reformatted and augmented version of the United States Nuclear Commission puiblication, dated July 12, 2011.

EXECUTIVE SUMMARY

The Near-Term Task Force was established in response to Commission direction to conduct a systematic and methodical review of U.S. Nuclear Regulatory Commission processes and regulations to determine whether the agency should make additional improvements to its regulatory system and to make recommendations to the Commission for its policy direction, in light of the accident at the Fukushima Dai-ichi Nuclear Power Plant. The Task Force appreciates that an accident involving core damage and uncontrolled release of radioactive material to the environment, even one without significant health consequences, is inherently unacceptable. The Task Force also recognizes that there likely will be more than 100 nuclear power plants operating throughout the United States for decades to come. The Task Force developed its recommendations in full recognition of this environment.

In examining the Fukushima Dai-ichi accident for insights for reactors in the United States, the Task Force addressed protecting against accidents resulting from natural phenomena, mitigating the consequences of such accidents, and ensuring emergency preparedness.

The accident in Japan was caused by a natural event (i.e., tsunami) which was far more severe than the design basis for the Fukushima Dai-ichi Nuclear Power Plant. As part of its undertaking, the Task Force studied the manner in which the NRC has historically required protection from natural phenomena and how the NRC has addressed events that exceed the current design basis for plants in the United States.

In general, the Task Force found that the current NRC regulatory approach includes:

- requirements for design-basis events with protection and mitigation features controlled through specific regulations or the general design criteria (Title 10 of the *Code of Federal Regulations* (10 CFR) Part 50, "Domestic Licensing of Production and Utilization Facilities," Appendix A, "General Design Criteria for Nuclear Power Plants")
- requirements for some "beyond-design-basis" events through specific regulations (e.g., station blackout, large fires, and explosions)
- voluntary industry initiatives to address severe accident features, strategies, and guidelines for operating reactors

This regulatory approach, established and supplemented piece-by-piece over the decades, has addressed many safety concerns and issues, using the best information and techniques available at the time. The result is a patchwork of regulatory requirements and other safety initiatives, all important, but not all given equivalent consideration and treatment by licensees or during NRC technical review and inspection. Consistent with the NRC's organizational value of excellence, the Task Force believes that improving the NRC's regulatory framework is an appropriate, realistic, and achievable goal.

The current regulatory approach, and more importantly, the resultant plant capabilities allow the Task Force to conclude that a sequence of events like the Fukushima accident is unlikely to occur in the United States and some appropriate mitigation measures have been implemented, reducing the likelihood of core damage and radiological releases. Therefore, continued operation and continued licensing activities do not pose an imminent risk to public health and safety.

However, the Task Force also concludes that a more balanced application of the Commission's defense-in-depth philosophy using risk insights would provide an enhanced regulatory framework that is logical, systematic, coherent, and better understood. Such a framework would support appropriate requirements for increased capability to address events of low likelihood and high consequence, thus significantly enhancing safety.

Excellence in regulation demands that the Task Force provide the Commission with its best insights and vision for an improved regulatory framework.

The Task Force finds that the Commission's longstanding defense-in-depth philosophy, supported and modified as necessary by state-of-the-art probabilistic risk assessment techniques, should continue to serve as the primary organizing principle of its regulatory framework. The Task Force concludes that the application of the defense-in-depth philosophy can be strengthened by including explicit requirements for beyond-designbasis events.

Many of the elements of such a regulatory framework already exist in the form of rules regarding station blackout, anticipated transient without scram, maintenance, combustible gas control, aircraft impact assessment, beyond-design-basis fires and explosions, and alternative treatment. Other elements, such as severe accident management guidelines, exist in voluntary industry initiatives. The Task Force has concluded that a collection of such "extended design-basis" requirements, with an appropriate set of quality or special treatment standards, should be established.

The Task Force further sees this approach, if implemented, as a more comprehensive and systematic application of defense-in-depth to NRC requirements for providing "adequate protection" of public health and safety. Implementation of this concept would require strong Commission support for a clear policy statement, rule changes, and revised staff guidance.

The Task Force notes that, after the attacks of September 11, 2001, the Commission established new security requirements on the basis of adequate protection. These new requirements did not result from any immediate or imminent threat to NRC-licensed facilities, but rather from new insights regarding potential security events. The Task Force concluded that the Fukushima Dai-ichi accident similarly provides new insights regarding low-likelihood, high-consequence events that warrant enhancements to defense-in-depth on the basis of redefining the level of protection that is regarded as adequate. The Task Force recommendation for an enhanced regulatory framework is intended to establish a coherent and transparent basis for treatment of the Fukushima insights. It is also intended to provide lasting direction to the staff regarding a consistent decisionmaking framework for future issues.

The Task Force has considered industry initiatives in this framework and sees that these could play a useful and valuable role. The Task Force believes that voluntary industry initiatives should not serve as a substitute for regulatory requirements but as a mechanism for facilitating and standardizing implementation of such requirements.

The Task Force applied this conceptual framework during its deliberations. The result is a set of recommendations that take a balanced approach to defense-in-depth as applied to low-likelihood, high-consequence events such as prolonged station blackout resulting from severe natural phenomena. These recommendations, taken together, are intended to clarify and strengthen the regulatory framework for protection against natural disasters, mitigation, and emergency preparedness, and to improve the effectiveness of the NRC's programs. The Task Force's overarching recommendations are:

Clarifying the Regulatory Framework
1) The Task Force recommends establishing a logical, systematic, and coherent regulatory framework for adequate protection that appropriately balances defense-in-depth and risk considerations. (Section 3)

Ensuring Protection
2) The Task Force recommends that the NRC require licensees to reevaluate and upgrade as necessary the design-basis seismic and flooding protection of structures, systems, and components for each operating reactor. (Section 4.1.1)
3) The Task Force recommends, as part of the longer term review, that the NRC evaluate potential enhancements to the capability to prevent or mitigate seismically induced fires and floods. (Section 4.1.2)

Enhancing Mitigation
4) The Task Force recommends that the NRC strengthen station blackout mitigation capability at all operating and new reactors for design-basis and beyond-design-basis external events. (Section 4.2.1)
5) The Task Force recommends requiring reliable hardened vent designs in boiling water reactor facilities with Mark I and Mark II containments. (Section 4.2.2)
6) The Task Force recommends, as part of the longer term review, that the NRC identify insights about hydrogen control and mitigation inside containment or in other buildings as additional information is revealed through further study of the Fukushima Dai-ichi accident. (Section 4.2.3)
7) The Task Force recommends enhancing spent fuel pool makeup capability and instrumentation for the spent fuel pool. (Section 4.2.4)
8) The Task Force recommends strengthening and integrating onsite emergency response capabilities such as emergency operating procedures, severe accident management guidelines, and extensive damage mitigation guidelines. (Section 4.2.5)

Strengthening Emergency Preparedness
9) The Task Force recommends that the NRC require that facility emergency plans address prolonged station blackout and multiunit events. (Section 4.3.1)
10) The Task Force recommends, as part of the longer term review, that the NRC pursue additional emergency preparedness topics related to multiunit events and prolonged station blackout. (Section 4.3.1)
11) The Task Force recommends, as part of the longer term review, that the NRC should pursue emergency preparedness topics related to decisionmaking, radiation monitoring, and public education. (Section 4.3.2)

Improving the Efficiency of NRC Programs
12) The Task Force recommends that the NRC strengthen regulatory oversight of licensee safety performance (i.e., the Reactor Oversight Process) by focusing more

attention on defense-in-depth requirements consistent with the recommended defense-in-depth framework. (Section 5.1)

The Task Force presents further details on its recommendations in this report and an implementation strategy in Appendix A. The strategy includes several rulemaking activities to establish new requirements. Recognizing that rulemaking and subsequent implementation typically take several years to accomplish, the Task Force recommends interim actions to enhance protection, mitigation, and preparedness while the rulemaking activities are conducted.

These recommendations are based on the best available information regarding the Fukushima Dai-ichi accident and a review of relevant NRC requirements and programs. The Task Force concludes that these are a reasonable set of actions to enhance U.S. reactor safety in the 21st century.

1. INTRODUCTION

In the days following the Fukushima Dai-ichi nuclear accident in Japan, the U.S. Nuclear Regulatory Commission (NRC) directed the staff to establish a senior-level agency task force (the Task Force) to conduct a methodical and systematic review of the NRC's processes and regulations to determine whether the agency should make additional improvements to its regulatory system and to make recommendations to the Commission for its policy direction. The Commission direction was provided in a tasking memorandum dated March 23, 2011, from Chairman Gregory B. Jaczko to the Executive Director for Operations. The tasking included objectives for a near-term and a longer term review. Appendix B provides a copy of the tasking memorandum.

In response to the Commission's direction, the Executive Director for Operations established an agency Task Force to conduct a near-term evaluation of the need for agency actions. The Task Force's charter, dated March 30, 2011, called for a methodical and systematic review of relevant NRC regulatory requirements, programs, and processes, and their implementation, and to recommend whether the agency should make near-term improvements to its regulatory system. The charter also directed the Task Force to identify topics for review and assessment for the longer term effort. Appendix C presents a copy of the Task Force charter.

The Task Force structured its review activities to reflect insights from past lessons-learned efforts. For example, after the 1979 accident at Three Mile Island (TMI), the NRC had not yet developed much of the decisionmaking framework that is in place today. In addition, the post-TMI review considered a number of actions that were proposed for general safety enhancement rather than being directed at specific safety weaknesses revealed by the TMI accident. As a result, some of the actions taken by the NRC after TMI were not subjected to a structured review and were subsequently not found to be of substantial safety benefit and were removed.

In establishing a systematic and methodical process for its review, the Task Force determined that it would focus its efforts on areas that had a nexus to the Fukushima Daiichi accident regarding the initiating event, the response of equipment and personnel, and the progression of the accident as the Task Force understands it from available information. The Task Force recognized that detailed information in each of these areas was, in many cases, unavailable, unreliable, or ambiguous because of damage to equipment at the site and because the Japanese response continues to focus on actions to stop the ongoing radioactive release and to achieve long-term core and spent fuel pool cooling. Even without a detailed understanding of all aspects of the Fukushima accident, the Task Force identified those key areas most relevant to the safety of U.S. reactors, such as external events that could damage large areas of the plant, protection against and mitigation of a prolonged station blackout, and management of severe accidents. Section 2 of this report presents the sequence of events at Fukushima, as relevant to the Task Force's deliberations. The Task Force did not address insights from the NRC's incident response activities related to the Fukushima accident as these are being addressed by the NRC's Office of Nuclear Security and Incident Response.

Consistent with its tasking and charter, the Task Force remained independent of industry efforts, while obtaining a broad range of inputs. The Task Force had full access to the NRC staff to obtain information on existing programs, received briefings from staff experts in the Headquarters offices, and solicited inputs from all four NRC regional offices. The Task Force also obtained valuable insights from the members of the NRC site team in Japan.

The Task Force requested information on the status of licensees' implementation of severe accident management guidelines (SAMGs); the regional offices collected this information through Temporary Instruction (TI) 2515/184, "Availability and Readiness Inspection of Severe Accident Management Guidelines (SAMGs)," dated April 29, 2011, and the Office of Nuclear Reactor Regulation compiled the information for the Task Force. During the implementation of this TI, members of the Task Force accompanied the inspectors at two nuclear power plant sites to gain an independent perspective and additional insights into licensee decisionmaking during severe accidents.

While maintaining its independence of industry efforts, members of the Task Force met with representatives of the Institute of Nuclear Power Operations to gather information on the industry's post-Fukushima actions. The Task Force also met with representatives of the Federal Emergency Management Agency (FEMA) to discuss offsite emergency preparedness and to obtain insights on the U.S. National Response Framework. Finally, the Task Force appropriately screened and considered information and suggestions received from internal and external stakeholders.

The Task Force monitored, directly or indirectly, related international activities of the International Atomic Energy Agency (IAEA), Nuclear Energy Agency (NEA), and other organizations.

In developing recommendations, the Task Force considered the existing approach for regulatory decisionmaking. This approach includes the existing technical requirements related to the licensing, operation, and maintenance of commercial nuclear power plants. It is informed by the Commission's Policy Statement on Safety Goals for the Operations of Nuclear Power Plants, which appeared in the *Federal Register* in August 1986 (51 FR 30028).

The approach includes the agency's historical commitment to a defense-in-depth philosophy that ensures that the design basis includes multiple layers of defense. In developing its recommendations, the Task Force was also guided by the NRC's Principles of Good Regulation, particularly as related to ensuring a clear nexus between the Commission's requirements and its goals and objectives.

In addition, the Task Force was appropriately informed by the "Regulatory Analysis Guidelines of the U.S. Nuclear Regulatory Commission" (NUREG/BR-0058, Revision 4, issued September 2004), which provide a framework for evaluating potential new requirements. The Policy Statement on Safety Goals sets forth two qualitative safety goals, which are supported by two quantitative supporting objectives. The following are the qualitative safety goals:

- Individual members of the public should be provided a level of protection from the consequences of nuclear power plant operation such that individuals bear no significant additional risk to life and health.
- Societal risks to life and health from nuclear power plant operation should be comparable to or less than the risks of generating electricity by viable competing technologies and should not be a significant addition to other societal risks.

The quantitative supporting objectives are as follows:

- The risk to an average individual in the vicinity of a nuclear power plant of prompt fatalities that might result from reactor accidents should not exceed one-tenth of one percent (0.1 percent) of the sum of prompt fatality risks resulting from other accidents to which members of the U.S. population are generally exposed.
- The risk to the population in the area near a nuclear power plant of cancer fatalities that might result from nuclear power plant operation should not exceed one-tenth of one percent (0.1 percent) of the sum of cancer fatality risks resulting from all other causes.

In the Policy Statement on Safety Goals, the Commission emphasized the importance of features such as containment, siting, and emergency planning as "integral parts of the defense-in-depth concept associated with its accident prevention and mitigation philosophy." A cursory review of documents discussing the agency's approach to defense-in-depth provides a range of explanations and applications.

The Commission's policy on probabilistic risk assessment (PRA) ("Use of Probabilistic Risk Assessment Methods in Nuclear Regulatory Activities," dated August 16, 1995), states the following:

- Defense-in-depth is a philosophy used by the NRC to provide redundancy for facilities with "active" safety systems, e.g. a commercial nuclear power [plant], as well as the philosophy of a multiple-barrier approach against fission product releases.

An instructive discussion of the defense-in-depth philosophy also appears in director's decisions relating to a petition on Davis-Besse (FirstEnergy Nuclear Operating Company (Davis-Besse Nuclear Power Station, Unit 1), DD-03-3, 58 NRC 151, 163 (2003)).

The decision described defense-in-depth as encompassing the following requirements:

1) require the application of conservative codes and standards to establish substantial safety margins in the design of nuclear plants;
2) require high quality in the design, construction, and operation of nuclear plants to reduce the likelihood of malfunctions, and promote the use of automatic safety system actuation features;
3) recognize that equipment can fail and operators can make mistakes and, therefore, require redundancy in safety systems and components to reduce the chance that malfunctions or mistakes will lead to accidents that release fission products from the fuel;
4) recognize that, in spite of these precautions, serious fuel-damage accidents may not be completely prevented and, therefore, require containment structures and safety features to prevent the release of fission products; and
5) further require that comprehensive emergency plans be prepared and periodically exercised to ensure that actions can and will be taken to notify and protect citizens in the vicinity of a nuclear facility.

The Task Force has found that the defense-in-depth philosophy is a useful and broadly applied concept. It is not, however, susceptible to a rigid definition because it is a philosophy. For the purposes of its review, the Task Force focused on the following application of the defense-in-depth concept:

- protection from external events that could lead to fuel damage
- mitigation of the consequences of such accidents should they occur, with a focus on preventing core and spent fuel damage and uncontrolled releases of radioactive material to the environment
- emergency preparedness (EP) to mitigate the effects of radiological releases to the public and the environment, should they occur

These levels of defense-in-depth are appropriate for significant external challenges to a facility. In applying these defense-in-depth features, the Task Force sought to ensure that the Commission's regulatory requirements, processes, and programs effectively address each layer of protection while maintaining appropriate balance among them. The Task Force notes that this approach is also consistent with Levels of Defense 3, 4, and 5 in IAEA Draft Safety Standard DS 414, "Safety of Nuclear Power Plants: Design," dated January 2010.

The framework of the Regulatory Analysis Guidelines (NUREG/BR-0058) informed the Task Force as it developed recommendations and evaluated potential new requirements. These guidelines provide a range of potential actions depending on the nature of the underlyingsafety issue and the means of addressing it. These potential actions include the following:

- actions necessary to bring a facility into compliance with existing requirements (Title 10 of the *Code of Federal Regulations* (10 CFR) 50.109(a)(4)(i))
- actions necessary to ensure adequate protection (10 CFR 50.109(a)(4)(ii))

- actions defining or redefining what level of protection of the public health and safety or common defense and security should be regarded as adequate (10 CFR 50.109(a)(4)(iii))
- actions that provide substantial additional protection and for which the direct and indirect costs are justified by the increased protection afforded (10 CFR 50.109(a)(3))

In developing its recommendations, the Task Force considered all of the above-mentioned guidance (defense-in-depth, the Policy Statement on Safety Goals, Regulatory Analysis Guidelines, and the backfit rule as codified in 10 CFR 50.109, "Backfitting"). In the Task Force's deliberations, it became apparent that the existing guidance does not present a completely clear and consistent framework for decisionmaking. The Policy Statement on Safety Goals and Regulatory Analysis Guidelines address only limited aspects of defense-in-depth. The safety goals policy addresses defense-in-depth by setting a "subsidiary numerical objective" (a third-level goal) for core damage frequency, in addition to the higher level health effects goals. In the Regulatory Analysis Guidelines, which provide guidance on implementation of the backfit rule, the phrase "defense-in-depth" occurs only twice in 46 pages of guidance; those references are limited to dealing with core damage frequency and containment performance in the screening criteria. The defense-in-depth concept is notably absent from the Regulatory Analysis Guidelines as part of the decision rationale.

Extensive efforts have been made in the past to address safety goals and their relationship to defense-in-depth. The most extensive attempt occurred as part of the technology-neutral framework effort described in NUREG-1860, "Feasibility Study for a Risk-Informed and Performance-Based Regulatory Structure for Future Plant Licensing," issued December 2007. The technology-neutral framework effort attempted to reconcile these issues in a single process in which defense-in-depth plays a fundamental role in addressing and compensating for uncertainties.

Ultimately, the Task Force chose a decision rationale built around the defense-in-depth concept in which each level of defense-in-depth (namely protection, mitigation, and EP) is critically evaluated for its completeness and effectiveness in performing its safety function. The Task Force has therefore developed a comprehensive set of recommendations to increase safety and redefine what level of protection of the public health is regarded as adequate. The Task Force's logic is that (1) these recommendations are intended to make each level of defense-in-depth complete and effective and (2) ensuring the completeness and effectiveness of each level of defense-in-depth is an essential element in the overall approach to ensuring safety, called "adequate protection." With this in mind, the Task Force has recommended what it concludes are significant reinforcements to NRC requirements and programs.

Finally, the Task Force considered its recommendations and the Commission's requirements for nuclear power plants in the context of the NRC's Principles of Good Regulation. In particular, the principle of "clarity" states: "Regulations should be coherent, logical, and practical. There should be a clear nexus between regulations and agency goals and objectives, whether explicitly or implicitly stated. Agency positions should be readily understood and easily applied." Also, the principle of "efficiency" states, in part, that "Regulatory activities should be consistent with the degree of risk reduction they achieve."

The principles of "independence" and "openness" focus on the importance of obtaining inputs from the full range of stakeholders, including consideration of many and possibly conflicting public interests, and open channels of communication. The duration and scope of the Task Force's effort have necessarily limited the degree of stakeholder interaction that was possible. The implementation of Task Force recommendations will require additional effort by the NRC staff to conduct stakeholder outreach through its normal processes (e.g., rulemaking, licensing, public meetings, and workshops).

2. SUMMARY OF EVENTS AT FUKUSHIMA DAI-ICHI

At 14:46 Japan standard time on March 11, 2011, the Great East Japan Earthquake—rated a magnitude 9.0—occurred at a depth of approximately 25 kilometers (15 miles), 130 kilometers (81 miles) east of Sendai and 372 kilometers (231 miles) northeast of Tokyo off the coast of Honshu Island. This earthquake resulted in the automatic shutdown of 11 nuclear power plants at four sites along the northeast coast of Japan (Onagawa 1, 2, and 3; Fukushima Dai-ichi 1, 2, and 3; Fukushima Dai-ni 1, 2, 3, and 4; and Tokai 2). The earthquake precipitated a large tsunami that is estimated to have exceeded 14 meters (45 feet) in height at the Fukushima Dai-ichi Nuclear Power Plant site. The earthquake and tsunami produced widespread devastation across northeastern Japan, resulting in approximately 25,000 people dead or missing, displacing many tens of thousands of people, and significantly impacting the infrastructure and industry in the northeastern coastal areas of Japan.

Fukushima Dai-ichi Units 1 through 4 are located in the southern part of the station and are oriented such that Unit 1 is the northernmost and Unit 4 is the southernmost. Fukushima Dai-ichi Units 5 and 6 are located farther north and at a somewhat higher elevation than the Unit 1–4 cluster, and Unit 6 is located to the north of Unit 5.

Source: GRS, 2011.

Figure 1. Nuclear Power Plants in Japan.

Reactors at the Fukushima Dai-Ichi Nuclear Power Plant

Unit	Net MWe*	Reactor, Containment, and Cooling Systems**
1	460	BWR-3, Mark I, IC, HPCI
2	784	BWR-4, Mark I, RCIC, HPCI
3	784	BWR-4, Mark I, RCIC, HPCI
4	784	BWR-4, Mark I, RCIC, HPCI
5	784	BWR-4, Mark I, RCIC, HPCI
6	1,100	BWR-5, Mark II, RCIC, HPCS

* MWe—megawatts electric
** IC—isolation condenser, HPCI—high-pressure coolant injection system, RCIC—reactor core isolation cooling system, HPCS—high-pressure core spray system

Figure 2. Fukushima Dai-ichi Nuclear Power Plant (status before earthquake).

On March 11, 2011, Units 1, 2, and 3 were in operation, and Units 4, 5, and 6, were shut down for routine refueling and maintenance activities; the Unit 4 reactor fuel was offloaded to the Unit 4 spent fuel pool.

As a result of the earthquake, all of the operating units appeared to experience a normal reactor trip within the capability of the safety design of the plants. The three operating units at Fukushima Dai-ichi automatically shut down, apparently inserting all control rods into the reactor. As a result of the earthquake, offsite power was lost to the entire facility. The emergency diesel generators started at all six units providing alternating current (ac) electrical power to critical systems at each unit, and the facility response to the seismic event appears to have been normal.

Approximately 40 minutes following the earthquake and shutdown of the operating units, the first large tsunami wave inundated the site followed by multiple additional waves. The estimated height of the tsunami exceeded the site design protection from tsunamis by approximately 8 meters (27 feet). The tsunami resulted in extensive damage to site facilities and a complete loss of ac electrical power at Units 1 through 5, a condition known as station blackout (SBO). Unit 6 retained the function of one of the diesel generators.

The operators were faced with a catastrophic, unprecedented emergency situation. They had to work in nearly total darkness with very limited instrumentation and control systems. The operators were able to successfully cross-tie the single operating Unit 6 air-cooled diesel generator to provide sufficient ac electrical power for Units 5 and 6 to place and maintain those units in a safe shutdown condition, eventually achieving and maintaining cold shutdown. Despite the actions of the operators following the earthquake and tsunami, cooling was lost to the fuel in the Unit 1 reactor after several hours, the Unit 2 reactor after about 71 hours, and the Unit 3 reactor after about 36 hours, resulting in damage to the nuclear fuel shortly after the loss of cooling. Without ac power, the plants were likely relying on batteries and turbine-driven and diesel-driven pumps. The operators were likely implementing their severe accident management program to maintain core cooling functions well beyond the normal capacity of the station batteries. Without the response of offsite assistance, which appears to have been hampered by the devastation in the area, among other factors, each unit eventually lost the capability to further extend cooling of the reactor cores.

The current condition of the Unit 1, 2, and 3 reactors is relatively static, but those units have yet to achieve a stable, cold shutdown condition. Units 1, 2, 3, and 4 also experienced explosions further damaging the facilities and primary and secondary containment structures. The Unit 1, 2, and 3 explosions were caused by the buildup of hydrogen gas within primary containment produced during fuel damage in the reactor and subsequent movement of that hydrogen gas from the drywell into the secondary containment. The source of the explosive gases causing the Unit 4 explosion remains unclear. In addition, the operators were unable to monitor the condition of and restore normal cooling flow to the Unit 1, 2, 3, and 4 spent fuel pools.

Below is a sequence of events early in the accident for the six Fukushima Dai-ichi reactors. Only information from the Japanese utility and official Japanese Government sources, including the "Report of the Japanese Government to the IAEA Ministerial Conference on Nuclear Safety," is included.

Unit 1 Sequence of Events	
March 11	
14:47	Earthquake, loss of offsite ac power, and plant trip
14:52	Isolation condenser operated to cool reactor
15:03	Isolation condenser stopped operating
15:37	Tsunami and total loss of ac power—SBO
15:37	Loss of ability to inject water to the reactor
~17:00	Water level below top of fuel
--:--	Partial core damage (several hours after tsunami)
March 12	
14:30	Vent primary containment
15:36	Explosion results in severe damage to the reactor building (secondarycontainment)

Figure 3. Damage to Unit 1.

More detail is expected to emerge as recovery from the accident continues and access to various locations, facilities, data, and staff improves. This sequence of events provides only the level of detail necessary for the near-term assessment of insights and the recommendation of actions for consideration at U.S. nuclear facilities. When available, times indicated are in Japan standard time.

Unit 2 Sequence of Events	
March 11	
14:47	Earthquake, loss of offsite ac power, and plant trip
~14:50	RCIC manually operated to inject water to reactor
15:41	Tsunami and total loss of ac power at site—SBO
March 13	
--:--	RCIC continued to be used to cool reactor
~11:00	Vent primary containment
March 14	
13:25	RCIC stopped operating
~18:00	Water level below top of fuel
--:--	Partial core damage (approximately 3 days after tsunami)
--:--	Blowout panel open on side of reactor building
March 15	
~06:00	Explosion; suppression chamber pressure decreased indicating the possibility that primary containment was damaged

Figure 4. Damage to Unit 2.

Unit 3 Sequence of Events	
March 11	
14:47	Earthquake, loss of offsite ac power, and plant trip
15:05	RCIC manually started to inject water into reactor
15:41	Tsunami and total loss of ac power at site—SBO
March 12	
11:36	RCIC stopped operating
12:35	HPCI automatically started injecting water into reactor
March 13	
02:42	HPCI stopped operating
~08:00	Water level below top of fuel
--:--	Partial core damage (approximately 2 days after tsunami)
March 14	
05:20	Vent primary containment
11:01	Explosion results in severe damage to the reactor building (secondarycontainment)

Figure 5. Damage to Unit 3.

Unit 4 Sequence of Events (Unit 4 reactor was defueled)	
March 11	
14:46	Earthquake and loss of offsite ac power
15:38	Tsunami and total loss of ac power at site—SBO
March 15	
~06:00	Explosion in reactor building

Figure 6. Damage to Unit 4.

Unit 5 and 6 Sequence of Events (Both units were shut down for periodic inspection)	
March 11	
14:46	Earthquake and loss of offsite ac power
15:41	Tsunami and total loss of ac power at site—SBO
March 20	
14:30	Unit 5 enters cold shutdown
19:27	Unit 6 enters cold shutdown
Protective Action Recommendations at Fukushima Dai-ichi	
March 11	Evacuation of residents within 3 kilometers (1.9 miles) and shelter-in-place for residents within 10kilometers (6.2 miles)
March 12	Evacuation of residents within 20kilometers (12.4 miles)
March 15	Evacuation of residents within 30 kilometers (18.6 miles)
April 11	"Planned Evacuation Areas" and "Evacuation Prepared Area" established in the areas beyond 20 kilometers (12.4 miles)
April 21	Restricted area within 20 kilometers (12.4 miles) established to allow temporary accessand exclusion area of 3 kilometers (1.9 miles) established for members of the public

As directed in the Chairman's tasking memorandum, the Task Force emphasizes the need for the staff to maintain awareness and develop further insights during the long-term followup of the Fukushima event. Additional information is expected to evolve and become better understood regarding (1) the condition of structures, systems, and components (SSCs) in Units 1 through 6, including the effects of the seismic and flooding events and the explosions, (2) the timing and success of the actions taken by facility staff, including the adequacy of procedures and SAMGs, and (3) the progression of the accidents in the Unit 1, 2, and 3 reactors and the Unit 1, 2, 3, and 4 spent fuel pools.

Figure 7. Fukushima Dai-ichi Units 1–4 following explosions.

3. REGULATORY FRAMEWORK FOR THE 21ST CENTURY

Background

The combination of the massive earthquake and devastating tsunami at Fukushima were well in excess of external events considered in the plant design. The Fukushima accident also challenged the plant's mitigation capabilities and EP.

With that in mind, this section addresses the elements of the NRC regulatory framework that play a part in providing protection from design-basis events, as well as events as severe and complex as the Fukushima accident. Those elements include protection against seismic and flooding events (characterized as design-basis events), protection for loss of all ac power (characterized as a beyond-design-basis event), and mitigation of severe accidents (addressing beyond-design-basis topics of core damage and subsequent containment performance), as well as EP. The Fukushima accident therefore highlights the full spectrum of considerations necessary for a comprehensive and coherent regulatory framework.

Similar issues were raised by the TMI accident, and many beyond-design-basis requirements, programs, and practices were derived from that experience and from the concurrent development of PRA as a practical tool. Other sections of this report address specific elements of protection, mitigation, and preparedness and evaluate their current capabilities, limitations, and potential enhancements. This section will evaluate the overall NRC regulatory approach for ensuring safety through a defense-indepth philosophy that includes design-basis requirements and additional risk reduction requirements and programs. The goal of this section is to identify possible ways to better integrate the fundamental design-basis concept with the beyond-design-basis considerations, including EP.

Design-basis events became a central element of the safety approach almost 50 years ago when the U.S. Atomic Energy Commission (AEC) formulated the idea of requiring safety systems to address a prescribed set of anticipated operational occurrences and postulated accidents. In addition, the design-basis requirements for nuclear power plants included a set of external challenges including seismic activity and flooding from various sources. That approach and its related concepts of design-basis events and design bases were used in licensing the current generation of nuclear plants in the 1960s and 1970s.

Frequently, the concept of design-basis events has been equated to adequate protection, and the concept of beyond-design-basis events has been equated to beyond adequate protection (i.e., safety enhancements). This vision of adequate protection has typically only led to requirements addressing beyond-design-basis concerns when they were found to be associated with a substantial enhancement in safety and justified in terms of cost.

Starting in the 1980s and continuing to the present, the NRC has maintained the design-basis approach and expanded it to address issues of concern. The NRC added requirements to address each new issue as it arose but did not change the fundamental concept of design-basis events or the list of those events; nor did the NRC typically assign the concept of adequate protection to these changes. The following paragraphs include discussion of the historical development of requirements to address issues beyond the design basis, including the potential loss of all ac power (i.e., SBO) and other issues. In reading these paragraphs, it is helpful to keep in mind that actions to address issues beyond the design basis were largely considered safety enhancements. They were considered to be beyond what was required for adequate protection.

In the early 1970s, the AEC began questioning applicants and licensees about the potential consequences of an anticipated operational occurrence (a design-basis event) with the beyond-design-basis failure of the shutdown system (a sequence called anticipated transient without scram (ATWS)). This issue was clearly outside the design basis of the plants, yet it remained a concern for many years, eventually resulting in a regulation (10 CFR 50.62, "Requirements for Reducing the Risk from Anticipated Transients without Scram (ATWS) Events for Light-Water-Cooled Nuclear Power Plants"). That regulation established several requirements to address ATWS concerns but did not expand the list of design-basis events to include ATWS.

In the mid-1980s, the Commission established the SBO rule (10 CFR 50.63, "Loss of All Alternating Current Power") to address concerns related to loss of all ac power. Again the rule established new requirements but did not alter the design-basis concept or list of design-basis events. SBO is not a design-basis event, nor is SBO-related equipment subject to the NRC's quality assurance requirements in Appendix B, "Quality Assurance Criteria for Nuclear Power Plants and Fuel Reprocessing Plants," to 10 CFR Part 50, "Domestic Licensing of Production and Utilization Facilities."

In addition to the established regulatory approach, the AEC commissioned and the NRC later published the first PRA of nuclear power plants in WASH-1400, "Reactor Safety Study: An Assessment of Accident Risks in U.S. Commercial Nuclear Power Plants," issued October 1975. That study addressed possible reactor accidents based on the frequency of initiating events and their likely consequences. The study proceeded without regard to classification of events as "anticipated operational occurrences" or "postulated accidents" and therefore without regard to event categorization as "design-basis events." The treatment of events based solely on frequency and consequences remains a characteristic of PRA and is one of its strengths in complementing the traditional regulatory approach.

Following the TMI accident, numerous lessons-learned efforts were commissioned. One of those studies (NUREG/CR-1250, "Three Mile Island; A Report to the Commissioners and to the Public," issued in 1980 and generally referred to as the Rogovin Report) evaluated the then-existing NRC regulatory approach (characterized in the report as "the so-called 'design basis accident' concept"). The report concluded that "More rigorous and quantitative methods of risk analysis have been developed and should be employed to assess the safety of design and operation," and "The best way to improve the existing design review process is by relying in a major way upon quantitative risk analysis." The report's recommendations to the Commission included "Expand the spectrum of design basis accidents..." and "On a selective basis, determine whether some design features to mitigate the effects of some Class Nine accidents [i.e., severe accidents in current terminology] should be required."

On the basis of all the recommendations developed by the NRC following the TMI accident, the Commission established numerous new requirements (approximately 120 actions per plant), some within and some beyond the design bases. In addition, the Commission considered action to address core damage scenarios, again beyond the design basis. Ultimately, the Commission encouraged licensees to use the newly developed PRA methodology to search for vulnerabilities (in the Individual Plant Examination (IPE) program and Individual Plant Examination for External Events (IPEEE) program) and requested information on their findings. The Commission also encouraged the development of SAMGs based on PRA insights and severe accident research. However, the Commission did not take action to require the IPEs, IPEEEs, or SAMGs. While the Commission has been partially responsive to recommendations calling for requirements to address beyond-design-basis accidents, the NRC has not made fundamental changes to the regulatory approach for beyond-design-basis events and severe accidents for operating reactors.

Currently, risk-informed regulation (i.e., regulation using PRAs) serves the limited roles of maintenance rule implementation, Regulatory Analysis Guidelines, the search for vulnerabilities (e.g., through the IPE and IPEEE programs), the Reactor Oversight Process (ROP) and its significance determination process, and voluntary license amendment applications (e.g., risk-informed inservice inspection).

In contrast, for new reactors, the Commission has moved further from a largely design-basis accident concept, requiring applicants for design certifications and combined licenses (COLs) under 10 CFR Part 52, "Licenses, Certification, and Approvals for Nuclear Power Plants," to perform a PRA and provide a description and analysis of design features for the prevention and mitigation of severe accidents (10 CFR 52.47(23) and 10 CFR 52.79(48)). Each design certification rule (10 CFR Part 52, Appendix A, "Design Certification Rule for the U.S. Advanced Boiling Water Reactor," and other Part 52 appendices) then codifies the severe accident features of each approved standard design.

Following the terrorist events of September 11, 2001, the NRC issued security advisories, orders, license conditions, and ultimately a new regulation (10 CFR 50.54(hh)) to require licensees to develop and implement guidance and strategies to maintain or restore capabilities for core cooling and containment and spent fuel pool cooling under the circumstances associated with the loss of large areas of the plant due to a fire or explosion. These requirements have led to the development of extensive damage mitigation guidelines (EDMGs) at all U.S. nuclear power plants. The NRC has inspected the guidelines and strategies that licensees have implemented to meet the requirements of 10 CFR 50.54(hh)(2). However, there are no specific quality requirements associated with these requirements, and the quality assurance requirements of 10 CFR Part 50, Appendix B, do not apply. The EDMGs are requirements for addressing events well beyond those historically considered to be the design basis and were implemented as adequate protection backfits. In order to address the changing security threat environment, the Commission effectively redefined what level of protection should be regarded as adequate. This is a normal and reasonable, albeit infrequent, exercise of the NRC's responsibilities of protecting public health and safety.

All of the above indicate the Commission's desire and commitment to act either through regulatory requirements or voluntary industry initiatives to address concerns related to the design basis or beyond the design basis where appropriate.

Task Force Evaluation

As presented above, the current NRC regulatory approach includes (1) requirements for design-basis events with features controlled through specific regulations or the general design criteria (GDC) (10 CFR Part 50, Appendix A, "General Design Criteria for Nuclear Power Plants") and the quality requirements of 10 CFR Part 50, Appendix B, (2) beyonddesign-basis requirements through specific rules (e.g., the SBO rule) with specified quality requirements, (3) voluntary industry initiatives to address severe accident features, strategies, and guidelines for operating reactors, and (4) specific requirements to address damage from fires and explosions and their mitigation.

The Task Force presents the following observations on the NRC regulatory approach:

- Although complex, the current regulatory approach has served the Commission and the public well and allows the Task Force to conclude that a sequence of events like those occurring in the Fukushima accident is unlikely to occur in the United States and could be mitigated, reducing the likelihood of core damage and radiological releases.
- Therefore, in light of the low likelihood of an event beyond the design basis of a U.S. nuclear power plant and the current mitigation capabilities at those facilities, the Task Force concludes that continued operation and continued licensing activities do not pose an imminent risk to the public health and safety and are not inimical to the common defense and security. Nonetheless, the Task Force is recommending building on the safety foundation laid in the 1960s and 1970s, and the safety improvements added from the 1980s to the present, to produce a regulatory structure well suited to licensing and overseeing the operation of nuclear power plants for decades to come. The Task Force sees these recommendations, not as a rejection of the past, but more as a fulfillment of past intentions.
- Adequate protection has been, and should continue to be, an evolving safety standard supported by new scientific information, technologies, methods, and operating experience. This was the case when new information about the security environment was revealed through the events of September 11, 2001. Licensing or operating a nuclear power plant with no emergency core cooling system or without robust security protections, while done in the past, would not occur under the current regulations. As new information and new analytical techniques are developed, safety standards need to be reviewed, evaluated, and changed, as necessary, to insure that they continue to address the NRC's requirements to provide reasonable assurance of adequate protection of public health and safety. The Task Force believes, based on its review of the information currently available from Japan and the current regulations, that the time has come for such change.
- In response to the Fukushima accident and the insights it brings to light, the Task Force is recommending actions, some general, some specific, that it believes would be a reasonable, well-formulated set of actions to increase the level of safety associated with adequate protection of the public health and safety.
- The Commission has come to rely on design-basis requirements and a patchwork of beyond-design-basis requirements and voluntary initiatives for maintaining safety. Design-basis requirements include consideration of anticipated operational occurrences and postulated accidents such as loss-of-coolant accidents. Beyond-design-basis considerations such as ATWS and SBO are discussed below. Voluntary initiatives have addressed some severe accident considerations (through the IPE and IPEEE programs), shutdown risk issues, containment vents for BWR Mark I designs, and SAMGs.
- The concept of beyond-design-basis requirements applies, for example, to ATWS, SBO, aircraft impact assessment (AIA), combustible gas control, and EDMGs. Since

fire protection is not based on a design-basis fire, it too can be considered beyond design basis. Although the phrase "beyond design basis" appears only once in the NRC regulations (i.e., in 10 CFR 50.150, "Aircraft Impact Assessment," known as the AIA rule), regulators and industry use it often. Unfortunately, the phrase "beyond design basis" is vague, sometimes misused, and often misunderstood. Several elements of the phrase contribute to these misunderstandings. First, some beyond-design-basis considerations have been incorporated into the requirements and therefore directly affect reactor designs. The phrase is therefore inconsistent with the normal meaning of the words. In addition, there are many other beyond-design-basis considerations that are not requirements. The phrase therefore fails to convey the importance of the requirements to which it refers.

- The Task Force has noted that other international regulatory systems also address considerations beyond the design basis. For example, while the NRC addresses regulatory requirements in five categories—three design basis (normal operation, anticipated operational occurrences, and postulated accidents) and two beyond design basis (one required and one voluntary)—Finland addresses regulatory requirements in six categories—four design basis (normal operation, anticipated operational occurrences, and two postulated accident categories), one "design extension condition," plus severe accidents. France also addresses both design-basis requirements and additional requirements in categories called "Risk Reduction Category 1" and "Risk Reduction Category 2." In addition, the phrase used in the IAEA Draft Safety Standard DS 414 addresses considerations beyond the design basis, referring to them as those addressing "design extension conditions." In this report, the Task Force will refer to past considerations beyond the design basis using that phrase (e.g., "beyond-designbasis events"). In the context of the Task Force recommendation for a new regulatory framework for the future, the Task Force will refer to such considerations as "extended design basis" requirements.

- The primary responsibility for safety rests with licensees, and the NRC holds licensees accountable for meeting regulatory requirements. In addition, voluntary safety initiatives by licensees can enhance safety if implemented and maintained effectively, but should not take the place of needed regulatory requirements. The NRC inspection and licensing programs give less attention to beyond-design-basis requirements and little attention to industry voluntary initiatives since there are no requirements to inspect against. Because of this, the NRC gives much more attention to design-basis events than to severe accidents.

- With the exception of a few special cases, licensees of operating reactors are not required to develop or maintain a PRA, although all licensees currently have a PRA. These PRAs are of varying scope and are generally not required to meet NRC-endorsed quality standards. New reactor applications must include a description of a design-specific PRA and its results and must address severe accident protection and mitigation features.

- The Commission has expressed its intent with respect to industry initiatives in the Regulatory Analysis Guidelines (NUREG/BR-0058, Revision 4). That document states, "It must be clear to the public that substituting industry initiatives for NRC

regulatory action can provide effective and efficient resolution of issues, will in no way compromise plant safety, and does not represent a reduction in the NRC's commitment to safety and sound regulation."
- Lastly, the Task Force observes that for new reactor designs, the Commission's expectations that beyond-design-basis and severe accident concerns be addressed and resolved at the design stage are largely expressed in policy statements and staff requirements memoranda, only reaching the level of rulemaking when each design is codified through design certification rulemaking.

In summary, the major elements of the NRC regulatory approach relevant to the Fukushima accident, or a similar accident in the United States, are seismic and flooding protection (well established in the design-basis requirements); SBO protection (required, but beyond the design-basis requirements); and severe accident mitigation (expected but neither the severe accident mitigation features nor the SAMGs are required). In addition, U.S. facilities could employ EDMGs as further mitigation capability. The Task Force observes that this collection of approaches is largely the product of history; it was developed for the purpose of reactor licensing in the 1960s and 1970s and supplemented as necessary to address significant events or new issues. This evolution has resulted in a patchwork regulatory approach.

The Fukushima accident clearly demonstrates the importance of defense-in-depth. Whether through extraordinary circumstances or through limited knowledge of the possibilities, plants can be challenged beyond their established design bases protection. In such circumstances, the next layer of defense-in-depth, mitigation, is an essential element of adequate protection of public health and safety. Mitigation is provided for beyond-designbasis events and severe accidents, both of which involve external challenges or multiple failures beyond the design basis. This beyond-design-basis layer of defense-in-depth is broadly consistent with the IAEA concept of "design extension conditions" (presented in Draft Safety Standard DS 414).

The Task Force concludes that the NRC's safety approach is incomplete without a strong program for dealing with the unexpected, including severe accidents. Continued reliance on industry initiatives for a fundamental level of defense-in-depth similarly would leave gaps in the NRC regulatory approach. The Commission has clearly established such defense-indepth severe accident requirements for new reactors (in 10 CFR 52.47(23), 10 CFR 52.79(38), and each design certification rule), thus bringing unity and completeness to the defense-indepth concept. Taking a similar action, within reasonable and practical bounds appropriate to operating plants, would do the same for operating reactors.

The Task Force therefore concludes that the future regulatory framework should be based on the defense-in-depth philosophy, supported and modified as necessary by state-of-the-art PRA techniques. The Task Force also concludes that the application of defense-in-depth should be strengthened by formally establishing, in the regulations, an appropriate level of defense-in-depth to address requirements for "extended" design-basis events. Many of the elements of such regulations already exist in the form of the SBO rule (10 CFR 50.63), ATWS rule (10 CFR 50.62), maintenance rule (10 CFR 50.65), AIA rule (10 CFR 50.150), the requirements for protection for beyond-design-basis fires and explosions (10 CFR 50.54(hh)), and the alternative treatment requirements (10 CFR 50.69) and new reactor policy regarding regulatory treatment of nonsafety systems as described in SECY-94-084, "Policy and Technical Issues Associated with the Regulatory Treatment of Nonsafety Systems in Passive Plant Designs," dated March 28, 1994. Other elements such as SAMGs exist in voluntary industry initiatives. The Task Force envisions this collection of beyonddesign-basis requirements as a coherent whole in a separate section of 10 CFR Part 50 (e.g., 10 CFR 50.200, 10 CFR 50.201) or as a dedicated appendix to 10 CFR Part 50. This separate section would have an appropriate set of quality standards, analogous to Appendix B to 10 CFR Part 50, plus a change process similar to the 10 CFR Part 52 "50.59-like" process codified in the rule for each certified design (e.g., 10 CFR Part 52, Appendix A, Section VIII, "Processes for Changes and Departures").

The Task Force envisions a framework in which the current design-basis requirements (i.e., for anticipated operational occurrences and postulated accidents) would remain largely unchanged and the current beyond-design-basis requirements (e.g., for ATWS and SBO) would be complemented with new requirements to establish a more balanced and effective application of defense-in-depth.

This framework, by itself, would not create new requirements nor eliminate any current requirements. It would provide a more coherent structure within the regulations to facilitate Commission decisions relating to what issues should be subject to NRC requirements and what those requirements ought to be. The Task Force envisions that implementation of a new regulatory framework would result in the addition of some currently unregulated issues (i.e., those important to defense-in-depth) to a category of "extended design-basis" requirements. The framework could also support shifting issues currently addressed as design-basis requirements to the "extended design-basis" category of requirements. Such changes would establish a more logical, systematic, and coherent set of requirements addressing defense-in-depth.

As discussed earlier, the Task Force believes that voluntary industry initiatives could play a useful and valuable role in the suggested framework. Voluntary industry initiatives would not serve as substitutes for regulatory requirements but as a mechanism for facilitating and standardizing implementation of such requirements. The development of symptom-based emergency operating procedures (EOPs) in the 1980s and development of the EDMGs following the events of September 11, 2001, are just two examples of notable industry contributions to effective implementation of regulatory initiatives.

A newly organized part of the regulations would not only strengthen mitigation of accidents as severe as the Fukushima accident, but could also help to resolve some longstanding regulatory issues. For example, it could provide a natural location for requirements such as reactor coolant system breaks beyond the transition break size (being considered in the revision to 10 CFR 50.46, "Acceptance Criteria for Emergency Core Cooling Systems for Light-Water Nuclear Power Reactors"). It would also be a logical location for a requirement for PRAs and IPE and IPEEE generic safety insights for operating reactors, should the Commission desire such a requirement.

In a new regulatory framework, risk assessment and defense-in-depth would be combined more formally. PRA would help ensure that the design-basis requirements address events of a specific frequency with strict quality standards (i.e., 10 CFR Part 50, Appendix B) and that beyond-design-basis requirements address less frequent, but nonetheless important, events through appropriate quality standards. The Task Force concludes that the new framework could be implemented on the basis of full-scope Level 1 core damage assessment PRAs and Level 2 containment performance assessment PRAs.

The current NRC approach to land contamination relies on preventing the release of radioactive material through the first two levels of defense-in-depth, namely protection and mitigation. Without the release of radioactive material associated with a core damage accident, there would be no significant land contamination. The Task Force also concludes that the NRC's current approach to the issue of land contamination from reactor accidents is sound. The Task Force's objective of ensuring that protection and mitigation provide strong and effective levels of defense-in-depth is therefore fully consistent with reducing the likelihood of land contamination without introducing any new safety concepts or methods. The Task Force also considered the value of requiring a Level 3 PRA (i.e., a probabilistic assessment of accident dose and health effects) as part of a new regulatory framework.

The Task Force concluded that for large light-water reactors, the metrics of core damage frequency and large early release provide very effective, relatively simple, well-documented and understood measures of safety for decisionmaking. Therefore, the Task Force has not recommended including Level 3 PRA as a part of a regulatory framework. However, some limited Level 3 PRA analyses, such as those done for a few selected plants and reported in NUREG1150, "Severe Accident Risks: An Assessment of Five U.S. Nuclear Power Plants," issued December 1990, could confirm that the selected frequency ranges for design-basis and beyond-design-basis requirements are consistent with the Commission's safety goals.

The Task Force considered the role of the IPEs and IPEEEs (mentioned above) in a new regulatory framework. If the new regulatory framework had been in place before the start of the IPE and IPEEE programs, they would likely have been different, perhaps being required rather than encouraged. However, the programs have been completed, the NRC reviewed the efforts to some extent, and the licensees have taken voluntary actions, in some cases, to address identified vulnerabilities. Given this reality, the Task Force concludes that the most appropriate step consistent with the new risk-informed, defense-in-depth regulatory framework would be to revisit the results of those efforts to identify any significant items of a generic nature and consider them for possible inclusion under design-basis or extended design-basis regulations. Similarly, this effort could identify significant plant-specific items as candidates for plant-specific regulatory requirements (e.g., license conditions).

Finally, a new and dedicated portion of the regulations would allow the Commission to recharacterize its expectations for safety features beyond design basis more clearly and more positively as "extended design-basis" requirements. The Task Force recognizes fully that a comprehensive reevaluation and restructuring of the regulatory framework would be no small feat. The Task Force also recognizes that strengthening the roles of defense-in-depth and risk assessment, emphasizing beyond-design-basis and severe accident mitigation, and establishing a clear, coherent, and well-integrated regulatory framework would be a significant accomplishment. Therefore, the Task Force concludes that additional steps would be prudent to further enhance the NRC regulatory framework to encompass the protections for accidents beyond the design basis.

Recommendation 1

The Task Force recommends establishing a logical, systematic, and coherent regulatory framework for adequate protection that appropriately balances defense-in-depth and risk considerations.

1.1. Draft a Commission policy statement that articulates a risk-informed defense-in-depth framework that includes extended design-basis requirements in the NRC's regulations as essential elements for ensuring adequate protection.
1.2. Initiate rulemaking to implement a risk-informed, defense-in-depth framework consistent with the above recommended Commission policy statement.
1.3. Modify the Regulatory Analysis Guidelines to more effectively implement the defense-indepth philosophy in balance with the current emphasis on risk-based guidelines.

- The Task Force believes that the Regulatory Analysis Guidelines could be modified by implementing some of the concepts presented in the technology-neutral framework (NUREG-1860) to better integrate safety goals and defense-in-depth.

1.4. Evaluate the insights from the IPE and IPEEE efforts as summarized in NUREG-1560, "Individual Plant Examination Program: Perspectives on Reactor Safety and Plant Performance," issued December 1997, and NUREG-1742, "Perspectives Gained from the Individual Plant Examination of External Events (IPEEE) Program," issued April 2002, to identify potential generic regulations or plant-specific regulatory requirements.

Subsequent sections of this report will evaluate issues relevant to the Fukushima accident and will propose recommendations to strengthen associated NRC programs and requirements. The objective of strengthening those programs and requirements is to make them fully effective in providing defense-in-depth, thus supporting this recommended framework

4. SAFETY THROUGH DEFENSE-IN-DEPTH

The key to a defense-in-depth approach is creating multiple independent and redundant layers of defense to compensate for potential failures and external hazards so that no single layer is exclusively relied on to protect the public and the environment. In its application of the defense-in-depth philosophy, the Task Force has addressed protection from design-basis natural phenomena, mitigation of the consequences of accidents, and EP.

4.1. Ensuring Protection from External Events

The first level of defense-in-depth is protection. Specifically, the Task Force examined the historical development of facility design bases for protection from external hazards that could cause the loss of large areas of a plant. The combined effects of the Great East Japan Earthquake of 2011 and the ensuing tsunami at the Fukushima Nuclear Power Plant site represent the most significant external event challenges that any commercial nuclear reactor has ever faced. The following section discusses the importance of establishing appropriate protection from design-basis natural phenomena. In evaluating protection from design-basis natural phenomena, the Task Force considered earthquakes, floods, high winds (due to hurricanes or tornadoes), and external fires. The Task Force concluded that earthquakes and flooding hazards warranted further Task Force consideration due, in part, to significant advancements in the state of knowledge and the state of analysis in these areas in the time period since the operating plants were sited and licensed. In addition, the earthquake and subsequent tsunami highlighted the need to evaluate concurrent related events, such as seismically induced fires and floods.

4.1.1. Protection from Design-Basis Natural Phenomena

Background

The NRC has long recognized the importance of protection from natural phenomena as a means to prevent core damage and to ensure containment and spent fuel pool integrity. The NRC established several requirements addressing natural phenomena in 1971 with GDC 2, "Design Bases for Protection Against Natural Phenomena," of Appendix A to 10 CFR Part 50. GDC 2 requires, in part, that SSCs important to safety be designed to withstand the effects of natural phenomena such as floods, tsunami, and seiches without loss of capability to perform their safety functions. GDC 2 also requires that design bases for these SSCs reflect (1) appropriate consideration of the most severe of the natural phenomena that have been historically reported for the site and surrounding region, with sufficient margin for the limited accuracy and quantity of the historical data and the period of time in which the data have been accumulated, (2) appropriate combinations of the effects of normal and accident conditions with the effects of the natural phenomena, and (3) the importance of the safety functions to be performed.

Since the establishment of GDC 2, the NRC's requirements and guidance for protection from seismic events, floods, and other natural phenomena have continued to evolve. The agency has developed new regulations, new and updated regulatory guidance, and several regulatory programs aimed at enhancements for previously licensed reactors.

In 1973, Appendix A, "Seismic and Geologic Siting Criteria for Nuclear Power Plants," to 10 CFR Part 100 was established to provide detailed criteria to evaluate the suitability of proposed sites and the suitability of the plant design basis established in consideration of the seismic and geologic characteristics of the proposed sites.

In 1977, the NRC initiated the Systematic Evaluation Program (SEP) to review the designs of older operating nuclear reactor plants in order to reconfirm and document their safety. The purpose of the review was to provide (1) an assessment of the significance of differences between then-current technical positions on safety issues and those that existed when a particular plant was licensed, (2) a basis for deciding how these differences should be resolved in an integrated plant review, and (3) a documented evaluation of plant safety. The plants selected for SEP review included several that were licensed before a comprehensive set of licensing criteria (i.e., the GDC) had been developed or finalized. The SEP covered topics including seismic events, floods, high winds, and tornadoes.

In 1980, the NRC was concerned that licensees had not conducted the seismic qualification of electrical and mechanical equipment in some older nuclear reactor plants in accordance with the licensing criteria for the seismic qualification of equipment acceptable at that time. As a result, the NRC established the Unresolved Safety Issue (USI) A-46, "Seismic Qualification of Mechanical and Electrical Equipment in Operating Nuclear Power Plants," program in December 1980. In February 1987, the agency issued Generic Letter (GL) 87-02,

"Verification of Seismic Adequacy of Mechanical and Electrical Equipment in Operating Reactors, Unresolved Safety Issue (USI) A-46," to address this concern. The objective of USI A-46 was to develop alternative seismic qualification methods and acceptance criteria that could be used to assess the capability of mechanical and electrical equipment in operating nuclear power plants to perform their intended safety functions. The scope of the review was limited to equipment required to bring each affected plant to hot shutdown and maintain it for a minimum of 72 hours.

In 1991, the NRC issued Supplement 4 to GL 88-20, "Individual Plant Examination of External Events (IPEEE) for Severe Accident Vulnerabilities, 10 CFR 50.54(f)." This GL requested that "each licensee perform an individual plant examination of external events to identify vulnerabilities, if any, to severe accidents and report the results together with any licensee determined improvements and corrective actions to the Commission." The external events considered in the IPEEE program include seismic events, internal fires, high winds, and floods. The primary goal of the IPEEE program was for each licensee to identify plant-specific vulnerabilities to severe accidents, if any, and to report the results, with any licensee-proposed improvements and corrective actions, to the NRC.

In 1996, the NRC established two new seismic regulations for applications submitted on or after January 10, 1997. These regulations were not applied to existing reactors. The first regulation, 10 CFR 100.23, "Geologic and Seismic Siting Criteria," sets forth the principal geologic and seismic considerations that guide the Commission in its evaluation of the suitability of a proposed site and adequacy of the design bases established in consideration of the geologic and seismic characteristics of the proposed site. The second regulation, Appendix S, "Earthquake Engineering Criteria for Nuclear Power Plants," to 10 CFR Part 50, requires that nuclear power plants be designed so that certain SSCs remain functional if the safe shutdown earthquake (SSE) ground motion occurs. These plant features are those necessary to ensure (1) the integrity of the reactor coolant pressure boundary, (2) the capability to shut down the reactor and maintain it in a safe shutdown condition, or (3) the capability to prevent or mitigate the consequences of accidents that could result in potential offsite exposures comparable to the guideline exposures of 10 CFR 50.34(a)(1) or 10 CFR 100.11, "Determination of Exclusion Area, Low Population Zone, and Population Center Distance."

In 1996, the staff also established a new requirement in 10 CFR 100.20, "Factors To Be Considered When Evaluating Sites," for the evaluation of the nature and proximity of man-related hazards, such as dams, for applications submitted on or after January 10, 1997. This regulation was not applied to existing reactors.

In 1975, the NRC published the Standard Review Plan (SRP) (NUREG/75-087, later published as NUREG-0800, "Standard Review Plan for the Review of Safety Analysis Reports for Nuclear Power Plants: LWR Edition"), which provides standardized review criteria to assist the staff in evaluating safety analysis reports submitted by license applicants. Since its first publication, the SRP has undergone several revisions to incorporate new developments in design and analysis technology. Since the last SRP update in 2007, the staff has established interim staff guidance (ISG) in three areas related to protection from natural phenomena:

(1) DC/COL-ISG-1, "Interim Staff Guidance on Seismic Issues of High Frequency Ground Motion," (2) DC/COLISG7, "Assessment of Normal and Extreme Winter Precipitation Loads on the Roofs of Seismic Category I Structures," and (3) DC/COL-ISG-

20, "Seismic Margin Analysis for New Reactors Based on Probabilistic Risk Assessment." This interim guidance has been applied only to new reactor reviews.

The staff has also published several regulatory guides (RGs) that address specific technical issues related to protection from natural phenomena. These documents provide guidance to licensees and applicants on implementing specific parts of the NRC's regulations, techniques used by the NRC staff in evaluating specific problems or postulated accidents, and data needed by the staff in its review of applications for permits or licenses. These guides include the following:

- RG 1.29, "Seismic Design Classification," issued in 1972 and updated in 1973, 1976, 1978, and 2007
- RG 1.59, "Design Basis Floods for Nuclear Power Plants," issued in 1973 and updated in 1976 and 1977
- RG 1.60, "Design Response Spectra for Seismic Design of Nuclear Power Plants," issued in 1973
- RG 1.102, "Flood Protection for Nuclear Power Plants," issued in 1975 and updated in 1976
- RG 1.125, "Physical Models for Design and Operation of Hydraulic Structures and Systems for Nuclear Power Plants," issued in 1977 and updated in 1978 and 2009
- RG 1.208, "A Performance-Based Approach To Define the Site-Specific Earthquake Ground Motion," issued in 2007

The NRC staff continually evaluates new information regarding natural phenomena, including operational experience, and its potential impact on risk and overall plant safety. These evaluations have led to new requirements or guidance as discussed above, updated regulatory guidance, generic communications, and plant-specific actions to address identified issues. Several examples are presented below.

Following the Sumatra earthquake and its accompanying tsunami in December 2004, the NRC staff initiated a study to examine tsunami hazards at nuclear power plant sites, to review offshore and onshore modeling of tsunami waves, to describe the effects of tsunami waves on nuclear power plant SSCs, to develop potential approaches for screening sites for tsunami effects, to identify the repository of historic tsunami data, and to examine ways for an NRC reviewer to approach site safety assessment for a tsunami. The study, NUREG/ CR-6966, "Tsunami Hazard Assessment at Nuclear Power Plant Sites in the United States of America," was published March 2009. The results of this study were incorporated in the 2007 update of SRP Section 2.4.6, "Probable Maximum Tsunami Hazards." As discussed in NUREG/CR-6966, the 1977 revision to RG 1.59 (Revision 2) was expected to include guidance for assessment of tsunamis as a flooding hazard, but that effort was not completed. The staff is in the process of updating RG 1.59 to address tsunamis and other advances in flooding analysis. Since 1977, flood estimation techniques have significantly improved with the availability of more accurate datasets and newer hydrologic, hydraulic, and hydrodynamic models. It should be noted that the current fleet of reactors was sited before RG 1.59, Revision 2, was issued.

In August 2010, the NRC initiated a proposed generic issue (GI) regarding flooding of nuclear power plant sites following upstream dam failures. The staff evaluation of this issue is ongoing.

Lastly, the NRC is evaluating seismic hazards based on new Electric Power Research Institute models used to estimate earthquake ground motion and updated models for earthquake sources in the Central and Eastern United States. The NRC is addressing this issue through the ongoing evaluation of GI-199, "Implications of Updated Probabilistic Seismic Hazard Estimates in Central and Eastern United States on Existing Plants," initiated June 9, 2005. The results of the GI-199 safety/risk assessment stage were summarized in Information Notice 2010-018, "Implications of Updated Probabilistic Seismic Hazard Estimates in Central and Eastern United States on Existing Plants," dated September 2, 2010. As discussed in Information Notice 2010-018, currently available seismic data and models show increased seismic hazard estimates for some operating nuclear power plant sites in the Central and Eastern United States. Determination of site-specific seismic hazards and associated plant risk are planned for the next phase of GI-199.

Task Force Evaluation

Current NRC regulations and associated regulatory guidance provide a robust regulatory approach for evaluation of site hazards associated with natural phenomena. However, this framework has evolved over time as new information regarding site hazards and their potential consequences has become available. As a result, the licensing bases, design, and level of protection from natural phenomena differ among the existing operating reactors in the United States, depending on when the plant was constructed and when the plant was licensed for operation. Over the years, the NRC has initiated several efforts to evaluate risks and potential safety issues resulting from these differences.

The SEP, mentioned earlier, was a one-time evaluation, and integrated plant safety assessments were published in the early 1980s for each of the plants included in the SEP. The SEP covered several technical topics, including protection from natural phenomena (i.e., floods, seismic events, tornadoes, high winds). Even that reassessment was conducted before satellite imaging, Doppler radar, and well-established theories of plate tectonics were available. It is clear that our current state of knowledge far exceeds that available to decisionmakers three decades ago.

With regard to the IPEEE program, the staff performed a limited review of the IPEEE submittals to determine whether the licensees' IPEEE processes were capable of identifying and addressing severe accident vulnerabilities caused by external events. The staff published a summary of the results of the IPEEE program in NUREG-1742, "Perspectives Gained from the Individual Plant Examination of External Events (IPEEE) Program," in April 2002. However, the NRC reviews did not attempt to validate or verify the licensees' IPEEE results or the acceptability of proposed improvements. Further, the IPEEE analyses did not document the potential safety impacts of proposed improvements, and plants were not required to report completion of proposed improvements to the NRC.

The SEP, IPEEE program, USI A-46, and other regulatory initiatives, including licensing actions to address vulnerabilities, have resulted in some plant-specific safety enhancements to address the risk of external events resulting from natural phenomena. However, the staff has not undertaken a comprehensive reestablishment of the design basis for existing plants that would reflect the current state of knowledge or current licensing criteria. As a result, significant differences may exist between plants in the way they protect against design-basis natural phenomena and the safety margin provided.

With regard to seismic hazards, as discussed above, available seismic data and models show increased seismic hazard estimates for some operating nuclear power plant sites. The state of knowledge of seismic hazards within the United States has evolved to the point that it would be appropriate for licensees to reevaluate the designs of existing nuclear power reactors to ensure that SSCs important to safety will withstand a seismic event without loss of capability to perform their intended safety function. As seismic knowledge continues to increase, new seismic hazard data and models will be produced. Thus, the need to evaluate the implications of updated seismic hazards on operating reactors will recur and need to be reevaluated at appropriate intervals.

With regard to flooding hazards, the assumptions and factors that were considered in flood protection at operating plants vary. In some cases, the design basis does not consider the probable maximum flood (PMF). In other cases, the PMF is calculated differently at units colocated at the same site, depending on the time of licensing, resulting in different design-basis flood protection. The Task Force has observed that some plants have an overreliance on operator actions and temporary flood mitigation measures such as sandbagging, temporary flood walls and barriers, and portable equipment to perform safety functions. In addition, potential dam failures have been addressed inconsistently in the establishment of the design-basis flood. In some cases, emphasis was placed on dam failures coincident with seismic events, while other mechanisms for dam failures were not fully considered. Lastly, while tsunami hazards are not expected to be the limiting flood hazard for operating plants sited on the Atlantic Ocean and the Gulf of Mexico, plants in these coastal regions do not currently include an analysis of tsunami hazards in their licensing basis. Tsunami hazards have been considered in the design basis for operating plants sited on the Pacific Ocean.

The Task Force has concluded that flooding risks are of concern due to a "cliff-edge" effect, in that the safety consequences of a flooding event may increase sharply with a small increase in the flooding level. Therefore, it would be very beneficial to safety for all licensees to confirm that SSCs important to safety are adequately protected from floods.

This reevaluation should consider all appropriate internal and external flooding sources, including the effects from local intense precipitation on the site, PMF on streams and rivers, storm surges, seiches, tsunamis, and dam failures. Similar to seismic hazards, new flooding hazard data and models will be produced from time to time. Thus, there would be a continuing benefit to having operating reactors reevaluate the implications of updated flooding hazards at appropriate intervals.

Protection from natural phenomena is critical for safe operation of nuclear power plants due to potential common-cause failures and significant contribution to core damage frequency from external events. Failure to adequately protect SSCs important to safety from appropriate design-basis natural phenomena with appropriate safety margins has the potential for common-cause failures and significant consequences as demonstrated at Fukushima.

Recommendation 2

The Task Force recommends that the NRC require licensees to reevaluate and upgrade as necessary the design-basis seismic and flooding protection of SSCs for each operating reactor.

The Task Force recommends that the Commission direct the following actions to ensure adequate protection from natural phenomena, consistent with the current state of knowledge

Recommendations for Enhancing Reactor Safety in the 21st Century

and analytical methods. These should be undertaken to prevent fuel damage and to ensure containment and spent fuel pool integrity:

2.1. Order licensees to reevaluate the seismic and flooding hazards at their sites against current NRC requirements and guidance, and if necessary, update the design basis and SSCs important to safety to protect against the updated hazards.
2.2. Initiate rulemaking to require licensees to confirm seismic hazards and flooding hazards every 10 years and address any new and significant information. If necessary, update the design basis for SSCs important to safety to protect against the updated hazards.
2.3. Order licensees to perform seismic and flood protection walkdowns to identify and address plant-specific vulnerabilities and verify the adequacy of monitoring and maintenance for protection features such as watertight barriers and seals in the interim period until longer term actions are completed to update the design basis for external events.

4.1.2. Protection from Concurrent Related Events

Background

The Task Force evaluated various related concurrent events and determined that fires and internal floods induced by design-basis earthquakes warranted further Task Force consideration.

Seismically induced fires are frequent after earthquakes in urban areas. Seismic events have also resulted in fires at nuclear power plants. Seismically induced fires have the potential to cause multiple failures of safety-related systems and could create fires in multiple locations at the site. Fire protection systems are not required to be functional after a seismic event; therefore, efforts to fight seismically induced fires may be impaired by degraded fire protection equipment. A seismic event may also impede offsite fire crews from reaching the site, further challenging the capability to respond to such an event.

This scenario occurred following the July 16, 2007, magnitude 6.6 Niigata-Chuetsu Oki earthquake that occurred 19 kilometers from the Kashiwazaki-Kariwa nuclear power plant, located in Niigata, Japan. Following the earthquake, a fire occurred in the Kashiwazaki-Kariwa Unit 3 electrical transformer. Sparks from a short circuit caused by large ground displacements of the transformer foundation caused the fire. The sparks ignited oil leaked from the transformer. Damage to the onsite fire protection equipment resulting from the seismic event included multiple failures of the firefighting water system in Units 1, 2, 3, and 4; failure of one of the fire water storage tanks; and failure of other fire suppression systems. Attempts by the plant fire brigade to extinguish the fire were unsuccessful. The local municipality fire brigade eventually extinguished the fire approximately 2 hours after it began. The fire was contained by fire protection walls and did not affect any plant safety equipment. However, the event provided important insights into vulnerabilities from seismically induced fires.

The 2007 Japanese earthquake event also revealed insights regarding seismically induced flooding. The plants experienced flooding from sloshing of the spent fuel pool, fire suppression piping failure outside the Unit 1 reactor building that flowed into the plant through cable penetrations, and a condenser flexible connection failure. While there were no safety consequences, these flooding failures led to water flow to various portions of the plant that could have caused SSC functional failures.

Task Force Evaluation

The staff initiated Generic Safety Issue (GSI)-172, "Multiple System Responses Program (MSRP)," to address 21 potential safety concerns that were raised by the Advisory Committee on Reactor Safeguards (ACRS) during the resolution of USI A-17, "Systems Interactions in Nuclear Power Plants"; USI A-46, "Seismic Qualification of Equipment in Operating Plants"; and USI A-47, "Safety Implications of Control Systems." GSI-172 included the ACRS concern that the resolution of USI A-46, other seismic requirements, or fire protection regulations did not adequately address seismically induced fires. This concern was identified as Item 7.4.16 in NUREG/CR-5420, "Multiple System Responses Program—Identification of Concerns Related to a Number of Specific Regulatory Issues," published October 1989. ACRS was also concerned that previous internal flooding studies had examined events such as pipe ruptures (and subsequent flooding) as single events and that the nature of a seismic event could cause such problems in multiple locations simultaneously. This concern was identified as Item 7.4.18 in NUREG/CR-5420.

The staff developed guidance for the review of the safety concerns of GSI-172 in the IPE and IPEEE programs. As a result, the IPEEE program subsumed the issues related to seismically induced fires and floods.

With regard to seismically induced fires, NUREG-1742 states the following:

> All of the IPEEE submittals reported that the licensees qualitatively examined seismically induced fire interaction issues as part of the treatment of Sandia fire risk scoping study issues. A few licensees performed a PRA study for seismically induced fire-initiating events; albeit the level of detail varied from a simplistic probabilistic analysis to inclusion in their plant's seismic or fire PRA.
>
> In most of the submittals, licensees included seismically induced fire considerations within the scope of their overall seismic walkdown. The level of effort, scope, and detail directed toward addressing seismically induced fire issues varied significantly among the IPEEE submittals. One licensee did not discuss seismically induced fire evaluations in their IPEEE submittal. In most other cases, licensees limited their seismically induced fire evaluations exclusively to assessing direct impacts on safe shutdown equipment.

Seismically induced flooding events can potentially cause multiple failures of safety-related systems. The rupture of small piping could provide flood sources with the potential to affect multiple safety-related components simultaneously. Similarly, nonseismically qualified tanks are a potential flood source of concern. While some licensees proposed plant improvements to address related issues, NUREG-1742 states that the level of effort, scope, and detail directed toward addressing seismically induced flooding issues varied significantly among the IPEEE submittals. Some plants did not provide any information in their IPEEE submittals to verify this issue.

The GSI-172 issue regarding seismically induced fires and floods was closed based on the IPEEE results, and the NRC established no new requirements to prevent or mitigate seismically induced fires or floods. The Task Force concludes that the agency should reevaluate the closure of GSI-172 in light of the plant experience at the Kashiwazaki-Kariwa nuclear plant and the potential for common-mode failures of plant safety equipment as the result of seismically induced fires and floods.

Recommendation 3

The Task Force recommends, as part of the longer term review, that the NRC evaluate potential enhancements to the capability to prevent or mitigate seismically induced fires and floods.

4.2. Mitigation

The second level of defense-in-depth is mitigation. The Great East Japan Earthquake of 2011 and the ensuing tsunami resulted in many mitigation systems at the Fukushima Daiichi Nuclear Power Plant being unable to operate. The subsequent challenges faced by the operators at Fukushima Dai-ichi were beyond any faced previously at a commercial nuclear reactor. The Task Force examined the U.S. regulations, guidance, and practices for mitigating the consequences of accidents similar to those that occurred at Fukushima Daiichi. The following sections discuss the Task Force evaluation of insights from Fukushima and provide recommendations for enhancing the mitigation capability of U.S. reactors with regard to prolonged loss of ac power, containment overpressure protection, combustible gas control, spent fuel pool safety, and onsite emergency actions.

4.2.1. Prolonged Loss of Alternating Current Power

Background

Alternating current (ac) electrical power is critically important to the safety of nuclear power plants. Many of the SSCs intended to cool the nuclear fuel in the reactor and in the spent fuel pools, to maintain radioactive containment systems, and to provide ventilation systems to minimize release of radioactive materials rely on ac power. These systems depend on electrical power to drive pumps, fans, and compressors, operate instrumentation and control systems, and run motors to open and close valves and dampers. For these reasons, the loss of all ac power both onsite and offsite, as occurred at Fukushima, is highly significant. With this in mind, the Task Force critically evaluated the design-basis protections to prevent loss of ac power, as discussed above, and the plants' ability to maintain safety functions following the loss of ac power as discussed below.

The NRC SBO rule (10 CFR 50.63) requires that each nuclear power plant must be able to cool the reactor core and maintain containment integrity for a specified duration of an SBO (defined in 10 CFR 50.2, "Definitions," as a complete loss of required onsite and offsite ac electrical power). The specified duration is based on the following factors:

- the redundancy of the onsite emergency ac power sources
- the reliability of the onsite emergency ac power sources
- the expected frequency of loss of offsite power
- the probable time needed to restore offsite power

RG 1.155, "Station Blackout," describes an acceptable means to comply with 10 CFR 50.63. It primarily addresses three areas: (1) maintaining highly reliable onsite ac electric power systems, (2) developing procedures and training to restore offsite and onsite emergency ac power should either one or both become unavailable, and (3) ensuring that plants can cope with an SBO for some period of time based on the probability of occurrence of an SBO, as well as the capability for restoring ac power to the site in a timely fashion. The RG provides an acceptable method for determining the specified duration for withstanding an SBO considering the four factors identified in the rule language (10 CFR 50.63(a)(1)(i)–(iv)). The method described in RG 1.155 results in a minimum acceptable SBO duration capability ranging from 2 to 16 hours. The result for all operating plants was a coping duration of 4 to 8 hours.

In evaluating the expected frequency of loss of offsite power, the guide addresses the expected frequency of high winds, including those from tornadoes and hurricanes, and the expected annual snowfall. The impact of other external hazards (e.g., seismic and flooding) on the frequency of loss of offsite power is not addressed. Nor does the guide address the concurrent consequences on the facility of the external hazards impacting offsite power. Consequently, common-cause failures of all onsite and offsite power resulting from a naturally occurring external event are not considered.

The analysis supporting the requirements of 10 CFR 50.54(hh) demonstrates, among other things, the potential for prolonged SBO conditions arising from terrorist actions including large aircraft impacts and high explosives.

In a letter from J.E. Dyer (NRC) to A. Pietrangelo (Nuclear Energy Institute (NEI)) dated December 22, 2006, the NRC endorsed industry-developed guidance (NEI 06-02, Revision 0, "License Amendment Request (LAR) Guidelines," issued December 2006) to demonstrate compliance with the requirements reflected in the NRC's 2002 Interim Compensatory Measures Order (and, subsequently, in 10 CFR 50.54(hh)(2)). To comply with the requirements, each nuclear power plant licensee expanded command and control capabilities and developed strategies and capability to provide cooling to fuel in the reactor and spent fuel pool and to mitigate releases without reliance on the site's ac electrical power distribution system. The following mitigation capabilities were addressed:

- for pressurized water reactors (PWRs): » additional sources of coolant water for the reactor and steam generators » methods to reduce pressure in and feed cooling water to the steam generators
  - methods to cool the reactor core and minimize releases of radioactive materials from containment
- for BWRs:
  - additional sources of coolant water for the reactor
  - methods to reduce reactor pressure and feed cooling water to the reactor
  - methods to cool the reactor core and reduce releases of radioactive materials from containment
- for spent fuel pools:
  - additional sources of coolant water for and methods to inject or spray to the spent fuel pools
  - methods to control leakage from damage to the spent fuel pools

- methods to reduce releases of radioactive materials from the spent fuel pools

The strategies, called EDMGs, implemented to meet the requirements of the 2002 Interim Compensatory Measures Order, subsequent facility-specific license conditions, and ultimately 10 CFR 50.54(hh)(2), did not address external natural hazards (e.g., seismic, flooding, tornadoes, hurricanes) or initiating events other than extensive damage to the facilities caused by large fires or explosions. The EDMGs were designed to assist in the mitigation of one particular beyond-design-basis scenario (i.e., loss of large areas of the facility due to fires or explosions) that typically could involve SBO. The implementing guidance for the EDMGs sets expectations that the amount and capacity of equipment to implement the strategies should be sufficient to mitigate the consequences of an event that affects only one unit. In addition, the implementing guidance for the EDMGs specifies that the required mitigation equipment used under the EDMGs should be stored in an area physically separated by more than 91 meters (300 feet) from the equipment that could have been damaged by a large fire or explosion. The equipment is not expected to be protected from design-basis or beyond-design-basis external events, such as floods, earthquakes, or high winds.

Finally, critical instrumentation and control systems typically depend on the availability of direct current (dc) electrical power at the facility. During a prolonged SBO, when ac power would not be available and the battery banks become depleted, functional failure would occur for nearly all instrumentation and control systems for monitoring critical parameters and operating critical systems that ensure the integrity of the fuel in the reactor and spent fuel pools and maintaining containment structures.

Task Force Evaluation

Information available at the time of this report indicates that the earthquake at Fukushima Dai-ichi on March 11, 2011, caused a loss of all offsite sources of ac power to the six units, and the ensuing tsunami caused failure of the emergency diesel generators for Units 1 through 4. It appears that Unit 1 also suffered damage to its onsite dc power source because of the tsunami. While most of the emergency diesel generators in Units 5 and 6 also failed due to the tsunami, Unit 6 had one air-cooled emergency diesel generator that was not lost; operators cross-tied that generator to essential Unit 5 and 6 systems, thus retaining the ability to cool the Unit 5 and 6 reactors and spent fuel pools. The scope of the damage to the offsite power infrastructure from the earthquake combined with the damage to the site from the tsunami resulted in the inability to restore any ac electrical power to Units 1 through 4 for many days. The onsite emergency ac power sources have not yet been restored and, while ac power from offsite has been rerouted to the facility, damage to the onsite electrical distribution and other critical equipment from the tsunami has not allowed full utilization of this offsite ac power for installed plant equipment in Units 1 through 4. These four units were in a prolonged SBO for many days and still are significantly challenged regarding the reliable distribution and use of ac electrical power.

Under these circumstances, factors that prevented restoration of power included (1) common-cause failure of onsite emergency ac sources due to flooding, (2) common-cause failure of ac electrical distribution due to flooding, (3) common-cause failure of offsite (nonemergency) ac power distribution due to earthquake ground motion, and (4) offsite infrastructure degradation from the earthquake and tsunami, which may have impeded efforts to restore offsite power.

The Commission's SBO requirements provide assurance that each nuclear power plant can maintain adequate core cooling and maintain containment integrity for its approved coping period (typically 4 or 8 hours) following an SBO. Also, if available, the equipment used for compliance with 10 CFR 50.54(hh)(2) would provide additional ability to cool either the core or the spent fuel pool and mitigate releases from primary and secondary containment during a prolonged SBO. The implementing guidance for SBO focuses on high winds and heavy snowfalls in assessing potential external causes of loss of offsite power, but does not consider the likelihood of loss of offsite power from other causes such as earthquakes and flooding. Also, the SBO rule does not require the ability to maintain reactor coolant system integrity (i.e., PWR reactor coolant pump seal integrity) or to cool spent fuel. Further, the SBO rule focuses on preventing fuel damage and therefore does not consider the potential for the buildup of hydrogen gas inside containment during a prolonged SBO condition and the potential need to power hydrogen igniters in certain containment designs to mitigate the buildup of hydrogen. Nor does it consider containment overpressure considerations and the need to vent the containment in certain designs. Finally, the SBO rule does not require consideration of the impact on the station, and particularly on the onsite ac generation and distribution, of the natural event that caused the loss of offsite ac electrical power.

During the prolonged SBO condition at the Fukushima Dai-ichi units, after the batteries were damaged or depleted and no ac power was available to operate equipment or recharge the batteries, the operators faced significant challenges in understanding the condition of the reactors, containments, and spent fuel pools because instrumentation was either lacking or not functioning properly.

The Task Force concludes that revising 10 CFR 50.63 to expand the coping capability to include cooling the spent fuel, preventing a loss-of-coolant accident, and preventing containment failure would be a significant benefit. The Task Force also concludes that a strategy is needed to provide these functions for a prolonged period without ac power from the normal offsite or emergency onsite sources without the vital ac distribution systems within the plant. The Task Force developed a three-part strategy to achieve this objective. First, licensees would need a coping capability to maintain these functions for at least 8 hours at each unit. This capability should minimize reliance on operator action during this period in recognition of the potential for adverse work conditions related to the cause of the prolonged SBO. Also, this 8-hour coping period would provide sufficient time to enable the operators to focus their efforts on restoring ac power and deploying onsite equipment for the extended coping period to follow. Second, licensees would need an extended coping capability to maintain these functions for at least 72 hours. The Task Force envisions that establishing this extended coping capability would involve extensive operator actions during the 8-hour coping period to deploy portable equipment maintained at the site in a manner that protects it from the severe natural phenomena that may cause it to be needed. The purpose of the extended coping capability is to provide a bridge to the third component, which would be a sustainable cooling capability that would utilize preplanned and prestaged equipment at an offsite location that could be delivered and installed within 72 hours. The planning would need to consider the potential for degraded transportation infrastructure resulting from severe natural phenomena. The Task Force envisions that several sites might share the same prestaged equipment, provided that those sites are not susceptible to severe damage from the same initiating event (e.g., earthquake or hurricane) requiring concurrent demand for the same equipment.

To achieve the goal of providing an effective level of defense-in-depth for SBOs caused by external events beyond the design basis, the SBO mitigation equipment would need to be protected from such events. Such protection was not available at Fukushima, where beyond-design-basis flooding caused a prolonged SBO.

In the Task Force's proposed risk-informed, defense-in-depth framework (Recommendation 1 in Section 3 of this report), the extent of the beyond-design-basis external event that would require effective SBO mitigation would be established based on the likelihood (i.e., estimated frequency) of such events. Extensive work on seismic events has demonstrated that significant margin exists beyond a well-formulated seismic design-basis SSE. Typically, a margin of 2 exists above an SSE. That is to say, plant equipment failures are unlikely unless seismic loads are about twice the design-basis SSE loads.

Such loads generally correspond to earthquake frequencies 5 to 10 times less likely than the design-basis SSE. The Task Force therefore concludes that SBO equipment designed to the SSE would likely be sufficiently robust to function following a reasonably foreseeable beyond-design-basis seismic event.

The Task Force has concluded that the situation is somewhat different in terms of beyond-design-basis flooding. First, flooding can be caused by a number of different phenomena: river flooding; dam failure; precipitation; storm surge; tsunami; or internal failures of pipes, pumps, or tanks within the plant. Second, flooding can have a cliff-edge effect; that is, a small increase in flooding level can produce a large effect in terms of equipment failure and potential plant damage. With respect to this issue, the experience at Fukushima Dai-ichi Units 5 and 6 appears more informative than that at Fukushima Dai-ichi Units 1, 2, 3, and 4. Units 5 and 6 are sited at an elevation of 13 meters (43 feet) above sea level and, based on the information available, the tsunami reached a level of 14 meters (46 feet), producing about 1 meter (3 feet) of flooding on the site. In contrast, Units 1 through 4 appear to have been inundated by about 5 meters (16 feet) of sea water. The extensive damage at Units 1 through 4 is therefore not surprising. However, Units 5 and 6 also experienced extensive damage of critical safety equipment as a result of about 1 meter (3 feet) of flooding, leaving the units at significant risk of core damage. Only one air-cooled diesel generator remained available at Unit 6 and functioned with significant operator action to maintain cooling at the two units. This circumstance illustrates the concept of a cliff-edge effect.

The Task Force also considered external fires, as well as tornado and hurricane winds, as they relate to the qualification of SBO equipment. The Task Force has concluded that the existing regulations for both fires and high-wind requirements include sufficient safety margins to obviate the need for additional special protection for SBO equipment. The Task Force concludes that neither external fires nor high winds should be characterized as "cliff-edge" phenomena.

Based on the preceding considerations, the Task Force concludes that, to have SBO equipment function effectively as a layer of defense-in-depth, it would need to be protected from flooding beyond the design basis. The Task Force has also concluded that the safety margin built into the design-basis flood would not be sufficient to provide the desired level of protection.

The Task Force considers the issue of flood protection for SBO equipment to be significant and recognizes that flooding protection of such equipment would require it to be located at a suitable elevation (above the design-basis flood plus a significant margin) or require it to have an effective watertight enclosure. Establishing such protections may be difficult at some sites. Nevertheless, the Task Force concludes that such protection of SBO equipment is essential to implementation of the recommended framework for reactor safety.

A beyond-design-basis flood could be established through extensive, probabilistic hazards analysis. As a practical matter, and to prevent undue delays in implementing additional SBO protections, the Task Force concludes that locating SBO mitigation equipment in the plant one level above flood level (about 5 to 6 meters (15 to 20 feet)) or in watertight enclosures would provide sufficient enhanced protection for this level of defense-in-depth.

These recommendations for revision to 10 CFR 50.63 would provide additional safety margins for a prolonged SBO as a part of the overall risk-informed, defense-in-depth regulatory framework providing adequate protection of public health and safety.

In addition, the EDMGs and associated equipment could be helpful and available promptly to the operators to mitigate accidents such as those that occurred at Fukushima. However, the two issues discussed above result in limited effectiveness of the EDMG strategies for naturally occurring events that typically affect more than one unit.

As an interim measure, the equipment to implement the EDMGs would need to be reasonably protected from external events (i.e., stored in existing locations that are reasonably protected from significant floods and involve robust structures with enhanced protection from seismic and wind-related events). In addition, this equipment would need to be expanded to provide sufficient capacity to allow for a multiunit event response.

Recommendation 4

The Task Force recommends that the NRC strengthen SBO mitigation capability at all operating and new reactors for design-basis and beyond-design-basis external events.

The Task Force recommends that the Commission direct the staff to begin the actions given below to further enhance the ability of nuclear power plants to deal with the effects of prolonged SBO conditions at single and multiunit sites without damage to the nuclear fuel in the reactor or spent fuel pool and without the loss of reactor coolant system or primary containment integrity.

4.1. Initiate rulemaking to revise 10 CFR 50.63 to require each operating and new reactor licensee to (1) establish a minimum coping time of 8 hours for a loss of all ac power, (2) establish the equipment, procedures, and training necessary to implement an "extended loss of all ac" coping time of 72 hours for core and spent fuel pool cooling and for reactor coolant system and primary containment integrity as needed, and (3) preplan and prestage offsite resources to support uninterrupted core and spent fuel pool cooling, and reactor coolant system and containment integrity as needed, including the ability to deliver the equipment to the site in the time period allowed for extended coping, under conditions involving significant degradation of offsite transportation infrastructure associated with significant natural disasters.

- The purpose of the 8-hour minimum coping capability is to enable operators to restore ac power or to establish the proposed 72-hour extended coping capability. Core and spent fuel pool cooling would need to be provided and primary containment isolation capability and reactor coolant system integrity maintained by equipment (including essential instrumentation and controls) independent of ac power (e.g., turbine-driven, diesel-driven, dc-operated, air-operated, or passive systems).

- The 8-hour coping systems and equipment would be protected from damage from all design-basis events and extended beyond-design-basis events by either locating the equipment one level (i.e., 5 to 6 meters (15 to 20 feet)) above the plant design-basis flooding level or in water-tight enclosures.

- The 8-hour coping strategy should ensure that core and spent fuel pool cooling is maintained and unmanageable leakage of coolant does not occur (e.g., from PWR reactor coolant pump seal failure).

- The 8-hour coping strategy should also ensure that containment integrity can be established if needed, including the capability to operate wetwell vents for BWR facilities with Mark I and Mark II containments, and one train of hydrogen igniters at BWR facilities with Mark III containments and at PWR facilities with ice condenser containments.

- The design of the systems supporting the 8-hour minimum coping time should be based on a conservative analysis of the capacity of ac-independent equipment and instrumentation. The 8-hour coping capability should only rely on permanently installed equipment. Operator actions relied upon to maintain this coping capability during this 8-hour period should be limited to those types of actions consistent with routine types of operational activities governed by established procedures and training. This would enable the operators to focus on actions needed to restore ac power and to deploy and operate equipment to be used for the extended coping period. The systems and procedures necessary for this function need not be single failure-proof, but they should be included in the plant's licensing basis (i.e., described in the final safety analysis report) and should be subject to the quality assurance requirements of Appendix B to 10 CFR Part 50.

- The design of the systems supporting the 72-hour extended coping time should cover the same scope of functions as the 8-hour minimum coping time, but it can be based on realistic analysis with reasonable operator action using portable or permanently installed equipment governed by established procedures and training. This extended coping time will be sufficient to allow time for the effective acquisition, transportation, installation, and use of preplanned and prestaged offsite resources for continued achievement of the goals of core and spent fuel pool cooling, and reactor coolant system and primary containment integrity.

- The prestaged equipment could be used to satisfy these requirements at multiple sites as long as the sites would not reasonably be expected to experience the same natural event at the same time.

- As part of the revision to 10 CFR 50.63, the NRC should require that the equipment and personnel necessary to implement the minimum and extended coping strategies shall include sufficient capacity to provide core and spent fuel pool cooling, and reactor cooling system and primary containment integrity for all units at a multiunit facility. The staff should also make the appropriate revisions to the definitions of "station blackout" and "alternate ac source" in 10 CFR 50.2.

4.2. Order licensees to provide reasonable protection for equipment currently provided pursuant to 10 CFR 50.54(hh)(2) from the effects of design-basis external events and to add equipment as needed to address multiunit events while other requirements are being revised and implemented.

- This existing equipment currently provides some of the coping capability that is recommended for the long term, but current storage requirements do not ensure that it will be available after a design-basis external event. This requirement would increase the likelihood that the equipment will be available if called upon.
- The staff should also consider conforming changes to the requirements in 10 CFR 50.54(hh)(2) to address multiunit response capacity

4.2.2. Containment Overpressure Protection

Background

BWRs have robust capability to provide cooling water to the reactor core through many diverse safety-related and nonsafety-related systems when ac power is available. In addition, BWRs typically have two ac-independent ways of providing cooling water. In October 1975, the NRC published NUREG-75/014, "Reactor Safety Study: An Assessment of Accident Risks in U.S. Commercial Nuclear Power Plants (WASH-1400)." One of the many insights developed through the study was that the risk of containment failure during severe accidents was higher at BWRs with Mark I containments because the containment volume of Mark I containment designs was significantly less than that of the other containment designs, approximately one-sixth the volume of large dry PWR containments.

In December 1990, the NRC published NUREG-1150, which documented a relatively high containment failure probability in the event of core damage at a BWR with a Mark I containment design because of the smaller containment volume. The failure probability was dominated by accident sequences involving a loss of feedwater with loss of decay heat removal (due to multiple failures of safety systems) resulting in core damage and subsequent containment failure. These sequences are often referred to as "TW" sequences. A prolonged SBO can also produce these failure sequences.

Concurrent with the development of NUREG-1150, the NRC completed the Containment Performance Improvement Program for Mark I Containments, identifying a number of recommendations to enhance the performance of these containment designs. The NRC staff described the improvement program recommendations in SECY-89-017, "Mark I Containment Performance Improvement Program," issued January 1989. The Commission evaluated the staff recommendations and determined that the containment improvements should be evaluated on a plant-specific basis through the IPE program, with the exception of the recommendation for hardened wetwell vents. Specifically, the Commission directed the staff to approve the installation of hardened vents under the provisions of 10 CFR 50.59, "Changes, Tests and Experiments," for licensees that, on their own initiative, elected to incorporate that improvement into their plants.

The staff issued GL 89-16, "Installation of a Hardened Wetwell Vent," on September 1, 1989, describing the safety benefits of the hardened vent modification and requesting licensees to provide information on their plans to install that modification, or to provide cost information should they choose not to install the modification. Eventually, all BWR facilities with Mark I containment designs voluntarily installed a hardened vent. No regulatory requirement was imposed. The designs of those vents varied from plant to plant. At some facilities, the hardened vent relied on ac-operated valves, some relied on dc-operated or air-operated valves, and some incorporated passive rupture disks along with isolation valves. Each different design has different operational complexities during a prolonged SBO scenario. The updated final safety analysis report for each facility includes a description of the hardened vent, but the vent is not a required design feature for that facility.

In BWRs with a Mark II containment design, the containment volume could be approximately 25 percent larger than the volume of Mark I containments. In the resolution of GSI157, "Containment Performance," the staff concluded that that the need for hardened vents at BWRs with Mark II containments should be evaluated on a plant-specific basis through the IPE program. Eight BWR units in the United States have Mark II containment designs. Three of these units have installed hardened vents, and the remaining five units at three sites have not installed hardened vents.

Task Force Evaluation

Information available at the time of this report indicates that, during the days following the Fukushima Dai-ichi prolonged SBO event, primary containment (drywell) pressure in Units 1, 2, and 3 substantially exceeded the design pressure for the containments. The operators attempted to vent containment, but they were significantly challenged operating the wetwell (suppression pool) vents because of complications from the prolonged SBO. Units 1, 2, 3, and 4 use the Mark I containment design; however, because Mark II containment designs are only slightly larger in volume than Mark I containment designs, it can reasonably be concluded that a Mark II under similar circumstances would have suffered similar consequences.

The process at Fukushima Dai-ichi Units 1, 2, 3, and 4 for venting the wetwell involves opening one ac-powered motor-operated valve to permit air pressure to open air-operated valves in the vent line, and then opening another ac-powered motor-operated valve in line with the air-operated valves, permitting containment pressure to impact a rupture disk designed to open if containment pressure is significantly above design pressure. If all of these actions are successful, the containment would vent directly to the plant stack, and containment integrity could be reestablished by closing either the in-line ac-powered motor-operated valve or the air-operated valves. In a prolonged SBO situation, these actions would not be possible from the control room because of the loss of ac power and the depletion of the batteries providing dc control power for the valves. It is unclear whether the operators were ever successful in venting the containment in Unit 1, 2, or 3. The operators' inability to vent the containments complicated their ability to cool the reactor core, challenged the containment function, and likely resulted in the leakage of hydrogen gas into the reactor building, precipitating significant explosions in Units 1, 3, and 4.

Ensuring that BWR Mark I and Mark II containments have reliable hardened venting capability would significantly enhance the capability of those BWRs to mitigate serious beyond-design-basis accidents. A reliable venting system could be designed to be independent of ac power and to operate with limited operator actions from the control room. Alternatively, a reliable venting capability could be provided through a passive containment venting design, such as rupture disks with ac-independent isolation valves to reestablish containment following rupture of the disk. The Task Force concludes that the addition or confirmation of a reliable hardened wetwell vent in BWR facilities with Mark I and Mark II containment designs would have a significantly safety benefit.

During the longer term review, the staff needs to reevaluate the design of other containment structures for operating reactors to reaffirm the past conclusion that hardened vents are not necessary to mitigate certain beyond-design-basis accident scenarios.

Recommendation 5
The Task Force recommends requiring reliable hardened vent designs in BWR facilities with Mark I and Mark II containments.

The Task Force recommends that the Commission direct the staff to take the following actions to ensure the effectiveness of hardened vents:

5.1. Order licensees to include a reliable hardened vent in BWR Mark I and Mark II containments.

- This order should include performance objectives for the design of hardened vents to ensure reliable operation and ease of use (both opening and closing) during a prolonged SBO.

5.2. Reevaluate the need for hardened vents for other containment designs, considering the insights from the Fukushima accident. Depending on the outcome of the reevaluation, appropriate regulatory action should be taken for any containment designs requiring hardened vents.

4.2.3 Combustible Gas Control

Background

The NRC regulations in 10 CFR 50.44, "Combustible Gas Control for Nuclear Power Reactors," require reactors either to operate with their containment atmosphere inerted, resulting in the lack of oxygen to support combustion, or to have the capability for controlling combustible gas generated from a metal-water reaction involving approximately three-quarters of the fuel cladding so that there is no impact on the containment structural integrity. RG 1.7, "Control of Combustible Gas Concentrations In Containment," provides further guidance on regulatory expectations for combustible gas control.

BWR facilities with Mark I and Mark II containment structures are required to operate their containments with inerted atmospheres. BWR facilities with Mark III containments and PWR facilities with ice condenser containments are required to have hydrogen igniters inside containment to control the buildup of hydrogen gas.

These igniters are operated in two redundant trains, with each train powered by one of the redundant safety-grade dc electrical power systems. GSI-189 raised questions about the effectiveness of these igniter systems during a prolonged SBO scenario.

In response to the issues raised in GSI-189, licensees operating BWRs with Mark III containments and PWRs with ice condenser containments voluntarily installed nonsafety-grade backup electrical power to one train of the igniters, independent of the safety-grade ac and dc onsite power systems. PWR facilities with large dry containments do not control hydrogen buildup inside the containment structure because the containment volume is sufficient to keep the pressure spike of potential hydrogen deflagrations within the design pressure of the structure.

Task Force Evaluation

Information available at the time of this report indicates that, during the days following the Fukushima prolonged SBO event, Units 1, 3, and 4 experienced explosions, causing significant damage to the reactor buildings for those units. It is believed that the explosions in Units 1 and 3 resulted from hydrogen gas that was liberated inside the drywell during high-temperature zirconium fuel cladding reactions with water and that hydrogen gas migrated to the reactor building.

The migration route of the hydrogen gas from the primary containment to reactor building has not yet been determined definitively; however, the failure to prevent, through containment venting, the primary containment pressure from significantly exceeding the design pressure likely contributed to the transport of hydrogen gas.

It is believed that the explosion in the Unit 4 reactor building also resulted from hydrogen gas, but the source of the gas in Unit 4 is not yet clear. Unit 2 may also have experienced a hydrogen explosion in its suppression pool inside containment. However, the mechanism for suppression pool failure remains unclear.

The method of combustible gas control in BWR Mark I and Mark II containments (i.e., containment inerting with nitrogen) will prevent hydrogen fires or explosions as long as containment remains isolated, but it will not eliminate the hydrogen resulting from an accident damaging the core. In contrast, other designs eliminate hydrogen through controlled burning (BWR Mark III and PWR ice condenser containment designs) or by accommodating an associated hydrogen explosion (PWR large dry containments).

This means that in a BWR Mark I or Mark II containment, the hydrogen must be kept in containment by controlling containment pressure without venting (i.e., through heat removal from the containment when possible) or by venting to a safe location.

Implementation of Task Force Recommendation 4, associated with prolonged SBO, would reduce the likelihood of core damage and hydrogen production. In addition, implementation of Recommendation 5 to enhance the containment venting capabilities for Mark I and Mark II containments, while primarily intended for overpressure protection, would also provide for the reliable venting of hydrogen to the atmosphere. These two steps would greatly reduce the likelihood of hydrogen explosions from a severe accident.

Sufficient information is not yet available for the Task Force to reasonably formulate any further specific recommendations related to combustible gas control based on insights from the Fukushima Dai-ichi accident.

Recommendation 6

The Task Force recommends, as part of the longer term review, that the NRC identify insights about hydrogen control and mitigation inside containment or in other buildings as additional information is revealed through further study of the Fukushima Dai-ichi accident.

4.2.4. Spent Fuel Pool Safety

Background

SSCs for spent fuel storage and handling have safety classifications that reflect their importance to safety. SSCs essential to retaining the inventory of spent fuel pool water covering the spent fuel and to maintaining a substantial margin to criticality are typically classified as safety related. Such safety-related SSCs include the spent fuel pool structure and penetrations, the spent fuel storage racks, the neutron-absorbing panels in the racks, and the spent fuel itself.

Some fuel handling equipment is also safety related. Because the consequences of many fuel handling events and loss of spent fuel forced cooling events have been evaluated and found to be small, these events are not classified as design-basis events.

Consequently, other spent fuel storage and handling equipment and spent fuel pool water inventory makeup and cooling systems may not be classified as safety related. At U.S. reactors, some of the spent fuel pool cooling and makeup systems are powered by safety-grade ac electrical power and some are powered by nonsafety-grade ac electrical power.

Licensees developed the EDMGs, described in Section 4.2.1 of this report, to maintain or restore spent fuel pool cooling and mitigate releases under the circumstances associated with the loss of large areas of the plant due to fire or explosion. These requirements arose from analyses conducted by the NRC staff after September 11, 2001, that demonstrated, among other things, the potential for prolonged SBO conditions.

The NRC regulations in 10 CFR 50.36, "Technical Specifications," describe the requirements for technical specifications included in each facility operating license. The technical specifications describe requirements, called limiting conditions for operation (LCOs), for the characteristics of safety systems and components that must be available during various reactor operating modes. Specifically for electrical power systems, when the reactor is operating, the LCOs typically require two independent onsite and at least two offsite ac electrical power systems to be operable to provide electrical power to the safety equipment. When the reactor is shut down and defueled for maintenance work and all of the fuel is placed in the spent fuel pool, the LCOs do not require any electrical power systems to be operable. In this condition, the heat load in the spent fuel pool is highest, and the time margin to boil could be as little as several hours immediately after transfer of the fuel from the reactor to the spent fuel pool.

The fuel could be at risk of uncovery in as a few as 10 hours without pool cooling; ac electrical power is important to the cooling the nuclear fuel in the spent fuel pools and to providing ventilation systems to minimize the release of radioactive materials. The regulation in 10 CFR 50.36(b) authorizes the NRC to include additional technical specifications as it finds appropriate.

The spent fuel pools at Fukushima Dai-ichi Units 1 through 4 contained many fewer assemblies than typically stored in U.S. reactor unit spent fuel pools. Unit 4 contained more assemblies than the other units because Unit 4 was in an extended outage and the reactor was defueled, transferring all assemblies to the spent fuel pool to facilitate maintenance activities associated with the reactor systems.

The storage capacity of U.S. reactor unit spent fuel pools ranges from less than 2,000 assemblies to nearly 5,000 assemblies, with an average storage capacity of approximately 3,000 spent fuel assemblies.

Fuel Assemblies in the Reactor Cores and Spent Fuel Pools at Fukushima Dai-ichi Units 1 through 4

	Reactor Core	Spent Fuel Pool
Unit 1	400	292
Unit 2	548	587
Unit 3	548	514
Unit 4	0	1,331

Typically, the U.S. spent fuel pools are filled with spent fuel assemblies up to approximately three-quarters of their capacity. In addition to the unit-specific spent fuel pools at the Fukushima Dai-ichi facility, a separate spent fuel storage building existed onsite with wet pool storage of spent fuel containing 6,291 spent fuel assemblies. U.S. reactor facilities do not typically have an additional spent fuel wet storage building like that at Fukushima Dai-ichi.

A spent fuel assembly just removed from a BWR after an operating cycle generates approximately 10 kilowatts of heat, and that heat level diminishes rapidly over time. Within a short period of time after removal from the reactor, spent fuel assemblies are coolable with water sprays, and within a few years, the assembly rate of heat generation is reduced to a few percent of its original heat generation rate. Consequently, the number of spent fuel assemblies in the spent fuel pool does not significantly affect the ability to cool the spent fuel in the pool.

Many U.S. reactors have dry spent fuel storage capability in addition to wet storage in the spent fuel pools. These dry storage facilities are called independent spent fuel storage installations, and fuel stored in such an installation first must be placed into a dry cask. The NRC reviews and certifies the designs for these dry casks. Typically, 5 years must pass from the time an assembly is removed from the reactor before it can be placed into a dry cask. After 5 years, the heat generation rate is very low.

In addition to responding to prolonged SBO conditions, the EDMGs also address contingencies for cases when the spent fuel pools are unable to retain water above the top of the fuel. This situation could also occur with significant beyond-design-basis seismic events. One effective strategy for mitigation is to blanket the spent fuel with a water spray.

Current spent fuel pool instrumentation provides limited indication and typically depends on the availability of dc electrical power at the facility. That power is provided either through inverters powered by ac electrical power or by the station's safety-grade redundant battery banks. Direct spent fuel pool level indication is rarely provided in the control room for the current nuclear fleet. Typically, level is measured using a level switch in the skimmer surge tank. During a prolonged SBO, ac power would not be available and the battery banks would be depleted, resulting in functional failure of nearly all instrumentation and control systems for monitoring spent fuel pool parameters and operating systems ensuring the integrity of the fuel in the spent fuel pools.

Task Force Evaluation

Information available at the time of this report indicates that the earthquake at Fukushima caused a loss of all offsite sources of ac power to the six units, and the ensuing tsunami caused the failure of the emergency diesel generators for Units 1 through 4. The scope of the damage to the offsite power infrastructure from the earthquake, combined with the damage to the site from the tsunami, resulted in the inability to restore any ac electrical power to Units 1 through 4 for many days.

During this protracted SBO condition, no ac power was available to operate equipment, and the batteries were depleted. This resulted in having no onsite capability to provide water inventory or cooling to the spent fuel pools, and the operators were significantly challenged in understanding the condition of the spent fuel pools because of the lack of instrumentation or because of instrumentation that was not functioning properly. Eventually, spent fuel cooling was provided by pumper trucks employing high booms to spray water from a distance into the spent fuel pools.

The reliability and availability of U.S. spent fuel pool makeup systems would be better ensured if the NRC had a requirement for those systems to have safety-related ac power that is controlled under a technical specification LCO.

Substantial additional defense-in-depth would be provided, and cooling the spent fuel in a prolonged SBO would have been substantially simplified, with an installed seismically qualified means to spray water into the spent fuel pools, including an easily accessible connection to supply the water (e.g., using a portable pump or pumper truck) at grade outside the building.

The lack of information on the conditions of the fuel in the Fukushima spent fuel pools was a significant problem in monitoring the course of the accident and contributed to a poor understanding of possible radiation releases and to confusion about the need and priorities for support equipment. The Task Force therefore concludes that reliable information on the conditions in the spent fuel pool is essential to any effective response to a prolonged SBO or other similarly challenging accident.

The Task Force concludes that clear and coherent requirements to ensure that the plant staff can understand the condition of the spent fuel pool and its water inventory and coolability and to provide reliable, diverse, and simple means to cool the spent fuel pool under various circumstances are essential to maintaining defense-in-depth. The Task Force sees significant value in ensuring that sufficient cooling capacity exists under various design-basis natural phenomena.

Final understanding of the detailed sequence of events and the condition of the spent fuel pools will not be fully developed for some time. Based on the information to date, it is clear that the two most cogent insights from the Fukushima accident related to spent fuel pool safety concern (1) the instrumentation to provide information about the condition of the pool and the spent fuel and (2) the plant's capability for cooling and water inventory management. The Task Force's recommendations address these two critical areas.

Recommendation 7

The Task Force recommends enhancing spent fuel pool makeup capability and instrumentation for the spent fuel pool.

The Task Force recommends that the Commission direct the staff to do the following:

7.1. Order licensees to provide sufficient safety-related instrumentation, able to withstand design-basis natural phenomena, to monitor key spent fuel pool parameters (i.e., water level, temperature, and area radiation levels) from the control room.
7.2. Order licensees to provide safety-related ac electrical power for the spent fuel pool makeup system.

7.3. Order licensees to revise their technical specifications to address requirements to have one train of onsite emergency electrical power operable for spent fuel pool makeup and spent fuel pool instrumentation when there is irradiated fuel in the spent fuel pool, regardless of the operational mode of the reactor.

7.4. Order licensees to have an installed seismically qualified means to spray water into the spent fuel pools, including an easily accessible connection to supply the water (e.g., using a portable pump or pumper truck) at grade outside the building.

7.5. Initiate rulemaking or licensing activities or both to require the actions related to the spent fuel pool described in detailed recommendations 7.1–7.4.

4.2.5. Onsite Emergency Actions

Background

A number of guidelines and procedures guide onsite emergency actions by reactor operators, depending on the nature and extent of events at the plant. As discussed in previous sections, nuclear reactors are designed to handle the loss of offsite electrical power with multiple onsite emergency diesel generators. Events such as a loss of offsite power are within the plants' design basis and are addressed by plant procedures (typically abnormal operating procedures, alarm response procedures, and EOPs). These procedures instruct the plant operators on the steps necessary to take the plant from full-power operation to a safe shutdown condition.

EOPs have long been part of the NRC's safety requirements. The NRC regulations address them through the quality assurance requirements of Criterion V, "Instructions, Procedures, and Drawings," and Criterion VI, "Document Control," in Appendix B to 10 CFR Part 50, and in the administrative controls section of the technical specifications for each plant. Numerous RGs and technical reports (e.g., NUREG-0660, "NRC Action Plan Developed as a Result of the TMI-2 Accident," issued May 1980; NUREG-0737, "Clarification of TMI Action Plan Requirements," issued November 1980; and NUREG-0711, "Human Factors Engineering Program Review Model," issued February 2004) also address EOPs. In addition, the EOPs are the subject of a national consensus standard (American National Standards Institute/ American Nuclear Society 3.21994, "Administrative Controls and Quality Assurance for the Operational Phase of Nuclear Power Plants"). The training and both the written and simulator exams for licensing reactor operators and senior reactor operators also include the EOPs. While implementing EOPs, the event command and control functions remain in the control room under the direction of the shift supervisor and plant manager, both of whom have senior reactor operator licenses.

An SBO is considered to be beyond the plant's design basis. This means that the regulatory requirements stated above do not apply. Instead, specialized requirements included within 10 CFR 50.63 cover SBO. In addition to addressing the loss of offsite electrical power, 10 CFR 50.63 requires reactor licensees to address the simultaneous loss of onsite and offsite electrical power (i.e., SBO) by providing an additional source of electrical power (referred to as an "alternate ac" source) or by showing that the plant could cope with a complete loss of ac power by removing decay heat for a specified period of time. In the case of an SBO, the operators would follow a set of procedures (usually abnormal operating procedures) required by 10 CFR 50.63(c)(ii) and (iii). These procedures would instruct the operators in maintaining safety functions using the alternate ac power source or through coping strategies. In addition, procedures would direct operators to take steps to restore the onsite and offsite sources of ac power.

In addition, the nuclear industry developed SAMGs during the 1980s and 1990s in response to the TMI accident and followup activities. These followup activities included extensive research and study (including several PRAs) on severe accidents and severe accident phenomena. The SAMGs are intended for use by plant technical support staff, usually located in the plant's Technical Support Center (TSC), and are meant to enhance the ability of the operators to manage accident sequences that progress beyond the point where EOPs and other plant procedures are applicable and useful. EOPs typically cover accidents to the point of loss of core cooling and initiation of inadequate core cooling (e.g., core exit temperatures in PWRs greater than 649 degrees Celsius (1,200 degrees Fahrenheit)). As stated in the Westinghouse SAMG documentation, "the SAMG is designed to fill the void between the EOPs and the E-Plan [the procedure and guidance for emergency response]." While implementing SAMGs, the accident command and control functions shift to the TSC and typically to the emergency coordinator or shift technical advisor or both.

In GL 88-20, Supplement 2, "Accident Management Strategies for Consideration in the Individual Plant Examination Process," dated April 4, 1990, the NRC encouraged but did not require licensees to develop and implement SAMGs. Since the SAMGs are voluntary and targeted to technical support staff, the formal training and licensing of plant operators does not address them.

Following the terrorist events of September 11, 2001, the NRC issued security advisories, orders, license conditions, and ultimately a new regulation (10 CFR 50.54(hh)) to require licensees to develop and implement guidance and strategies intended to maintain or restore core cooling and containment and spent fuel pool cooling capabilities under the circumstances associated with the loss of large areas of the plant due to fire or explosion. These requirements have led to the development of EDMGs at all U.S. nuclear power plants. The guidelines and strategies included in the EDMGs are NRC requirements, and the NRC inspected EDMG implementation following the events at Fukushima under TI 2515/183, "Followup to the Fukushima Daiichi Nuclear Station Fuel Damage Event," dated March 23, 2011. The results of this TI are available on the NRC Web site at http://www.nrc.gov/NRR/OVERSIGHT/ASSESS/follow-up-rpts.html. In addition, the NRC added the requirements of 10 CFR 50.54(hh) to the agency's routine inspection program as part of the triennial fire protection inspections.

As stated in the industry's guidance document NEI 06-12, "B.5.b Phase 2&3 Submittal Guideline," Revision 2, issued December 2006 (Agencywide Documents Access and Management System (ADAMS) Accession No. ML070090060), "the initial EDMGs are not a type of emergency operating procedures (EOPs), nor are they intended to be a replacement for EOPs. They are, in fact, intended to be used when the normal command and control structure is disabled and the use of EOPs is not feasible." In terms of command and control, either control room, plant, TSC, or emergency operations facility (EOF) staff could make EDMG decisions. The EDMGs do not play a large role in the formal training and licensing of plant operators.

Task Force Evaluation

The accidents at Fukushima highlight the importance of having plant operators who are well prepared and well supported by technically sound and practical procedures, guidelines, and strategies. In addition, it is clear that a preplanned approach to command and control and decisionmaking during an emergency is vital.

Each of the onsite emergency action programs (the abnormal operating procedures, alarm response procedures, EOPs, SAMGs, and EDMGs) contributes to overall emergency response capability of plant and operators to mitigate accidents. It is clear that the SAMGs and EDMGs complement the EOPs in an important way. The NRC and industry have established the command and control responsibilities for each of these programs, although not necessarily in a consistent manner. Each of these programs was developed at a different time to serve a different purpose, and each of these programs is treated differently in the NRC's regulations, inspection program, and licensing process, as well as in licensee programs and organizations.

Soon after its establishment, the Task Force considered whether to include the SAMGs as a regulatory requirement and whether to require the integration of the SAMGs into a coherent and holistic program for onsite emergency response activities. This was based on the important role the SAMGs would play in onsite emergency response—just as important as that of EOPs and EDMGs, both required programs. To gain insights into the current implementation of the SAMGs, the Task Force requested that NRC inspectors collect information on how each licensee had implemented that industry voluntary initiative. The inspectors collected information on the initial implementation, ongoing training, and maintenance of the SAMGs under TI 2515/184. The results of the inspection under the SAMG TI reinforced the value of making SAMGs a requirement. The inspectors observed inconsistent implementation of SAMGs and attributed it to the voluntary nature of this initiative. The results of this TI are available on the NRC Web site at http://www.nrc.gov/ NRR/OVERSIGHT/ASSESS/ SAMGs.html.

In order to ensure the effectiveness of these onsite emergency action programs and to support the effectiveness of mitigation, sound training as well as other readiness measures are important. The inspections under TI 2515/184 identified that some licensee programs include extensive classroom and simulator training and testing on SAMGs, while others do not.

The Task Force concludes that all U.S. plants have addressed all of the elements of onsite emergency actions that need to be accomplished by reactor operators. However, the overall effectiveness of those programs could be substantially enhanced through further integration, including clarification of transition points, command and control, decisionmaking, and through rigorous training that includes conditions that are as close to real accident conditions as feasible.

The Task Force also concludes that action is warranted to confirm, augment, consolidate, simplify, and strengthen current regulatory and industry programs in a manner that produces a single, comprehensive framework for accident mitigation, built around NRCapproved licensee technical specifications. These modified technical specifications would consolidate EOPs, SAMGs, EDMGs, and other important elements of emergency procedures, guidance, and tools in a manner that would clarify command and control and decisionmaking during accidents.

Integration of these accident support functions in a logical and coherent manner and with appropriate regulatory treatment to ensure the effectiveness of operator actions during events would substantially increase the effectiveness of the overall event mitigation. Since the current requirements in this area apply only to normal operation and emergencies within the plant's design basis, they appear outdated and inconsistent with Commission decisions in policy statements and rulemakings to regulate accident mitigation in other areas beyond the plant's design basis. The Task Force concludes that an expansion of the regulatory requirements to include procedures for beyond-design-basis events is warranted, and that such an expansion would redefine the scope of such activities to include them in the regulatory framework to provide defense-in-depth and to ensure adequate protection of public health and safety.

The new treatment of accident procedures would also include the authority to implement SAMGs and EDMGs as necessary and as described or referenced in the plant technical specifications without the need to seek NRC permission or to invoke 10 CFR 50.54(x) and (y). This change would further clarify authority, streamline decisionmaking, and prevent potential delays in taking important emergency actions.

The effectiveness of onsite emergency actions is a very important part of the overall safety of nuclear power plants. The NRC could strengthen the current system substantially by requiring more formal, rigorous, and frequent training of reactor operators and other onsite emergency response staff on realistic accident scenarios with realistic conditions.

Recommendation 8

The Task Force recommends strengthening and integrating onsite emergency response capabilities such as EOPs, SAMGs, and EDMGs.

8.1. Order licensees to modify the EOP technical guidelines (required by Supplement 1, "Requirements for Emergency Response Capability," to NUREG-0737, issued January 1983 (GL 82-33), to (1) include EOPs, SAMGs, and EDMGs in an integrated manner, (2) specify clear command and control strategies for their implementation, and (3) stipulate appropriate qualification and training for those who make decisions during emergencies.
- The Task Force strongly advises that the NRC encourage plant owners groups to undertake this activity rather than have each licensee develop its own approach. In addition, the Task Force encourages the use of the established NRC practice of publishing RG (rather than NUREGs, supplements to NUREGs, or GLs) for endorsing any acceptable approaches submitted by the industry.

8.2. Modify Section 5.0, "Administrative Controls," of the Standard Technical Specifications for each operating reactor design to reference the approved EOP technical guidelines for that plant design.

8.3. Order licensees to modify each plant's technical specifications to conform to the above changes.

8.4. Initiate rulemaking to require more realistic, hands-on training and exercises on SAMGs and EDMGs for all staff expected to implement the strategies and those licensee staff expected to make decisions during emergencies, including emergency coordinators and emergency directors.

4.3. Emergency Preparedness

If mitigation is not successful in preventing a release of radioactive materials from the plant, EP ensures that adequate protective actions are in place to protect public health and safety. Protective actions are taken to avoid or reduce radiation dose. As a condition of their license, operators of nuclear power plants must develop and maintain EP plans that meet comprehensive NRC EP requirements.

Following the TMI accident in 1979, the NRC revised its regulations to substantially enhance EP requirements. The regulations in 10 CFR 50.47, "Emergency Plans," include the 16 planning standards of 10 CFR 50.47(b), and Appendix E, "Emergency Planning and Preparedness for Production and Utilization Facilities," to 10 CFR Part 50 describes information needed to demonstrate compliance with EP requirements. The NRC considers the evaluation criteria in NUREG-0654, "Criteria for Preparation and Evaluation of Radiological Emergency Response Plans and Preparedness in Support of Nuclear Power Plants," Revision 1, issued November 1980, to be guidance and an acceptable means for demonstrating compliance with the Commission's regulations.

After the events of September 11, 2001, the NRC staff reviewed the EP basis for nuclear power plants, considering the impact of hostile actions unanticipated at the time the basis was established. The staff concluded that the EP basis remains valid. The staff based its conclusion on studies that confirmed that the timing and magnitude of releases related to hostile actions would be no more severe than those associated with the other accident sequences considered in the EP basis. However, hostile actions could present unique challenges to EP programs since they differ from operational events for which licensees and offsite response organizations typically plan, train, and exercise. The accident at Fukushima provides its own unique challenges to EP; however, they are rooted in more traditional accident progression sequences.

The agency is in the final stages of a comprehensive rulemaking effort to revise EP regulations, as outlined in SECY-11-0053, "Final Rule: Enhancements to Emergency Preparedness Regulations (10 CFR Part 50 and 10 CFR Part 52)," dated April 8, 2011. These revisions codify the hostile-action-based enhancements, among others. The Task Force has reviewed the draft final rule, particularly the provisions that provide enhancements that would also address challenges to EP programs caused by an accident like that at Fukushima. The subsections below discuss these provisions.

In analyzing the accident and its impact on EP in the United States, the Task Force focused primarily on EP considerations for multiunit and prolonged SBO events, as discussed in the following section. Section 4.3.2 captures other EP insights beyond that focus.

4.3.1. Emergency Preparedness Considerations for Multiunit Events and Prolonged Station Blackout

The accident at Fukushima has shown that prolonged SBO and multiunit events are realities that must be addressed as part of EP. While of low probability, these events have the potential for severe consequences that require an effective EP response. The Task Force's evaluation in this section focuses on a licensee's capability to respond during these types of events.

Currently, the United States has 29 single-unit sites, 33 dual-unit sites, and 3 triple-unit sites. The agency is currently reviewing new reactor applications that may add units to existing sites; however, no applicant has requested to bring the total number of units at a single site to more than four. In most cases, proposed quadruple-unit sites have physical separation between the two existing and the two proposed units.

Background

Requirements for emergency response personnel, staffing, and emergency worker protection are codified in 10 CFR 50.47(b)(1), 10 CFR 50.47(b)(2), and 10 CFR 50.47(b)(11).

The proposed EP rulemaking amends Appendix E to 10 CFR Part 50 to address concerns about the assignment of tasks or responsibilities to on-shift emergency response organization (ERO) personnel that would potentially overburden them and prevent the timely performance of their functions under the emergency plan. Licensees must have enough on-shift staff to perform specified tasks in various functional areas of emergency response 24 hours a day, 7 days a week.

The regulation in 10 CFR 50.47(b)(2) requires adequate on-shift staffing levels but gives no clear definition of "adequate." This provides some flexibility in how licensees assign emergency plan implementation duties to on-shift personnel. The proposed EP rule better ensures sufficient on-shift staffing in the threat environment after September 11, 2001, by limiting the assignment of responsibilities that on-shift ERO members would likely perform concurrently with their emergency plan functions.

The regulations in 10 CFR 50.47(b)(1) and 10 CFR 50.47(b)(2) require the assignment and definition of emergency response responsibilities to address decisionmaking and command and control.

Dose assessment, or dose projection, as required by 10 CFR 50.47(b)(9), is the primary means for assessing the potential consequences of a radiological emergency. Appendix E to 10 CFR Part 50 describes the required content of emergency plans, including assessment of the impact of the release of radioactive materials.

After declaration of an emergency, licensees must notify the NRC and State and local response organizations. In addition, licensees are responsible for providing notification and instruction to the public within the plume exposure pathway emergency planning zone (EPZ), as required in 10 CFR 50.27(b)(5) and Section IV.D.3 of Appendix E to 10 CFR Part 50. The predominant method used in the United States for alerting the public is an alert and notification system based on sirens to provide an acoustic warning signal. Some sites employ other means, such as tone alert radios and route alerting, as either primary or supplemental alerting methods. The public then typically receives information about an event and offsite protective actions via emergency alert system broadcasts or other means, such as mobile loudspeakers. The State and local governments are responsible for activating systems to alert and notify the public, and FEMA evaluates this capability.

The regulations in 10 CFR 50.47(b)(6) and 10 CFR 50.47(b)(8) cover the communications equipment needed during an emergency.

As a result of the TMI accident, the NRC and others recognized a need to substantially improve the NRC's ability to acquire data on plant conditions during emergencies. The Commission has defined the NRC's role in the event of an emergency primarily as one of monitoring the licensee to ensure that appropriate recommendations are made with respect to offsite protective actions. Other aspects of the NRC role include supporting the licensee with technical analysis and logistic support, supporting offsite authorities (including confirming the licensee's recommendations to offsite authorities), keeping other Federal agencies and entities informed of the status of the incident, and keeping the media informed based on the NRC's knowledge of the status of the incident, including coordination with other public affairs groups.

To fulfill its role, the NRC requires accurate and timely data on four types of parameters:

(1) core and coolant system conditions must be known well enough to assess the extent or likelihood of core damage, (2) conditions inside the containment building must be known well enough to assess the likelihood and consequence of its failure, (3) radioactivity release rates must be available promptly to assess the immediacy and degree of public danger, and (4) data from the plant's meteorological tower are necessary to assess the likely patterns of potential or actual impact on the public.

Experience with the voice-only emergency communications link, previously used for data transmission, has demonstrated that excessive amounts of time are needed for the routine transmission of data and for verification or correction of data that appear questionable. Therefore, the NRC selected the Emergency Response Data System (ERDS) to fulfill the agency's data collection needs. ERDS allows for the direct electronic transmission of selected parameters from the electronic data systems that are currently installed at licensee facilities. ERDS was designed for use only during emergencies and would be activated by the licensees during declared emergencies classified at the Alert lever or higher to begin transmission to the NRC Operations Center. ERDS would be supplemented with voice transmission for essential data not available on the licensee's systems, rather than require a modification to the existing system to transmit that data.

Section IV of Appendix E to 10 CFR Part 50 codifies the requirements for ERDS. The NRC requires power reactor licensees to transmit ERDS data to a server at NRC Headquarters. Many licensees currently use analog modulator/demodulators (modems) to establish point-to-point data connections. Although this technology was state of the art when ERDS was first implemented, it is now obsolete, and replacement equipment is no longer readily available. In addition, the use of modems inherently introduces a cyber security vulnerability to the systems to which the modems are attached.

As part of the current effort to modernize the ERDS infrastructure, the NRC has been working with individual licensees to develop an acceptable solution to replace the existing modems. The NRC chose virtual private network (VPN) technology to create a secure point-to-point data pathway between the licensee site and NRC Headquarters. This technology permits all ERDS-enabled facilities to connect to the NRC simultaneously, thereby enhancing the NRC's ability to respond to incidents that may affect multiple licensees simultaneously, such as grid instability events. Some licensees are currently in the process of replacing the existing analog modems with VPN devices on a voluntary basis, while others have yet to commit to the initiative.

The regulation in 10 CFR 50.47(b)(14) requires periodic drills and exercises to develop key skills and evaluate major portions of emergency response capabilities, and 10 CFR 50.47(b) (15) requires radiological emergency response training. NUREG-0654 includes further detail on the implementation of these regulations.

The regulation in 10 CFR 50.47(b)(8) requires the provision and maintenance of adequate emergency facilities and equipment to support the emergency response. Studies of the TMI accident identified the need for extensive improvements in the overall response to accidents at nuclear plants, including enhanced facilities and systems to support the control room in mitigating the consequences of accidents and to support the licensee's capability to respond to abnormal plant conditions. NUREG-0696, "Functional Criteria for Emergency Response Facilities," issued February 1981, describes the facilities and systems that licensees can use to improve emergency response to accidents, such as the TSC, operational support center

(OSC), and EOF. The document also provides guidance on the functional criteria for these facilities and on the integrated support these facilities offer to the control room.

Licensees must have the capability to augment the on-shift staff within a short time after the declaration of an emergency. To accomplish this, licensees typically staff an onsite TSC, which relieves the control room of emergency response duties and allows operators to focus on reactor plant safety. Responders also staff an onsite OSC to provide an assembly area for damage repair teams. Finally, licensees establish an EOF to function as the center for evaluation and coordination activities related to the emergency and as the focal point for providing information to Federal, State, Tribal, and local authorities involved in the response.

The proposed EP rulemaking amends Section IV.E.8 of Appendix E to 10 CFR Part 50 to address concerns about ERO augmentation during hostile action by requiring licensees to identify alternative facilities as staging areas for responding staff. This alternate site must have the capability for communication with the EOF, control room, and plant security; the capability to perform offsite notifications; and the capability for engineering assessment activities, including damage control team planning and preparation.

Licensees have submitted several requests to the NRC to consolidate EOFs for plants they operate within a State or in multiple States. Previous regulatory standards did not address the capabilities and functional requirements for a consolidated EOF, such as capabilities for handling simultaneous events at two or more sites. The NRC is revising, via the proposed EP rule, the regulations and associated guidance to reflect a performance-based approach for EOFs and to provide functional requirements for these facilities.

Task Force Evaluation

The events in Japan have highlighted the importance of the human element during response to an emergency. The current regulatory approach provides for staffing and protection of staff during postulated reactor accidents. External events on the scale of Fukushima cause concerns that the existing framework would present challenges to personnel and their safety. In particular, the presence of staff onsite during the initiation of the emergency condition, staff needed to augment the current onsite staff, and staff needed for crew relief poses significant challenges during large external events.

The proposed EP rulemaking will require an analysis of the duties of on-shift personnel to ensure the fulfillment of all required functions. The accident at Fukushima supports an expansion of this analysis to include whether enough responders are available for multiunit events. During traditional accident scenarios, most required response personnel would be summoned to the site within a certain required time. During a catastrophic natural disaster, the local infrastructure may challenge the timely augmentation of on-shift personnel. Should licensees choose not to add more on-shift personnel, they would need to have a viable notification and transportation strategy for ensuring that the staff needed to augment the site response would be available to respond effectively. In addition, since more responders are needed during a multiunit event, additional protective equipment would be needed.

Through discussions with inspectors and technical experts, the Task Force has found that the current framework for command and control during an accident has been developed and practiced over the years and that authorities for decisionmaking during an event are well defined. However, in this area as well, multiunit events create a nuance to the command and control structure that is not yet fully developed.

During an accident like that at Fukushima, it may be necessary to make difficult decisions to prioritize limited response resources. The EOF remains the primary facility for interaction with offsite authorities, and the TSC remains the primary facility for technical response to the accident.

Currently, during a General Emergency, the licensee's emergency director assigned with the authority to lead the licensee response is located in the EOF. An emergency director in the TSC remains in command of the technical assessment and damage control aspects of the response. During a multiunit event, the lead TSC official would be in the best position to address the triage and prioritization of resource requirements for each unit.

Ensuring that the response framework contains the correct level of authority, knowledge, and experience is paramount to successful response. In light of the Fukushima accident, the staff should explore concepts such as whether decisionmaking authority is in the correct location (i.e., at the facility), whether currently licensed operators need to be integral to the ERO outside of the control room (i.e., in the TSC), and whether licensee emergency directors should have a formal "license" qualification for severe accident management in addition to their existing qualification requirements, and different than a reactor operator license.

The accident at Fukushima also presented challenges with respect to dose assessment capability because of the multiunit nature of the release. While monitoring the accident, dose assessors at the NRC had to use makeshift, ad hoc methods to consider the source term from these multiple concurrent releases and overlay the release points to arrive at a final sitewide dose projection. The difficulty of conducting this dose assessment highlights the gap in capability for U.S. plants to perform multiunit dose assessment. Currently, dose assessment software (such as the NRC's RASCAL) is not designed to model multiunit accidents. The presence of releases from multiple units and spent fuel pools at Fukushima has highlighted the need for the ability to project doses from releases at multiple units.

In the absence of a software solution, licensees would need to develop emergency plan guidance that outlines how to conduct a multiunit dose assessment, including spent fuel pools as release points, to ensure that this capability exists.

Following a large natural disaster, such as the accident at Fukushima, the ability to notify both government authorities and the public could be challenged. Licensees use traditional telephones, cellular telephones, satellite telephones, short wave radio, and the Internet to communicate with the NRC and State and local governments. The Task Force believes that licensees have enough redundant and diverse methods to communicate with the NRC and State and local governments that it is reasonable to expect the successful communication of a declared emergency onsite. Because of the diverse nature of these methods, it is unlikely that a common-cause failure would disable all means of communication.

With respect to alerting the public within the plume exposure pathway EPZ, the Task Force finds that the provisions being incorporated by the EP rulemaking will enhance the existing public alerting framework. The proposed final rule addresses provisions for a backup to the primary alert and notification system. The backup measures would be implemented if the primary means of alert and notification were unavailable during an emergency. These enhancements will provide an additional layer of preparedness that will be useful during a large-scale natural disaster.

Communications equipment plays a critical role in the effective conduct of any incident response effort. Currently, licensees use an array of different telecommunications devices to communicate onsite, including hardwired telephones, cellular telephones, satellite telephones, radios, and pagers. Since many of these devices depend on electrical power, most by battery, their use during a prolonged SBO would be limited by battery life. Additionally, since hardwired telephones and cellular telephones rely upon offsite infrastructure (i.e., phone switches and cell towers) that could be damaged or destroyed by the event, their use may be limited. Onsite radios may be hampered by a lack of power to radio repeaters.

During the accident at Fukushima, numerous organizations assessed the evolution of the situation onsite and sought data to aid decisionmakers during the response. Having accurate, real-time data from the site allows for the performance of a multitude of analyses. In addition, the more data that can be provided using automated sources, the less burden placed on the licensee to provide information. Having data provided directly from automated sources at the site also gives confidence to government authorities and the public that the plant operator is not filtering the details of an evolving accident. However, the current regulatory approach and requirements do not ensure that ERDS data would be available during a prolonged SBO or during other natural disasters when power supplies could be lost and transmission capability may be affected.

Another challenge evident from Fukushima is the need for archived data to aid in the reconstruction of events after an accident. When ERDS data are transmitted to the NRC servers, the NRC stores the incoming data. Ensuring that licensees have reliable power sources and transmission methods will therefore ensure that data are archived for accident reconstruction.

Effective onsite and offsite response necessitates abundant communication. During a prolonged SBO, an awareness of plant conditions becomes even more critical. Ensuring that the NRC and State stakeholders continue to receive plant data, especially during the most severe accidents, adds another layer of both technical assessment capability and confidence that onsite conditions are being communicated in a timely and accurate way.

Effective and timely ERDS modernization is necessary to ensure that during multiunit events, the NRC is able to receive data from all affected nuclear units. Given the current limited modem connections available for simultaneous use, the NRC should ensure that licensees upgrade to the VPN solution in an expedient manner. Once the current modernization effort is complete, the staff should then evaluate additional modernization to address redundant transmission capability, completeness of data, and continuous monitoring.

The conduct of training and exercises provides confidence that emergency plans are workable and that personnel would be successful in mitigating the consequences of an accident. However, EP drills and exercises currently do not consider prolonged SBO or multiunit accident scenarios. Therefore, training and exercises should explore and practice the concepts of command and control, decisionmaking, prioritization, and contingency planning under these conditions. Since licensees will likely rely heavily on offsite support during this type of event, exercising the steps necessary to identify and acquire offsite equipment and support is an important element to practice.

Both prolonged SBO and multiunit events present new challenges to EP facilities that were not considered when the NRC issued NUREG-0696. The accident at Fukushima has clearly shown that these events are a reality. While several utilities have implemented combined EOFs that are capable of handling multiunit events, licensee onsite TSCs and OSCs have not been designed or drilled for multiunit events. TSCs and OSCs are not as conducive to consolidation since most job functions in these facilities would be specific to a particular unit, and attempts to have one person manage the technical response for multiple units could introduce opportunities for errors. The proposed EP rulemaking requires the identification of alternate facilities.

During a multiunit event, licensees could use both the normal and alternate facilities to provide enough capacity for response. The proposed EP rulemaking codifies performance-based requirements for combined EOFs. EOFs are more suited to handling multiunit events since they represent the interface with offsite responders, regardless of the number of onsite units in emergency status. The NRC should use a performance-based approach to TSCs, OSCs, and EOFs to ensure flexibility for licensees.

Recommendation 9

The Task Force recommends that the NRC require that facility emergency plans address prolonged SBO and multiunit events.

The Task Force recommends that the Commission direct the staff to do the following:

9.1. Initiate rulemaking to require EP enhancements for multiunit events in the following areas:
- personnel and staffing
- dose assessment capability
- training and exercises
- equipment and facilities
- communications capability
- ERDS capability
- training and exercises
- equipment and facilities

9.2. Initiate rulemaking to require EP enhancements for prolonged SBO in the following areas:
- communications capability
- ERDS capability
- training and exercises
- equipment and facilities

9.3. Order licensees to do the following until rulemaking is complete:
- Determine and implement the required staff to fill all necessary positions for responding to a multiunit event.
- Add guidance to the emergency plan that documents how to perform a multiunit dose assessment (including releases from spent fuel pools) using the licensee's site-specific dose assessment software and approach.
- Conduct periodic training and exercises for multiunit and prolonged SBO scenarios. Practice (simulate) the identification and acquisition of offsite resources, to the extent possible.
- Ensure that EP equipment and facilities are sufficient for dealing with multiunit and prolonged SBO scenarios.
- Provide a means to power communications equipment needed to communicate onsite (e.g., radios for response teams and between facilities) and offsite (e.g., cellular telephones, satellite telephones) during a prolonged SBO.
- Maintain ERDS capability throughout the accident.

9.4. Order licensees to complete the ERDS modernization initiative by June 2012 to ensure multiunit site monitoring capability.

Recommendation 10

The Task Force recommends, as part of the longer term review, that the NRC should pursue additional EP topics related to multiunit events and prolonged SBO.
The Task Force recommends that the Commission direct the staff to do the following:

10.1. Analyze current protective equipment requirements for emergency responders and guidance based upon insights from the accident at Fukushima.
10.2. Evaluate the command and control structure and the qualifications of decisionmakers to ensure that the proper level of authority and oversight exists in the correct facility for a long-term SBO or multiunit accident or both.
- Concepts such as whether decisionmaking authority is in the correct location (i.e., at the facility), whether currently licensed operators need to be integral to the ERO outside of the control room (i.e., in the TSC), and whether licensee emergency directors should have a formal "license" qualification for severe accident management.

10.3. Evaluate ERDS to do the following:
- Determine an alternate method (e.g., via satellite) to transmit ERDS data that does not rely on hardwired infrastructure that could be unavailable during a severe natural disaster.
- Determine whether the data set currently being received from each site is sufficient for modern assessment needs.
- Determine whether ERDS should be required to transmit continuously so that no operator action is needed during an emergency.

4.3.2. Other Emergency Preparedness Insights

In addition to prolonged SBO and multiunit events, the Task Force has identified other EP insights from the accident at Fukushima. An overarching lesson is that major damage to infrastructure in the area surrounding the plant might challenge an effective emergency response. In addition, the NRC should learn from the real-world implementation of protective actions and further develop concepts such as recovery and reentry. A third lesson relates to the need for the public to be educated on radioactivity and radiological hazards before an incident occurs.

Background

Natural disasters, such as hurricanes, floods, large fires, and tornados, occur often in the United States. State and local governments constantly manage these types of events and ensure that emergency plans are workable. Likewise, the NRC works closely with FEMA to ensure that the state of offsite preparedness continues to ensure reasonable assurance that the public can be protected should an accident occur. While these disasters do not significantly impact nuclear plants because of the plants' robust design features, they often cause significant damage in the surrounding community and could challenge the effective implementation of an offsite emergency plan should it be required. These natural disasters may alter the preplanned emergency framework by changing evacuation routes (e.g., bridge washed out or tree down in the roadway), disabling emergency sirens, or making evacuation dangerous (e.g., icy roads). Local government decisionmakers take factors such as these into consideration when formulating protective action decisions to determine how best to protect the public. A catastrophic natural disaster would create additional challenges beyond those routinely experienced by state and local emergency planners.

Currently, if a nuclear power plant shuts down as a result of a natural disaster and the disaster is of such severity that damage or changes to the offsite emergency response infrastructure may be substantial or are in question, the NRC and FEMA determine the status of offsite EP and coordinate approval of plant restart activities.

Evacuation time estimates (ETEs) are used as a tool to (1) develop and improve evacuation plans in advance of an accident and (2) to decide whether sheltering or evacuation is the more protective response during an accident. Evacuation is preferred if a dose in excess of protective action guides is probable, but it is not always more effective in reducing public exposure. ETEs are a planning tool and do nothing to affect conditions during an actual evacuation. Draft NUREG/CR-7002, "Criteria for Development of Evacuation Time Estimate Studies," issued May 2010, provides the latest guidance for licensees to develop a comprehensive set of ETEs.

Infrastructure damage could also affect the ability of licensees to bring equipment from offsite sources to the site. The regulation in 10 CFR 50.47(b)(3) requires licensees to maintain agreements with offsite organizations needed to support emergency response. Typically, this includes local fire departments, law enforcement, and medical support. As part of the requirements of 10 CFR 50.54(hh)(2)(i), licensees must identify and seek readily available agreements for additional offsite resources (both local and regional) that could support fire fighting, electrical power, core cooling, and other needs.

The regulation in 10 CFR 50.47(b)(10) requires licensees to make protective action recommendations. To facilitate a preplanned strategy for protective actions during an emergency, two EPZs surround each nuclear power plant. The exact size and shape of each EPZ is determined through detailed planning that includes consideration of the specific conditions at each site, unique geographical features of the area, and demographic information. This preplanned strategy for an EPZ provides a substantial basis to support activity beyond the planning zone in the extremely unlikely event it would be needed. The plume exposure pathway EPZ has a radius of about 16 kilometers (10 miles) from the reactor site. Predetermined protective action plans in place for this EPZ are designed to avoid or reduce dose from potential exposure to radioactive materials. These action plans include sheltering, evacuation, and the use of potassium iodide (KI) where appropriate. The ingestion exposure pathway EPZ has a radius of about 80 kilometers (50 miles) from the reactor site. Predetermined protective action plans in place for this EPZ are designed to avoid or reduce dose from the potential ingestion of radioactive materials. These action plans include a ban of contaminated food and water.

NUREG-0396, "Planning Basis for the Development of State and Local Government Radiological Emergency Response Plans in Support of Light Water Nuclear Power Plants," issued December 1978, establishes the concept and basis for the 10-mile and 50-mile EPZs, describes the basis for the types of reactor accidents that should be considered in an emergency plan, states that emergency planning is not based on probability but on public perceptions of the problem and what could be done to protect public health and safety (as a matter of prudence rather than necessity), and concludes that the objective of an emergency plan should be to provide dose savings for a spectrum of accidents that could produce offsite doses in excess of the U.S. Environmental Protection Agency's (EPA's) protective action guides.

The regulations in 10 CFR 50.47(b)(13) also address general plans for recovery and reentry and the means by which decisions to relax protective measures (e.g., allow reentry into an evacuated area) are reached. While requirements for the licensees, States, and local governments appear in 10 CFR 50.47(b)(13) and NUREG-0654, the approach of the U.S. Government to recovery and reentry involves numerous other Federal partners.

Appendix E to 10 CFR Part 50 and 10 CFR 50.47(b)(9) require radiation monitoring, which refers to the measurement of actual radiation dose. NUREG-0654 provides guidance to licensees and offsite response organizations on topics including field monitoring, monitoring equipment, and airborne plume tracking.

In January 2001, the Commission published a rule change to the NRC EP regulations to include consideration of the use of KI. If taken properly, KI may help reduce the dose of radiation to the thyroid gland from radioactive iodine and thus reduce the risk of thyroid cancer. If a person takes in radioactive iodine after consuming KI, the radioactive iodine will be rapidly excreted from the body. The NRC has supplied KI tablets to States requesting it for the population within the 10-mile EPZ. If warranted, KI is to be used to supplement evacuation or sheltering, not to take the place of these actions.

The population closest to the nuclear power plant that is within the 10-mile EPZ is at greatest risk of exposure to radiation and radioactive materials. When the population is evacuated from the area and potentially contaminated foodstuffs are removed from the market, the risk from further radioactive iodine exposure to the thyroid gland is essentially eliminated. Beyond the 10-mile EPZ, the major risk of radioiodine exposure is from the ingestion of contaminated foodstuffs, particularly milk products. Both EPA and the Food and Drug Administration have published guidance to protect consumers from contaminated foods. These protective actions are preplanned in the 50-mile ingestion pathway EPZ.

In the unlikely event of a nuclear power plant accident, it is important to follow the direction of State or local governments in order to make sure that protective actions, such as taking KI pills, are implemented safely and effectively for the affected population. While use of KI at the correct time and dosage can help prevent the uptake of radioactive iodine in the thyroid gland, it does not offer any protection from other radioisotopes or for other organs. KI is a medical tool for a limited, targeted situation.

Task Force Evaluation

The current regulatory approach for the evaluation of offsite EP following a natural disaster is robust and has proven its effectiveness following recent hurricanes, including Hurricane Katrina. An NRC task force examined the lessons learned from the active 2005 hurricane season in a report dated March 30, 2006 (ADAMS Accession No. ML060900005).

ETEs are currently recalculated when the population around a nuclear plant either increases or decreases significantly. As supported by the proposed EP rule, the scenarios described in NUREG/CR-7002 provide a basis for licensees to develop a comprehensive set of ETEs.

Performing additional time estimates for natural disasters with unpredictable damage would offer no corresponding benefit to licensee personnel in providing appropriate protective action recommendations to offsite officials or to offsite emergency planners in developing evacuation and other protective action strategies. With regard to seismic events impacting a plant site and causing a severe accident, consideration of the estimated time to evacuate the area would require assessment of the overall condition of dwellings, buildings, roadways, and other critical infrastructure at the time of the event. Additionally, when dwellings and other buildings are compromised and can no longer provide effective sheltering, evacuation would be conducted regardless of the time needed. If sheltering is not an option, ETE values are not relevant to decisionmaking. With regard to extreme weather conditions such as significant hurricanes, evacuation might involve an area much larger than a nuclear power plant site and begins days in advance of landfall. Therefore, the evacuation of the population in the plant vicinity would likely be completed well before the hurricane affects that area.

The accident at Fukushima has illustrated the potential increased need for offsite assistance to the licensee. In the case of large natural disasters such as earthquakes, hurricanes, and floods, the phenomena challenging the plant will also have affected the local community. In these cases, prearranged resources may not be available because of their inability to reach the plant site, other (potentially lifesaving) priorities within the community, or the destruction of those resources.

During the emergency at Fukushima, conditions deteriorated such that Japanese officials required additional protective actions up to and beyond a 20-kilometer (16-mile) area around Fukushima (i.e., beyond the equivalent of the U.S. plume exposure pathway EPZ). The possibility of making protective action recommendations for areas beyond the plume exposure pathway EPZ has been a program consideration since the inception of the EPZ concept in the United States. The emergency planning basis for U.S. plants, as discussed in NUREG-0654, states, "...detailed planning within 10 miles would provide a substantial base for expansion of response efforts in the event that this proved necessary." NUREG-0654 goes on to state that it would be unlikely that any protective actions for the plume exposure pathway would be required beyond the plume exposure pathway EPZ. It further stated that the plume exposure EPZ is of sufficient size for actions within this zone to provide for substantial reduction in early severe health effects (injuries or deaths) in the event of a worst case core melt accident.

While the U.S. EP framework has always noted that the plume exposure pathway EPZ provides a basis for expansion, insights from real-world implementation at Fukushima, including the realities of multiunit events, might further enhance U.S. preparedness for such an event. The Task Force acknowledges that every situation will differ, so detailed preplanning in this area is not plausible. As information and insights emerge about the challenges faced by Japanese officials while implementing protective actions around Fukushima, the NRC and its partners should evaluate those insights to identify enhancements to the decisionmaking framework in the United States.

Similarly, licensees and States are required to have plans for recovery and reentry; however, these plans remain largely conceptual and are rarely practiced. Since recovery and reentry have proven to present challenges at Fukushima, the NRC should continue work in this area to forward the U.S. Government approach.

In the area of radiation monitoring, licensees have numerous fixed radiation monitors located inside the plant on the property of the site. During an emergency, licensee field teams, in addition to Federal, State, and local teams, are dispatched to take real-time radiation readings offsite. While multiunit events do not specifically change radiation monitoring concepts, a long-term SBO could challenge radiation monitors that rely upon an external power supply. As long as field teams are adequately staffed, equipped, and capable of transit given the nature of the natural disaster, field monitoring remains an effective method to acquire radiation data. In additional, real-time radiation monitoring helps to validate dose projections, quantify actual dose, and provide confidence to the public and stakeholders that the conditions around the site are being accurately characterized. During a radiological release, accurate and timely dose data are critical to validating dose projections and ensuring dose reduction for the public. Having publicly available dose data provides a level of public confidence. The staff should explore the concepts of ac independence, survivability of equipment during a natural hazard, and ability to transmit real-time radiation readings publicly via the Internet. The concepts of radiation and radiation safety continue to be challenging topics to teach to those not involved in nuclear fields. This is underscored by the invisible nature of radiation and the potential chronic, in addition to acute, health affects that could be attributed to radiation exposure. While the NRC and various other Federal, State, and local government agencies and other medical organizations have conducted education on the uses, benefits, and drawbacks of KI, recent events have shown a continued gap in the public knowledge with respect to KI.

Based on the observed gaps in public awareness following the accident at Fukushima, an effort to increase education and outreach in the vicinity of each nuclear power plant is warranted. Misinformation and hysteria during a nuclear emergency challenge the agency's goal of public confidence. Training should be targeted to the areas surrounding each nuclear power plant in order to reach those who could be affected should an emergency at a nuclear power plant occur. In addition to public participation, the NRC should make extra effort to involve local response personnel, health officials, decisionmakers, media, and local politicians.

Recommendation 11

The Task Force recommends, as part of the longer term review, that the NRC should pursue EP topics related to decisionmaking, radiation monitoring, and public education.

The Task Force recommends that the Commission direct the staff to do the following:

11.1. Study whether enhanced onsite emergency response resources are necessary to support the effective implementation of the licensees' emergency plans, including the ability to deliver the equipment to the site under conditions involving significant natural events where degradation of offsite infrastructure or competing priorities for response resources could delay or prevent the arrival of offsite aid.

11.2. Work with FEMA, States, and other external stakeholders to evaluate insights from the implementation of EP at Fukushima to identify potential enhancements to the U.S. decisionmaking framework, including the concepts of recovery and reentry.

11.3. Study the efficacy of real-time radiation monitoring onsite and within the EPZs (including consideration of ac independence and real-time availability on the Internet).

11.4. Conduct training, in coordination with the appropriate Federal partners, on radiation, radiation safety, and the appropriate use of KI in the local community around each nuclear power plant.

5. IMPLICATIONS FOR NRC PROGRAMS

Section 3 of this report presented the most significant Task Force finding and recommendation relative to NRC programs (i.e., the NRC regulatory framework and how it could be strengthened). This section will discuss impacts on the NRC inspection program, the management of NRC records and information, and NRC participation in international activities.

5.1. NRC Inspection Program

Background

For many decades, the NRC has had a vigorous reactor inspection and oversight program for operating reactors and vendor inspection program for new plant construction. The ROP is a formal process integrating the NRC's inspection, assessment, and enforcement programs, and it has been in place for the last decade. The ROP evaluates the overall safety performance of operating nuclear power reactors and communicates this information to licensee management, members of the public, and other stakeholders. In addition, since 2004, the NRC has included safety culture in the ROP for operating reactor licensees. Over the past three decades, the safety performance of the nuclear fleet in the United States has improved, as a result in some part of the effectiveness of the NRC's inspection, assessment, and enforcement programs.

Regarding reactor protection and mitigation systems, a fundamental characteristic of the ROP is that inspection activities or "samples" are selected for the relative risk significance of the activity or equipment being examined based on its effect on core damage frequency. Further, the NRC evaluates inspection findings in these areas and uses the significance determination process to determine significance based on risk. The ROP's reliance on risk undervalues the safety benefit of defense-in-depth and consequently reduces the level of NRC resources focused on inspecting defense-indepth characteristics that contribute to safety.

In addition, the ROP does not consider the industry's voluntary safety enhancements. Consequently, the staff devotes limited inspection effort to voluntary initiatives such as the implementation and adequacy of SAMGs or the implementation of the Groundwater Protection Initiative. If it inspects them at all, the agency would likely evaluate voluntary initiatives through nonrecurring inspections guided by TIs. Finally, the structure of the risk-based inspection program under the ROP focuses on licensee compliance with regulations and requirements and leaves very limited opportunity for inspection staff to evaluate the adequacy of the licensing basis at a given facility.

Task Force Evaluation

Following the Fukushima accident, the NRC recognized the more general relevance and importance of the SAMGs and EDMGs that had been developed, and later required, following the accident at TMI and the terrorist events of September 11, 2001. Therefore, the NRC issued TI 2515/183 to its resident inspectors to ensure licensee compliance with existing requirements and to collect information on the readiness of these measures for use under various external challenges.

The Task Force has had the benefit of the results of the inspections under TI 2515/183 and concludes that the effort was well planned and worthwhile. In addition, in an April 22, 2011, memorandum from Charles L. Miller to Eric J. Leeds, "Task Force Request Regarding Inspection of Severe Accident Management Guidelines," the Task Force asked that inspectors collect information on the implementation of the voluntary SAMG initiative. In response, the NRC issued TI 2515/184. The Task Force has factored the information from both of these staff efforts into its evaluation and recommendations.

Through these two inspection activities, the Task Force also had the opportunity to compare industry activities under a required program and a similar voluntary initiative (i.e., EDMGs and SAMGs). Both programs had been effectively implemented, including initial program formulation and licensee staff training. Those programs are now 10 to 20 years old, and some licensees have maintained both programs in a manner expected for an important safety activity, including in terms of maintenance, configuration control, training, and retraining. However, some licensees have treated the industry voluntary initiative (the SAMG program) in a significantly less rigorous and formal manner, so much so that the SAMG inspection would have resulted in multiple violations had it been associated with a required program. The results of the SAMG inspection do not indicate, nor does the Task Force conclude that, the SAMGs would not have been effective if needed. However, indications of programmatic weaknesses in the maintenance of the SAMGs are sufficient to recommend strengthening this important activity.

On the basis of its evaluation, the Task Force concludes that enhancements to the inspection program would improve its focus on safety. Since these modifications are all staff activities not involving any backfit considerations, the NRC can pursue them based solely on their value in improving the staff's safety focus.

Recommendation 12

The Task Force recommends that the NRC strengthen regulatory oversight of licensee safety performance (i.e., the ROP) by focusing more attention on defense-in-depth requirements consistent with the recommended defense-in-depth framework.

The Task Force recommends the Commission direct the staff to strengthen the ROP by doing the following:

12.1. Expand the scope of the annual ROP self assessment and biennial ROP realignment to more fully include defense-in-depth considerations.
12.2. Enhance NRC staff training on severe accidents, including training resident inspectors on SAMGs.

5.2. Management of NRC Records and Information

Background

In the 1990s, the NRC decided to prepare for a transition from paper records management to electronic records management and began a process that resulted in the deployment of ADAMS in the late 1990s and early 2000s. At present, essentially every document generated by the agency is effectively integrated into a powerful electronic records management system that is searchable in a variety of ways. However, at the time of the original transition to

ADAMS, individual offices decided what records generated before the deployment of ADAMS would be incorporated into the electronic system and what records would remain in paper and microfiche format.

In SECY-06-0164, "The NRC Knowledge Management Program," dated July 25, 2006, the staff described to the Commission the plans for developing and implementing an agency knowledge management program. The program recognized that the agency is a knowledge-centric organization that depends on its staff to make sound regulatory decisions to accomplish the agency's mission of protecting people and the environment. The staff informed the Commission about the NRC's ongoing programs for maintaining explicit, implicit, and tacit knowledge and new initiatives to leverage information technology solutions to transfer knowledge.

The knowledge management program focused on a variety of areas to enhance identifying, retaining, transferring, and using critical information and knowledge in the agency's ongoing work. The staff updated the Commission on the implementation status of knowledge management initiatives in SECY-07-0138, "NRC Knowledge Management Program Status Update," dated August 14, 2007.

Task Force Evaluation

During the course of data collection and analysis, the Task Force searched for and reviewed hundreds of documents, including some issued 40 or more years ago. The Task Force also interacted with scores of NRC staff and other individuals to understand issues and evaluate insights from the Fukushima event.

During the course of these activities, the Task Force struggled to access electronically a variety of critical historical documents, including Commission papers and staff requirements memoranda, GLs, bulletins, NUREGs, RGs, and other key documents that significantly contribute to the knowledge base for technical and regulatory evaluation and decisions made by the agency.

Many documents dated before 2000 are not available electronically. Consequently, from the perspective of integrated knowledge management, it would be equally difficult for staff to access these foundational documents without personal paper files.

In addition, during a variety of interviews with staff from multiple offices on similar subjects, it became clear that organizationally influenced knowledge gaps may exist, in that staff members in one organization may not be aware of information in another organization that is relevant to their work. In addition, staff members working on operating reactor licensing noted that, in order to support a licensing action or decision, they often need to read, evaluate, and refer to critical documents that must be viewed on microfiche.

The NRC has made great strides in electronic document management. Because of financial constraints, legacy documents are not all accessible electronically through ADAMS, and no strategy exists to further enhance the availability of historical documents underpinning agency positions and decisions. The Task Force believes that the staff should strongly consider continued retrofitting of its electronic document library in a methodical and coherent way to incorporate all key legacy documents.

Further, the Task Force believes that the NRC would enhance its organizational and technical capacity by establishing an electronic framework, similar to Wikipedia and managed by staff technical experts, that links data on various subjects so that the staff members could access the information easily, allowing them to develop the well-founded knowledge required to accomplish their tasks and support their regulatory decisions.

As time passes, maintaining historical institutional knowledge becomes more dependent on a comprehensive and accessible information management system. The Task Force therefore encourages the staff to do the following:

- Add key legacy documents to the electronic records system (ADAMS).
- Develop an information management platform to enhance organizational and technical capacity by providing subject matter in an electronic format managed by staff technical experts.

5.3. International Cooperation and Coordination Background

The NRC is actively involved in numerous international activities related to the Fukushima accident, both bilaterally and multilaterally, through such organizations as IAEA, NEA, and the Multinational Design Evaluation Program (MDEP). The regulatory authority of Japan (the Nuclear and Industrial Safety Agency with its support organization, the Japan Nuclear Energy Safety Organization) is also a member of each of these international organizations.

Through each of the venues, the NRC has received information on the accident in Japan and on the followup activities of each nation.

In addition to its frequent contacts through the NRC Operation Center, the NRC staff has participated in the following activities, all of which included discussions of the Fukushima accident and followup actions planned or underway:

- April 2011 NEA Steering Committee meeting
- April 2011 MDEP Steering Technical Committee meeting
- May 2011 MDEP EPR reactor design working group meeting
- May 2011 NEA Committee on Nuclear Regulatory Activities (CNRA) planning meeting
- June 2011 CNRA discussions on Fukushima
- June 2011 NEA, IAEA, France G20-G8 Forum on the Fukushima Accident
- June 2011 IAEA Ministerial Meeting on Fukushima

These international interactions have helped the world's nuclear safety authorities share information and develop plans to enhance safety following the Fukushima accident. In part because of these interactions, the nuclear regulatory authorities around the world have developed a consistent understanding of the important elements of the accident and similar roadmaps forward, each appropriate to the individual country and its regulatory approach.

The staff has also been well informed of the activities of the European regulatory authorities in the Western European Nuclear Regulators' Association and the European Nuclear Safety Regulators Group through discussions within MDEP, NEA/CNRA, and IAEA.

Task Force Evaluation

The NRC's longstanding commitment to international cooperation has benefitted the agency during the monitoring and followup activities related to the Fukushima accident. It is clear that the NRC's active participation in international activities has served and continues to serve nuclear safety in the United States and worldwide. It is also clear that the NRC's long-term activities, such as further information collection, event analysis, and comparisons of the effectiveness of actions taken, would benefit from international cooperation both in terms of effectiveness and cost efficiency.

International cooperation to date has been very effective in collecting and sharing information and in developing and confirming an understanding of the important elements of the Fukushima accident relevant to the activities of the Task Force.

NRC participation in these international efforts also contributes to the safety of nuclear reactors throughout the world by providing forums for sharing the agency's best understanding of events and issues and effectively addressing them. These international forums also enable the NRC to provide leadership in the resolution of important safety concerns. In addition, participation in international efforts generally requires a minimal commitment of resources and in some cases, such as the collection and analysis of accident data, actually results in a resource savings.

The Task Force endorses continued international cooperation and coordination, including the following:

- participation in collaborative, international efforts to determine and analyze the Fukushima accident sequence of events
- participation in international efforts to update IAEA Fundamental Safety Standard (NSR-1) and other related standards to reflect insights from the Fukushima event
- continued cooperation and coordination with other national regulatory authorities on insights from the Fukushima event as well as their plans, actions, and findings

6. SUMMARY OF OVERARCHING RECOMMENDATIONS

This section presents the Task Force's recommendations for improving the safety of both operating and new nuclear reactors. It also addresses recommended improvements in the NRC programs for the oversight of reactor safety. The recommendations are based on the Task Force's evaluations of the relevant issues identified from the Fukushima accident.

Appendix A of this report proposes an implementation strategy and offers further details on these recommendations. The Task Force makes the following overarching recommendations, as stated in the preceding sections of this report:

Clarifying the Regulatory Framework

1. The Task Force recommends establishing a logical, systematic, and coherent regulatory framework for adequate protection that appropriately balances defense-in-depth and risk considerations. (Section 3)

Ensuring Protection

2. The Task Force recommends that the NRC require licensees to reevaluate and upgrade as necessary the design-basis seismic and flooding protection of SSCs for each operating reactor. (Section 4.1.1)
3. The Task Force recommends, as part of the longer term review, that the NRC evaluate potential enhancements to the capability to prevent or mitigate seismically induced fires and floods. (Section 4.1.2)

Enhancing Mitigation

4. The Task Force recommends that the NRC strengthen SBO mitigation capability at all operating and new reactors for design-basis and beyond-design-basis external events. (Section 4.2.1)
5. The Task Force recommends requiring reliable hardened vent designs in BWR facilities with Mark I and Mark II containments. (Section 4.2.2)
6. The Task Force recommends, as part of the longer term review, that the NRC identify insights about hydrogen control and mitigation inside containment or in other buildings as additional information is revealed through further study of the Fukushima Dai-ichi accident. (Section 4.2.3)
7. The Task Force recommends enhancing spent fuel pool makeup capability and instrumentation for the spent fuel pool. (Section 4.2.4)
8. The Task Force recommends strengthening and integrating onsite emergency response capabilities such as EOPs, SAMGs, and EDMGs. (Section 4.2.5)

Strengthening Emergency Preparedness

9. The Task Force recommends that the NRC require that facility emergency plans address prolonged SBO and multiunit events. (Section 4.3.1)
10. The Task Force recommends, as part of the longer term review, that the NRC pursue additional EP topics related to multiunit events and prolonged SBO. (Section 4.3.1)
11. The Task Force recommends, as part of the longer term review, that the NRC should pursue EP topics related to decisionmaking, radiation monitoring, and public education. (Section 4.3.2)

Improving the Efficiency of NRC Programs

The Task Force recommends that the NRC strengthen regulatory oversight of licensee safety performance (i.e., the ROP) by focusing more attention on defense-in-depth requirements consistent with the recommended defense-in-depth framework. (Section 5.1)

7. APPLICABILITY AND IMPLEMENTATION STRATEGY FOR NEW REACTORS

The Task Force has considered the applicability and implementation of its recommendations for new reactors, including certified designs, designs in the certification process, certified designs applying for renewal, early site permits, and applications for operating licenses and COLs. Since no new reactors are currently licensed, the recommendations involving orders are not applicable. However, the Task Force has assessed the rulemaking recommendations, and they would be equally applicable to new reactors.

Recommendation 8 for the integration of EOPs, SAMGs, and EDMGs and for controlling accident decisionmaking under technical specifications would be applicable to COLs. For near-term COLs (i.e., those expected to be licensed before the NRC completes the proposed rulemakings), the Task Force recommends that the agency impose those requirements through inspections, tests, analyses, and acceptance criteria (ITAAC). The Task Force recognizes that, with the sole exception of fire protection programs, the Commission has expressed (in the staff requirements memorandum dated September 11, 2002, for SECY02-0067, "Inspections, Tests, Analyses, and Acceptance Criteria (ITAAC) for Operational Programs (Programmatic ITAAC)," dated April 5, 2002) a desire to resolve programmatic issues (e.g., training, quality assurance, fitness for duty) before COL issuance and handle the issues through existing oversight programs rather than resolve them through the ITAAC process. Specifically, the Commission stated (in the staff requirements memorandum for SECY-02-0067) that, "They [ITAAC] should encompass only those matters that, by their nature, cannot be resolved prior to construction." Further, the Commission stated, "...the Commission is not prepared to dismiss the possibility that programmatic ITAAC may be necessary in some very limited areas." The Task Force suggests that this would be one of those areas in which it is not practical to resolve the issue before COL issuance, in that the integration of EOPs, SAMGs, and EDMGs could require a few years of effort by licensees, the industry, and the NRC staff. However, this strategy would ensure implementation and NRC oversight before plant operation. The Task Force concludes that all of the current early site permits already meet the requirements of detailed recommendation 2.1, relating to the design-basis seismic and flooding analysis, and all of the current COL and design certification applicants are addressing them adequately in the context of the updated state-of-the-art and regulatory guidance used by the staff in its reviews.

The Task Force concludes that Recommendation 4, with new requirements for prolonged SBO mitigation, and Recommendation 7, about spent fuel pool makeup capability and instrumentation, should apply to all design certifications or to COL applicants if the recommended requirements are not addressed in the referenced certified design. The Task Force recommends that design certifications and COLs under active staff review address this recommendation before licensing.

The Task Force notes that the two design certifications currently in the rulemaking process (i.e., the AP1000 and the economic simplified boiling-water reactor (ESBWR)) have passive safety systems. By nature of their passive designs and inherent 72-hour coping capability for core, containment, and spent fuel pool cooling with no operator action required, the ESBWR and AP1000 designs have many of the design features and attributes necessary to address the Task Force recommendations. The Task Force supports completing those design certification rulemaking activities without delay. However, COL applicants referencing these designs would have to address prestaging of any needed equipment for beyond 72 hours, and ITAAC should be established to confirm effective implementation of minimum and extended coping, as described in detailed recommendation 4.1. Since the Task Force recommends the SBO additions on the basis of adequate protection, the NRC should impose them as new requirements in accordance with 10 CFR 52.59(b)(1) as part of the staff's review of the recently docketed Advanced Boiling-Water Reactor design certification renewal applications. The recommendations related to expanding 10 CFR 50.54(hh) and the EP requirements to fully address multiunit accidents and SBO conditions should apply to COL applicants. Near-term COLs could implement these recommendations through ITAAC. For the two plants with reactivated construction permits (Watts Bar Unit 2 and Bellefonte Unit 1), the Task Force recommends that those operating license reviews and the licensing itself include all of the near-term actions and any of the recommended rule changes that have been completed at the time of licensing. Any additional rule changes would be imposed on the plants in the same manner as for other operating reactors.

APPENDIX A: SUMMARY OF DETAILED RECOMMENDATIONS BY IMPLEMENTATION STRATEGY

In this appendix, the Task Force proposes an integrated strategy for implementing its recommendations in a coherent manner. The structure of this process includes (1) a policy statement, (2) rulemaking activities, (3) orders, (4) staff actions, and (5) actions for long-term evaluation. As described in Section 3 of the report, in light of the low likelihood of an event beyond the design basis of a U.S. nuclear power plant and the current mitigation capabilities at those facilities, the Task Force concludes that continued operation of these plants and continued licensing activities do not pose an imminent risk to the public health and safety. Further, the Task Force concludes that the current regulatory approach and regulatory requirements continue to serve as a basis for the reasonable assurance of adequate protection of public health and safety until the actions set forth below have been implemented.

Policy Statement

Draft a Commission policy statement that articulates a risk-informed defense-indepth framework that includes extended design-basis requirements in the NRC's regulations as essential elements for ensuring adequate protection. (Section 3—detailed recommendation 1.1)

Recommended Rulemaking Activities

The Task Force recommends that the Commission direct the staff to initiate these important rulemaking activities, including concurrent development of associated guidance, and complete them as a soon as possible.

- Initiate rulemaking to implement a risk-informed, defense-in-depth framework consistent with the above recommended Commission policy statement. (Section 3—detailed recommendation 1.2)
- Initiate rulemaking to require licensees to confirm seismic hazards and flooding hazards every 10 years and address any new and significant information. If necessary, update the design basis for SSCs important to safety to protect against the updated hazards. (Section 4.1.1—detailed recommendation 2.2)
- Initiate rulemaking to revise 10 CFR 50.63 to require each operating and new reactor licensee to (1) establish a minimum coping time of 8 hours for a loss of all ac power, (2) establish the equipment, procedures, and training necessary to implement an "extended loss of all ac" coping time of 72 hours for core and spent fuel pool cooling and for reactor coolant system and primary containment integrity as needed, and (3) preplan and prestage offsite resources to support uninterrupted core and spent fuel pool cooling, and reactor coolant system and containment integrity as needed, including the ability to deliver the equipment to the site in the time period allowed for extended coping, under conditions involving significant degradation of offsite transportation infrastructure associated with significant natural disasters. (Section 4.2.1—detailed recommendation 4.1)
- Initiate rulemaking or licensing activities or both to require the actions related to the spent fuel pool described in detailed recommendations 7.1–7.4. (Section 4.2.5—detailed recommendation 7.5)
- Initiate rulemaking to require more realistic, hands-on training and exercises on SAMGs and EDMGs for all staff expected to implement the strategies and those licensee staff expected to make decisions during emergencies, including emergency coordinators and emergency directors. (Section 4.2.6—detailed recommendation 8.4)
- Initiate rulemaking to require EP enhancements for multiunit events in the following areas: personnel and staffing, dose assessment capability, training and exercises, and equipment and facilities. (Section 4.3.1—detailed recommendation 9.1)
- Initiate rulemaking to require EP enhancements for prolonged SBO in the following areas: communications capability, ERDS capability, training and exercises, and equipment and facilities. (Section 4.3.1—detailed recommendation 9.2)

Recommended Orders

The Task Force recommends that the Commission use orders to ensure that licensees take the near-term actions described below. In some cases, these are interim actions to be taken until requirements associated with future rulemakings can be implemented.

- Order licensees to reevaluate the seismic and flooding hazards at their sites against current NRC requirements and guidance, and, if necessary, update the design basis and SSCs important to safety to protect against the updated hazards. (Section 4.1.1—detailed recommendation 2.1)
- Order licensees to perform seismic and flood protection walkdowns to identify and address plant-specific vulnerabilities and verify the adequacy of monitoring and

maintenance for protection features such as watertight barriers and seals in the interim period until longer term actions are completed to update the design basis for external events. (Section 4.1.1—detailed recommendation 2.3)
- Order licensees to provide reasonable protection for equipment currently provided pursuant to 10 CFR 50.54(hh)(2) from the effects of design-basis external events and to add equipment as needed to address multiunit events while other requirements are being revised and implemented. (Section 4.2.1—detailed recommendation 4.2)
- Order licensees to include a reliable hardened vent in boiling-water reactor (BWR) Mark I and Mark II containments. (Section 4.2.3—detailed recommendation 5.1)
- Order licensees to provide sufficient safety-related instrumentation, able to withstand design-basis natural phenomena, to monitor key spent fuel pool parameters (i.e., water level, temperature, and area radiation levels) from the control room. (Section 4.2.5— detailed recommendation 7.1)
- Order licensees to provide safety-related ac electrical power for the spent fuel pool makeup system. (Section 4.2.5—detailed recommendation 7.2)
- Order licensees to revise their technical specifications to address requirements to have one train of onsite emergency electrical power operable for spent fuel pool makeup and spent fuel pool instrumentation when there is irradiated fuel in the spent fuel pool, regardless of the operational mode of the reactor. (Section 4.2.5—detailed recommendation 7.3)
- Order licensees to have an installed, seismically qualified means to spray water into the spent fuel pools, including an easily accessible connection to supply the water (e.g., using a portable pump or pumper truck) at grade outside the building. (Section 4.2.5—detailed recommendation 7.4)
- Order licensees to modify the EOP technical guidelines (required by Supplement 1, "Requirements for Emergency Response Capability," to NUREG-0737, issued January 1983 (GL 82-33), to (1) include EOPs, SAMGs, and EDMGs in an integrated manner, (2) specify clear command and control strategies for their implementation, and (3) stipulate appropriate qualification and training for those who make decisions during emergencies. (Section 4.2.6—detailed recommendation 8.1)
- Order licensees to modify each plant's technical specifications to conform with detailed recommendation 8.2. (Section 4.2.6—detailed recommendation 8.3)
- Order licensees to do the following until rulemaking is complete: determine and implement the required staff to fill all necessary positions for responding to a multiunit event, conduct periodic training and exercises for multiunit and prolonged SBO scenarios, ensure that EP equipment and facilities are sufficient for dealing with multiunit and prolonged SBO scenarios, provide a means to power communications equipment needed to communicate onsite and offsite during a prolonged SBO, and maintain ERDS capability throughout the accident. (Section 4.3.1—detailed recommendation 9.3)
- Order licensees to complete the ERDS modernization initiative by June 2012 to ensure multiunit site monitoring capability. (Section 4.3.1—detailed recommendation 9.4)

Recommended Staff Actions

The Task Force recommends that the staff begin the actions given below.

- Modify the Regulatory Analysis Guidelines to more effectively implement the defense-in-depth philosophy in balance with the current emphasis on risk-based guidelines. (Section 3—detailed recommendation 1.3)
- Evaluate the insights from the IPE and IPEEE efforts as summarized in NUREG1560, "Individual Plant Examination Program: Perspectives on Reactor Safety and Plant Performance," issued December 1997, and NUREG-1742, "Perspectives Gained from the Individual Plant Examination of External Events (IPEEE) Program," issued April 2002, to identify potential generic regulations or plant-specific regulatory requirements. (Section 3—detailed recommendation 1.4)
- Modify Section 5.0, "Administrative Controls," of the Standard Technical Specifications for each operating reactor design to reference the approved EOP technical guidelines for that plant design. (Section 4.2.6—detailed recommendation 8.2)
- Expand the scope of the annual ROP self assessment and biennial ROP realignment to more fully include defense-in-depth considerations. (Section 5.1—detailed recommendation 12.1)
- Enhance NRC staff training on severe accidents, including training resident inspectors on SAMGs. (Section 5.1—detailed recommendation 12.2)

Recommended Actions for Long-Term Evaluation

The Task Force recommends that the staff pursue the longer term review activities described below to further evaluate insights from the Fukushima event and to enhance the safety of U.S. plants.

- Evaluate potential enhancements to the capability to prevent or mitigate seismically induced fires and floods. (Section 4.1.2—detailed recommendation 3)
- Reevaluate the need for hardened vents for other containment designs, considering the insights from the Fukushima accident. Depending on the outcome of the reevaluation, appropriate regulatory action should be taken for any containment designs requiring hardened vents. (Section 4.1.3—detailed recommendation 5.2)
- Identify insights about hydrogen control and mitigation inside containment or in other buildings as additional information is revealed through further study of the Fukushima Dai-ichi event. (Section 4.1.4—detailed recommendation 6)
- Analyze current protective equipment requirements for emergency responders and guidance based upon insights from the accident at Fukushima. (Section 4.3.1—detailed recommendation 10.1)
- Evaluate the command and control structure and the qualifications of decisionmakers to ensure that the proper level of authority and oversight exists in the correct facility

for a long-term SBO or multiunit accident or both. (Section 4.3.1—detailed recommendation 10.2)
- Evaluate ERDS to do the following: determine an alternate method (e.g., via satellite) to transmit ERDS data that does not rely on hardwired infrastructure that could be unavailable during a severe natural disaster, determine whether the data set currently being received from each site is sufficient for modern assessment needs, and determine whether ERDS should be required to transmit continuously so that no operator action is needed during an emergency. (Section 4.3.1—detailed recommendation 10.3)
- Study whether enhanced onsite emergency response resources are necessary to support the effective implementation of the licensees' emergency plans, including the ability to deliver the equipment to the site under conditions involving significant natural events where degradation of offsite infrastructure or competing priorities for response resources could delay or prevent the arrival of offsite aid. (Section 4.3.2—detailed recommendation 11.1)
- Work with FEMA, States, and other external stakeholders to evaluate insights from the implementation of EP at Fukushima to identify potential enhancements to the U.S. decisionmaking framework, including the concepts of recovery and reentry. (Section 4.3.2—detailed recommendation 11.2)
- Study the efficacy of real-time radiation monitoring onsite and within the EPZs (including consideration of ac independence and real-time availability on the Internet). (Section 4.3.2—detailed recommendation 11.3)
- Conduct training, in coordination with the appropriate Federal partners, on radiation, radiation safety, and the appropriate use of KI in the local community around each nuclear power plant. (Section 4.3.2—detailed recommendation 11.4)

APPENDIX B: TASKING MEMORANDUM

March 23, 2011

MEMORANDUM TO:	R. W. Borchardt Executive Director for Operations
FROM:	Chairman Jaczko /RA/
SUBJECT:	TASKING MEMORANDUM – COMGBJ-11-0002 – NRC ACTIONS FOLLOWING THE EVENTS IN JAPAN

The staff should establish a senior level agency task force to conduct a methodical and systematic review of our processes and regulations to determine whether the agency should make additional improvements to our regulatory system and make recommendations to the Commission for its policy direction. The review should address the following near term and then longer term objectives.

Near Term Review

- This task force should evaluate currently available technical and operational information from the events that have occurred at the Fukushima Daiichi nuclear complex in Japan to identify potential or preliminary near term/immediate operational or regulatory issues affecting domestic operating reactors of all designs, including their spent fuel pools, in areas such as protection against earthquake, tsunami, flooding, hurricanes; station blackout and a degraded ability to restore power; severe accident mitigation; emergency preparedness; and combustible gas control.
- The task force should develop recommendations, as appropriate, for potential changes to inspection procedures and licensing review guidance, and recommend whether generic communications, orders, or other regulatory requirements are needed.
- The task force efforts should be informed by some stakeholder input but should be independent of industry efforts.
- The report would be released to the public per normal Commission processes (including its transmission to the Commission as a Notation Vote Paper).

To ensure the Commission is both kept informed of these efforts and called upon to resolve any policy recommendations that surface, the task force should, at a minimum, be prepared to brief the Commission on a 30 day quick look report; on the status of the ongoing near term review at approximately the 60 day point; and then on the 90 day culmination of the near term efforts. Additional specific subject matter briefings and additional voting items that request Commission policy direction may also be added during the Commission's agenda planning meetings.

(EDO) (SECY Suspense: 30, 60, & 90 days)

- The task force's longer term review should begin as soon as NRC has sufficient technical information from the events in Japan with the goal of no later than the completion of the 90 day near term report, and the task force should provide updates on the beginning of the longer term review at the 30 and 60 day status updates.
- This effort would include specific information on the sequence of events and the status of equipment during the duration of the event.
- The task force should evaluate all technical and policy issues related to the event to identify potential research, generic issues, changes to the reactor oversight process, rulemakings, and adjustments to the regulatory framework that should be conducted by NRC.
- The task force should evaluate potential interagency issues such as emergency preparedness.
- Applicability of the lessons learned to non-operating reactor and non-reactor facilities should also be explored.
- During the review, the task force should receive input from and interact with all key stakeholders.
- The task force should provide a report with recommendations, as appropriate, to the Commission within six months from the start of the evaluation for Commission policy direction.
- The report would be released to the public per normal Commission processes (including its transmission to the Commission as a Notation Vote Paper).
- Before beginning work on the longer term review, staff should provide the Commission with estimated resource impacts on other regulatory activities.
- The ACRS should review the report as issued in its final form and provide a letter report to the Commission.

(EDO) (SECY Suspense: 9 months, if needed)

cc: Commissioner Svinicki
Commissioner Apostolakis
Commissioner Magwood
Commissioner Ostendorff
OGC
CFO
OCA
OPA
Office Directors, Regions, ACRS, ASLBP (via E-Mail)
PDR

APPENDIX C: MEMO TRANSMITTING CHARTER FOR THE NUCLEAR REGULATORY COMMISSION TASK FORCE TO CONDUCT A NEAR-TERM EVALUATION OF THE NEED FOR AGENCY ACTIONS FOLLOWING THE EVENTS IIN JAPAN

March 30, 2011

MEMORANDUM TO: Martin J. Virgilio
Deputy Executive Director
for Reactor and Preparedness Programs Executive Director for Operations
Charles L. Miller, Director
Office of Federal and State Materials
and Environmental Management Programs

FROM: R. W. Borchardt /RA/
Executive Director for Operations

SUBJECT: AGENCY TASK FORCE TO CONDUCT NEAR-TERM EVALUATION OF THE NEED FOR AGENCY ACTIONS FOLLOWING THE EVENTS IN JAPAN

On March 11th, 2011, Japan experienced a severe earthquake resulting in the shutdown of multiple reactors. It appears that the reactors' response to the earthquake went according to design. At the Fukushima Daiichi site, the earthquake caused the loss of normal AC power. In addition, it appears that the ensuing tsunami caused the loss of emergency AC power at the Fukushima Daiichi site. Subsequent events caused damage to fuel and radiological releases offsite.

The purpose of this memorandum is to task the Deputy Executive Director for Reactor and Preparedness Programs (DEDR) to convene an agency task force of U.S. Nuclear Regulatory (NRC) senior leaders and experts. The task force should conduct a methodical and systematic review of relevant NRC regulatory requirements, programs, and processes, and their implementation, to recommend whether the agency should make near-term improvements to our regulatory system. The task force should also identify a framework and topics for review and assessment for the longer-term effort.

Attached is a charter for the task force. The charter defines the objective, scope, coordination and communication, expected products, schedule, staffing, and Executive Director for Operations interface. The task force should update the Commission on the near-term review at approximately 30 and 60 days, and provide its observations, findings, and recommendations in the form of a written report and briefing at the completion of the near-term effort occurring at approximately 90 days.

The review should be conducted in accordance with Tasking Memorandum – COMGBJ-11-0002, "NRC Actions Following the Events in Japan."

Enclosure: As stated
CONTACT: Nathan T. Sanfilippo, OEDO
301-415-3951

CHARTER FOR THE NUCLEAR REGULATORY COMMISSION TASK FORCE TO CONDUCT A NEAR-TERM EVALUATION OF THE NEED FOR AGENCY ACTIONS FOLLOWING THE EVENTS IN JAPAN

Objective

The objective of this task force is to conduct a methodical and systematic review of relevant NRC regulatory requirements, programs, and processes, and their implementation, to recommend whether the agency should make near-term improvements to our regulatory system. This task force will also identify a framework and topics for review and assessment for the longer-term effort.

Scope

The task force review will include the following:
a. A near-term review to:

- Evaluate currently available technical and operational information from the events that have occurred at the Fukushima Daiichi nuclear complex in Japan to identify potential or preliminary near-term/immediate operational or regulatory actions affecting domestic reactors of all designs, including their spent fuel pools. The task force will evaluate, at a minimum, the following technical issues and determine priority for further examination and potential agency action:
- External event issues (e.g. seismic, flooding, fires, severe weather)
- Station blackout
- Severe accident measures (e.g., combustible gas control, emergency operating procedures, severe accident management guidelines)
- 10 CFR 50.54 (hh)(2) which states, "Each licensee shall develop and implement guidance and strategies intended to maintain or restore core cooling, containment, and spent fuel pool cooling capabilities under the circumstances associated with loss of large areas of the plant due to explosions or fire, to include strategies in the following areas: (i) Fire fighting; (ii) Operations to mitigate fuel damage; and (iii) Actions to minimize radiological release." Also known as B.5.b.
- Emergency preparedness (e.g., emergency communications, radiological protection, emergency planning zones, dose projections and modeling, protective actions)
- Develop recommendations, as appropriate, for potential changes to NRC's regulatory requirements, programs, and processes, and recommend whether generic communications, orders, or other regulatory actions are needed.

b. Recommendations for the content, structure, and estimated resource impact for the longer-term review.

Coordination and Communications

The near-term task force will:

- Solicit stakeholder input as appropriate, but remain independent of industry efforts.
- Coordinate and cooperate where applicable with other domestic and international efforts reviewing the events in Japan for additional insights.
- Provide recommendations to the Commission for any immediate policy issues identified prior to completion of the near-term review.
- Provide recommendations to program offices for any immediate actions not involving policy issues, prior to completion of the near-term review.
- Identify resource implications of near-term actions.
- Consider information gained from Temporary Instruction 2515/183, "Followup to the Fukushima Daiichi Nuclear Station Fuel Damage Events."
- Develop a communications plan.
- Update and brief internal stakeholders, as appropriate.

Expected Product and Schedule

The task force will provide its observations, conclusions, and recommendations in the form of a written report to the Deputy Executive Director for Reactor and Preparedness Programs at the completion of the 90-day near-term review.

During the development of its report, the task force will brief the Commission on the status of the review at approximately the 30- and 60-day points.

The report will be transmitted to the Commission via a SECY paper, and the task force will brief the Commission on the results of the near-term effort at approximately the 90- day point. The report will be released to the public via normal Commission processes.

The task force will recommend a framework for a longer-term review as a part of the near-term report. The longer-term review will begin as soon as the NRC has sufficient technical information from the events in Japan (with a goal of beginning by the end of the near-term review).

Staffing

The task force will consist of the following members:

Leader	Charles Miller	FSME
Senior Managers	Daniel Dorman	NMSS
	Jack Grobe	NRR
	Gary Holahan	NRO
Senior Staff	Amy Cubbage	NRO
	Nathan Sanfilippo	OEDO
Administrative Assistant	Cynthia Davidson	OGC

Additional task force members will be added as needed. For the near-term review, other staff members may be consulted on a part-time basis.

EDO Interface

The task force will keep agency leadership informed on the status of the effort and provide early identification of significant findings. The task force will report to Martin J. Virgilio, Deputy Executive Director for Reactor and Preparedness Programs.

ACKNOWLEDGMENT

Over the past 4 months, the Near-Term Task Force has devoted many long hours and an extensive amount of thought, deliberation, and collaboration to produce this report. The recommendations presented herein will likely require the same by those who will make decisions as to whether they should be endorsed or not. That is as it should be. The Task Force members comprise over 135 years of regulatory experience as a collective body. I have valued greatly their wisdom and dedication in completing this task. It has been my privilege to serve as their leader. So to:

Amy Cubbage Cynthia Davidson
Dan Dorman Jack Grobe
Gary Holahan Nathan Sanfilippo
I say thank you,
Dr. Charles L. Miller

Chapter 2

STATEMENT OF GREGORY B. JACZKO, CHAIRMAN, UNITED STATES NUCLEAR REGULATORY COMMISSION. HEARING ON "REVIEW OF THE NRC'S NEAR-TERM TASK FORCE RECOMMENDATIONS FOR ENHANCING REACTOR SAFETY IN THE 21ST CENTURY"

August 2, 2011

Chairman Boxer, Ranking Member Inhofe, Chairman Carper, Ranking Member Barrasso, and Members of the Committee, we appreciate the opportunity to appear before you to provide a summary of the findings of the NRC's Near-Term Task Force review of the Fukushima Dai-ichi nuclear accident.

I first want to thank, on behalf of the Commission, Dr. Charles Miller and the other members of the Task Force for all of their work in conducting the 90-day review. I also want to acknowledge the numerous other NRC staff who were available to the Task Force as a resource in conducting its review, as well as the Federal Emergency Management Agency, which engaged the Task Force in discussions of offsite emergency preparedness and provided insights on the U.S. National Response Framework, the Institute of Nuclear Power Operations – which shared information on the industry's post-Fukushima actions, and other groups and individuals who shared their views with the Task Force.

In my testimony today, I would like to provide you with a summary of the Task Force findings and recommendations. My colleagues and I are in the process of developing the Commission's direction to the NRC staff on addressing the Task Force recommendations.

OVERVIEW

The Near-Term Task Force was established in response to unanimous Commission direction to conduct a systematic and methodical review of NRC processes and regulations to determine whether the agency should make additional improvements to its regulatory system.

The six-member Task Force, who collectively have over 135 years of regulatory experience, was responsible for making recommendations to the Commission for its policy direction in light of the accident at the Fukushima Dai-ichi Nuclear Power Plant. With its 90-day review completed, the Task Force issued its report to the Commission on July 12, 2011. The Commission made the report publicly available on July 13, 2011. The Task Force briefed the Commission on its findings on July 19, 2011.

Overall, the Task Force found that continued operation and continued licensing activities do not pose an imminent risk to public health and safety. The Task Force concluded that a sequence of events like the Fukushima Dai-ichi accident is unlikely to occur in the United States, and that some appropriate mitigation measures have been implemented, reducing the likelihood of core damage and radiological releases. The Task Force was clear, however, that any accident involving core damage and uncontrolled radioactive releases of the magnitude of Fukushima Dai-ichi—even one without significant health consequences—is inherently unacceptable.

The Task Force also concluded that a more balanced application of the Commission's defense-in-depth philosophy using risk insights would provide an enhanced regulatory framework. Such a framework would support appropriate requirements for increased capability to address events of low likelihood and high consequence, such as prolonged station blackout resulting from severe natural phenomena. This concept is the basis for the Task Force's proposal to redefine the level of protection regarded as adequate and provides the foundation for the Task Force's recommendations.

The Task Force report included a comprehensive set of twelve overarching recommendations. The Task Force recommendations are intended to clarify and strengthen the regulatory framework for nuclear power plants, and are structured around the focus areas of the NRC's defense-in-depth philosophy as applied to protection from natural phenomena; mitigation of prolonged station blackout events; and emergency preparedness. The Task Force also provided recommendations to improve the effectiveness of the NRC's programs.

In addition to these overarching recommendations, the Task Force report also includes a number of detailed recommendations that provide an integrated implementation strategy. The detailed recommendations are grouped into five categories: 1) a policy statement; 2) rulemakings; 3) orders; 4) staff actions; and 5) long-term evaluation topics. The longer-term evaluation topics are those issues about which sufficient information was not yet available for the near-term Task Force to make specific recommendations, and these topics were therefore deferred for possible consideration as part of the longer-term review.

Recognizing that conducting a rulemaking and the subsequent implementation typically takes several years to accomplish, the Task Force recommended interim actions to be taken in the near-term. The recommended orders are intended to provide those interim safety enhancements for protection, mitigation, and preparedness while the rulemaking activities are conducted.

REGULATORY FRAMEWORK

The Task Force's first recommendation is for the Commission to establish a logical, systematic and coherent regulatory framework for adequate protection that appropriately balances defense-in-depth and risk considerations. In the Task Force's view, the NRC's existing regulatory framework does not apply defense-in-depth and risk insights consistently.

For example, beyond design basis events and severe accident issues have sometimes been addressed with new requirements such as the station blackout rule and in other cases have been addressed by voluntary industry initiatives such as severe accident management guidelines (SAMGs) which were not included in NRC requirements. The Task Force concluded that the proposed regulatory framework would serve all stakeholders well to facilitate staff and Commission decision-making, provide transparency and clarity for public stakeholders, and provide stability and predictability for the industry's business decisions on meeting regulatory requirements.

PROTECTION RECOMMENDATIONS

With regard to protection of equipment from natural phenomena, the Task Force concluded that protection of important plant equipment from the appropriate external hazards is a key foundation of safety and that it is essential for nuclear plants to be protected against the appropriate design basis external events.

Design basis external hazards were established during the construction permit phase for operating U.S. plants, and they are not typically revisited through the life of the plant. The last construction permit for an operating U.S. plant was issued in 1978, and for many plants, this was completed in the 1960s. Since that time, there have been significant advancements in the state of knowledge and state of analysis methods for seismic and flooding hazards.

Through the years, various NRC programs have been initiated to evaluate the risk from external hazards, and actions were taken to address plant vulnerabilities that were identified. However, the hazards were not comprehensively reevaluated for all sites and the design basis was not necessarily updated.

The Task Force concluded that the state of knowledge of seismic and flooding hazards has evolved to the point that it is appropriate for licensees to reevaluate the designs of existing nuclear power reactors to ensure that structures, systems and components important to safety will withstand such events without loss of capability to perform their intended safety function.

On this basis, the Task Force made its second recommendation, which is for the Commission to require licensees to reevaluate the design basis seismic and flooding hazards and as necessary, upgrade the protection of plant structures, systems and components. In its third recommendation, the Task Force also recommended, as part of the longer-term review, that the NRC evaluate potential enhancements to the capability to prevent or mitigate seismically- induced fires and floods.

The Task Force recognized that the proposed analysis and potential modifications would take time to implement. Therefore, as an interim action, the Task Force recommended seismic and flooding protection walkdowns be completed over the next several months to identify and address plant-specific vulnerabilities and verify the adequacy of monitoring and maintenance for protection features such as watertight barriers and seals.

MITIGATION RECOMMENDATIONS

The Task Force also provided recommendations covering several aspects of mitigation of low frequency events. These include mitigation of prolonged station blackout events, containment overpressure prevention, hydrogen control, spent fuel pool cooling, and onsite emergency response capabilities.

STATION BLACKOUT

In order to strengthen the ability of nuclear power plants to deal with the effects of prolonged station blackout events, the Task Force made its fourth recommendation: the development of a comprehensive integrated approach to provide uninterrupted core and spent fuel cooling, and provide integrity of the reactor coolant system and containment. The proposed approach is divided into three phases: (1) an eight hour minimum coping phase; (2) a 72-hour extended coping phase; (3) and an offsite support phase. As an interim measure, the Task Force recommended that licensees be ordered to take reasonable action to protect existing mitigation equipment and to ensure that adequate capability is available to mitigate multiunit accidents.

CONTAINMENT OVERPRESSURE

All boiling water reactors with Mark I containments voluntarily installed hardened wetwell vents in the early 1990's. The wetwell vents are intended to ensure containment integrity is maintained by preventing containment overpressure.

The Task Force recommended that Mark I wetwell vents be a requirement and that the wetwell vent designs be enhanced to provide capability to open and to reclose as needed during prolonged station blackout scenarios. Eight boiling water reactor units in the United States have Mark II containment designs.

Three of these units have installed hardened vents, and the remaining five units at Columbia, Limerick and Susquehanna have not installed hardened vents. The Task Force concluded that a Mark II under similar circumstances as Fukushima Dai-ichi units 1, 2 and 3, would have suffered similar consequences. Therefore, in its fifth recommendation, the Task Force recommended that reliable hardened wetwell vents be required at all boiling water reactors with Mark II containments.

Additionally, the Task Force also recommended that the NRC staff reevaluate other containment designs as part of the long-term review to ensure that hardened vents are not necessary to mitigate beyond design basis accidents at other facilities.

HYDROGEN CONTROL

With regard to hydrogen control, the Task Force recommendation regarding enhanced mitigation of prolonged station blackout would, if implemented, reduce the likelihood of core damage and hydrogen production. This recommendation also includes provisions for backup power for hydrogen igniters in containment designs that require those features. In addition, while primarily aimed at containment overpressure prevention, enhanced wetwell vents for Mark I and Mark II containments designs would provide a reliable means for venting hydrogen to the atmosphere. These steps would greatly reduce the likelihood of hydrogen explosions from a severe accident.

Sufficient information from the detailed sequence of events and cause of hydrogen explosions at the Fukushima Dai-ichi plants was not available, however, for the Task Force to reasonably formulate any further specific recommendations related to combustible gas control. Therefore, in its sixth recommendation, the Task Force recommended that the NRC staff identify insights about hydrogen control and mitigation in primary containment and other buildings as part of the longer-term review.

SPENT FUEL SAFETY

In the area of spent fuel pool safety, the Task Force concluded that the two most important insights from the Fukushima Dai-ichi accident relate to instrumentation to provide information about the condition of the pool and the spent fuel and the plant's capability for spent fuel cooling.

To address both of these insights, the Task Force made its seventh recommendation to enhance spent fuel pool makeup capability and instrumentation for the spent fuel pool. Specifically, the Task Force recommended that spent fuel pool instrumentation be required to provide reliable information on the conditions in the spent fuel pool. Additionally, the Task Force recommended a requirement for spent fuel makeup to have safety-related backup power, and lastly, the Task Force recommended a requirement for a seismically qualified flow path to spray water into the spent fuel pools.

ONSITE EMERGENCY RESPONSE

The Task Force's eighth and final recommendation for enhanced mitigation capability is in the area of onsite emergency response. The Task Force recommended that the onsite emergency response capabilities be strengthened and integrated for a seamless response to severe accidents.

EMERGENCY RESPONSE RECOMMENDATIONS

In addition to protection and mitigation measures, the Task Force examined how the insights from the accident at Fukushima Dai-ichi might inform both onsite and offsite emergency planning in the U.S. While the Task Force believes that the emergency planning basis in the U.S. provides radiological protection to members of the public, the Task Force identified two aspects of the Fukushima Dai-ichi accident that it concluded warrant additional consideration in the U.S. These two aspects are emergency planning for prolonged station blackout events and emergency planning for multiple unit events. In its ninth recommendation, the Task Force recommended that licensees be required to address prolonged station blackout and multiunit events in their facility's emergency plans. Examples of the proposed requirements include backup power supplies for communications equipment, and ensuring adequate staffing is available to respond to an event affecting more than one unit on a multiunit site.

In its tenth and eleventh recommendations, the Task Force proposed several topics that it believes warrant further evaluation during the longer-term review. These topics include protective equipment for emergency responders, qualifications for emergency decisionmakers, off-site radiation monitoring capability, and training for decisionmakers and the public on radiation safety and the appropriate use of potassium iodide.

NRC Programs

Finally, the Task Force identified one recommendation to enhance NRC programs. The Task Force concluded that enhancements to the NRC inspection program would improve its focus on safety. Specifically, in its twelfth recommendation, the Task Force recommended that the NRC strengthen regulatory oversight of licensee safety performance by balancing the use of risk by providing additional emphasis on defense-in-depth requirements.

Conclusion

In summary, the Task Force identified a number of important recommendations that touch on a broad range of issues. These recommendations seek to clarify the NRC's regulatory framework, to enhance safety through interim actions, orders, and rulemakings, and lastly, to provide recommended topics for long-term evaluation.

With the Task Force report now in hand, the Commission is considering the recommendations and deliberating on the path forward. We have a shared interest in stakeholder participation, including questions and feedback received at the Task Force's public meeting on July 28th. I look forward to ongoing dialogue and exchange of ideas among my colleagues and me in the coming weeks.

Chairman Boxer, Ranking Member Inhofe, Chairman Carper, Ranking Member Barrasso, and Members of the Committee, this concludes my formal testimony today. On behalf of the Commission, thank you for the opportunity to appear before you. We look forward to continuing to work with you to advance the NRC's important safety mission. We would be pleased to respond to any questions you may have.

In: Reactor Safety Recommendations
Editors: Kenton I. Vinson and Rupert E. Gilliam
ISBN: 978-1-61942-645-0
© 2012 Nova Science Publishers, Inc.

Chapter 3

RECOMMENDED ACTIONS TO BE TAKEN WITHOUT DELAY FROM THE NEAR-TERM TASK FORCE REPORT

R. W. Borchardt

September 9, 2011

PURPOSE

The purpose of this paper is to provide, for Commission consideration, the recommendations of the U. S. Nuclear Regulatory Commission (NRC) staff, regarding those Near-Term Task Force (NTTF) recommendations that can and, in the staff's judgment, should be initiated, in part or in whole, without delay.

In the Commission notation vote paper due on October 3, 2011, the staff plans to provide the prioritization of the NTTF recommendations to (1) reflect regulatory actions to be taken by the staff in response to the Fukushima lessons learned; (2) identify implementation challenges; (3) include technical and regulatory bases for the prioritization; (4) identify additional recommendations, if any; and (5) include a schedule and milestones with recommendations for appropriate stakeholder engagement and involvement of the Advisory Committee for Reactor Safeguards (ACRS).

BACKGROUND

The NTTF was established to complete the near-term review required by the Chairman's tasking memorandum of March 23, 2011 (COMGBJ-11-0002). In SECY-11-0093, "Near-Term Report and Recommendations for Agency Actions Following the Events in Japan," dated July 12, 2011, the NTTF provided its recommendations to the Commission. The staff requirements memorandum (SRM) for SECY-11-0093, dated August 19, 2011, directed the staff, by September 9, 2011, to "identify and make recommendations regarding any NTTF recommendations that can, and in the staff's judgment, should be implemented, in part or in whole, without unnecessary delay."

Contact: David Skeen, NRR/DE 301-415-3298.

DISCUSSION

As directed by SRM-SECY-11-0093, the staff reviewed the NTTF recommendations within the context of the NRC's existing framework and considered the various regulatory vehicles available to the NRC to implement the recommendations. This review was conducted by an ad hoc team consisting of NRC senior management representatives and technical experts. The staff determined the near-term regulatory actions based on its judgment of the potential and relative safety enhancement of each of the recommendations. Additionally, the staff developed this paper by focusing on those NTTF recommendations that can, and in the staff's judgment, should be initiated without delay in whole or in part. This is a subset of the total NTTF recommendations. The staff initially focused on Recommendations 2, 4, 5, 7, 8 and 9, because the other recommendations proposed longer-term reviews by the NRC staff. The staff believes that all the NTTF's overarching recommendations, if adopted, would enhance safety and the staff agrees with moving forward with each of these recommendations. As such, the staff will continue to evaluate approaches to implement all other NTTF recommendations. The process used by the staff to identify near-term actions should not be interpreted as a lack of support for other NTTF recommendations; prioritization is necessary to better manage the work and resources discussed below.

To further inform this process, the staff sought external stakeholder feedback regarding the NTTF recommendations that stakeholders consider to be most important and that the NRC should undertake in the near-term. To accomplish this, the NRC staff conducted a public meeting on August 31, 2011, to discuss the six NTTF recommendations under consideration for inclusion in this paper. The meeting minutes and transcript are available in the Agencywide Documents Access and Management System (ADAMS) at ML112490382. In addition, written stakeholder comments were received and are available in ADAMS at ML11249A161. The stakeholder panelists expressed a desire for stakeholder involvement in the regulatory process going forward regardless of the regulatory vehicle used. Additionally, the industry, the Federal Emergency Management Agency, and nongovernmental participants agreed in concept with the six recommendations discussed at the meeting, although various viewpoints emerged concerning the pace of implementation and associated regulatory vehicles.

To determine and recommend near-term regulatory actions that can and should be initiated without delay, the staff considered whether any of the NTTF recommendations identified an imminent hazard to public health and safety. The staff agrees with the NTTF that none of the recommendations rise to this level. While the staff recognizes that the NTTF raises important issues for consideration, it does not have sufficient resources to initiate actions on all recommendations in the near-term. The staff identified a subset of actions that the staff concludes has the greatest potential for safety improvement in the near-term. The remaining recommendations will be evaluated and prioritized, along with this subset, as part of the notation vote paper due on October 3, 2011.

The near-term actions identified are the following:

2.1 Seismic and flood hazard reevaluations
2.3 Seismic and flood walkdowns
4.1 Station blackout regulatory actions
4.2. Equipment covered under Title 10 of the *Code of Federal Regulations* (10 CFR) 50.54(hh)(2)
5.1 Reliable hardened vents for Mark I containments
8 Strengthening and integration of emergency operating procedures, severe accident management guidelines, and extensive damage mitigation guidelines
9.3 Emergency preparedness regulatory actions

In addition, the staff provided a discussion in the *enclosure* of NTTF Recommendation 9.4 regarding the modernization of the Emergency Response Data System (ERDS). This discussion provides a status of ongoing industry actions in this area. The staff concluded that additional regulatory action is not necessary at this time to ensure implementation of the ERDS modernization.

The staff concluded that additional review is needed to identify specific regulatory actions related to NTTF Recommendation 7 regarding enhanced spent fuel pool makeup capacity and instrumentation for spent fuel pools. For example, the resolution strategy for Recommendation 2.1 may influence the seismic qualification of potential instrumentation for spent fuel pools.

Relative to Recommendations 4.2 and 5.1, the staff is proposing to issue Orders that would redefine the level of protection of public health and safety that should be regarded as adequate. While the basis for the staff's recommendation is provided in the *enclosure,* the supporting rationale for these Orders will be more fully developed as the technical and regulatory basis is formulated.

For the remaining recommendations discussed in this paper, the staff is proposing initiating this subset of actions as safety improvements. As such, the final regulatory action taken will depend on Commission direction, the supporting basis, and whether the applicable action is supportable under agency procedures and applicable backfitting requirements, including the potential to redefine what level of protection of public health and safety should be regarded as adequate.

For all the NTTF recommendations identified as potential near-term actions, the staff performed a more focused assessment to further define the regulatory activities that would be required, and to gain a sense of the resource impacts that could be incurred. This process, while principally centered on safety, gave consideration to the staff's estimate of the current supporting regulatory basis, the need for stakeholder engagement, and technical and scheduler dependencies (i.e., practical feasibility of undertaking action immediately). Enclosed are the assessments for each of the NTTF recommendations the staff proposes can and should be initiated without delay.

In general, the NTTF identified a specific regulatory vehicle (e.g., Order or rulemaking) for each recommendation. Initially, the staff assessed each recommendation independent of the regulatory vehicle proposed by the NTTF.

This allowed the staff to determine the actions that should be taken to assess, develop, or complete the supporting technical and regulatory bases. In many cases, external stakeholder engagement is recommended to inform these efforts so that the regulatory action and licensee actions taken effectively resolve the identified issues and implementation challenges are identified in advance. In developing the proposed regulatory vehicle for each staff recommendation in the enclosure, the staff considered the wide range of regulatory tools available.

As discussed above, the staff recommends issuance of Orders as the appropriate regulatory vehicle in those cases where the staff believes that sufficient basis exists to support the initiation of the development of new requirements in the near-term to redefine what level of protection of public health and safety should be regarded as adequate. The technical and regulatory basis for these Orders will be fully established as the Orders are developed. In cases where the staff determined that more information is required before taking additional regulatory action, the staff recommends issuance of requests for information pursuant to 10 CFR 50.54(f). In the remaining cases, the staff proposes to initiate rulemaking.

While not explicitly stated in the enclosed recommendations, the staff will evaluate licensee responses, document staff reviews, and oversee licensee implementation through inspections, consistent with our well-established regulatory processes.

The staff agrees with the NTTF assessment of the approach that should be taken for Watts Bar Unit 2 and Bellefonte Units 1 and 2. Those operating license reviews and the licensing itself should include all of the recommended regulatory actions and rule changes that have been completed at the time of licensing. Any additional rule changes would be imposed on the plants in the same manner as for other operating reactors.

With regard to near-term combined license reviews, the staff discusses options in SECY-11-0110, "Staff Statement In Support of the Uncontested Hearing for Issuance of Combined Licenses and Limited Work Authorizations for Vogtle Electric Generating Plant, Units 3 and 4 (Docket Nos. 52-025 and 52-026), dated August 9, 2011, and SECY-11-0115, "Staff Statement in Support of the Uncontested Hearing for Issuance of Combined Licenses for the Virgil C. Summer Nuclear Station, Units 2 and 3 (Docket Nos. 52-027 and 52-028)," dated August 19, 2011.

The remainder of the NTTF recommendations, with the exception of NTTF Recommendation 1 as directed by the Commission, will be evaluated further in the notation vote paper due on October 3, 2011. Included in that evaluation will be any elements of the NTTF recommendations that were evaluated as part of the short-term effort and were concluded to be longer-term regulatory actions (e.g., NTTF Recommendation 2.2).

Within schedule constraints and practical limitations given the limited understanding of the ultimate regulatory action that might be taken, the staff will provide its estimate for the supporting schedules and milestones with recommendations for appropriate stakeholder engagement and involvement of the ACRS in the notation vote paper due on October 3, 2011.

RECOMMENDATIONS

The staff recommends that the Commission provide direction to the staff to take the actions as described in the enclosure. The *enclosure* provides further description of each recommendation discussed above.

RESOURCES

For each of the recommended near-term actions, the staff performed an initial assessment to identify the skill sets, applicable organizations, and estimated resources that are needed to support the actions. There will be resource impacts associated with the recommended actions. The notation paper due on October 3, 2011, will provide a further discussion of the resources needed to accomplish the activities proposed in this paper, and staff activities that may be delayed or deferred as a result.

The Office of the General Counsel has reviewed this paper and has no legal objection. The Office of the Chief Financial Officer has reviewed this paper for resource implications and has concurred.

/RA/
R. W. Borchardt Executive Director for Operations
Enclosure: Staff Assessment of Near-Term Task Force Recommendations

STAFF ASSESSMENT OF NEAR-TERM TASK FORCE RECOMMENDATIONS

As directed by SRM-SECY-11-0093, U. S. Nuclear Regulatory Commission (NRC) staff reviewed the Near-Term Task Force (NTTF or Task Force) recommendations within the context of the NRC's existing framework and gave consideration to the various regulatory vehicles available to the NRC to implement the recommendations. The staff determined the near-term regulatory actions based on the staff's judgment of the potential and relative safety enhancement of each of the recommendations.

Each of the following assessments includes the recommendation as presented in the NTTF report, the associated regulations and guidance, the staff's assessment of the recommendation, and the staff's recommendations for regulatory actions to be initiated without delay.

NTTF RECOMMENDATION 2.1

The Task Force recommends the NRC require licensees to reevaluate and upgrade as necessary the design-basis seismic and flooding protection of SSCs [structures, systems, and components] for each operating reactor.

2.1 Order licensees to reevaluate the seismic and flooding hazards at their sites against current NRC requirements and guidance, and if necessary, update the design basis and SSCs important to safety to protect against the updated hazards.

REGULATIONS AND GUIDANCE

1. General Design Criterion (GDC) 2, "Design Bases for Protection Against Natural Phenomena," of Appendix A, "General Design Criteria for Nuclear Power Plants," to Title10 of the *Code of Federal Regulations* (10 CFR) Part 50, "Domestic Licensing of Production and Utilization Facilities," requires, in part, that SSCs important to safety be designed to withstand the effects of natural phenomena such as floods, tsunami, and seiches without loss of capability to perform their safety functions. Plants that received construction permits before issuance of GDC 2 in 1971 meet the intent of the GDC.
2. 10 CFR Part 100, "Reactor Site Criteria," Appendix A, "Seismic and Geologic Siting Criteria for Nuclear Power Plants," was established to provide detailed criteria to evaluate the suitability of proposed sites and the suitability of the plant design basis established in consideration of the seismic and geologic characteristics of the proposed sites.
3. Regulatory Guide (RG) 1.29, "Seismic Design Classification," issued June 1972 and updated August 1973, February 1976, September 1978, and March 2007.
4. RG 1.59, "Design Basis Floods for Nuclear Power Plants," issued August 1973 and updated April 1976 and August 1977.
5. RG 1.60, "Design Response Spectra for Seismic Design of Nuclear Power Plants," issued October 1973 and updated December 1973.
6. RG 1.102, "Flood Protection for Nuclear Power Plants," issued October 1975 and updated September 1976.
7. RG 1.125, "Physical Models for Design and Operation of Hydraulic Structures and Systems for Nuclear Power Plants," issued March 1977 and updated October 1978 and March 2009.
8. RG 1.208, "A Performance-Based Approach To Define the Site-Specific Earthquake Ground Motion," issued March 2007.

STAFF ASSESSMENT OF NTTF RECOMMENDATION 2.1

The staff's assessment of this recommendation indicates that plants may differ in the way they ensure safety against natural phenomena. The staff concluded that sufficient regulatory guidance currently exists to permit licensee reevaluations. However, the staff noted that results of inspections of SSCs at Fukushima Daiichi and Daini Nuclear Power Stations may help inform the implementation of this recommendation. To the extent practical, the new information on the events at Fukushima Daiichi and Daini should be incorporated into the reevaluations. The staff also noted that the implementation of this recommendation would require significant resources for both licensees and NRC, as well as specialized expertise to review licensee reevaluations and to document results of staff evaluations.

Seismic hazards. The state of knowledge of seismic hazards within the United States has evolved to the point that it would be appropriate for licensees to reevaluate the designs of existing nuclear power reactors to ensure that SSCs important to safety will withstand a seismic event without loss of capability to perform their intended safety function. The staff notes that ongoing activities to resolve Generic Issue 199, "Implications of Updated Probabilistic Seismic Estimates in Central and Eastern United States on Existing Plants," are directly related to this issue and will be considered in the resolution of Recommendation 2.1.

Flooding hazards. The assumptions and factors that were considered in flood protection at operating plants vary. In some cases, the design bases did not consider the effects from the local intense precipitation and related site drainage. In other cases, the probable maximum flood is calculated differently at units co-located at the same site, depending on the time of licensing, resulting in different design-basis flood protection. The NTTF and the staff noted that some plants rely on operator actions and temporary flood mitigation measures such as sandbagging, temporary flood walls and barriers, and portable equipment to perform safety functions. For several sites, the staff noted that all appropriate flooding hazards are not documented in the Updated Final Safety Analysis Report. The NTTF and the staff also noted that flooding risks are of concern because of a "cliff-edge" effect, in that the safety consequences of a flooding event may increase sharply with a small increase in the flooding level. Therefore, all licensees should confirm that SSCs important to safety are adequately protected from floods.

STAFF RECOMMENDATIONS

The staff recommends that the NRC, as a near-term action, undertake regulatory activities to:

1. Continue stakeholder interactions to discuss the technical basis and acceptance criteria for conducting a reevaluation of site specific seismic hazards. This would include implementation considerations of the hazard and risk methodologies described in draft Generic Letter (GL) 2001-XX, "Seismic Risk Evaluations for Operating Reactors," issued for public comment on September 1, 2011, (Agencywide Documents Access and Management System (ADAMS) Accession No. ML111710783).
2. Initiate stakeholder interaction to discuss application of the present-day regulatory guidance and methodologies being used for early site permit and combined license reviews to the reevaluation of flooding hazards at operating reactors.
3. Develop and issue a request for information to licensees pursuant to 10 CFR 50.54(f) to (1) reevaluate site specific seismic hazards using the methodology discussed in item 1 above, and (2) identify actions that have been taken or are planned to address plant-specific vulnerabilities associated with the updated seismic hazards.
4. Develop and issue a request for information to licensees pursuant to 10 CFR 50.54(f) to (1) reevaluate site specific flooding hazards using the methodology discussed in

item 2 above, and (2) identify actions that have been taken or are planned to address plant-specific vulnerabilities associated with the updated flooding hazards.
5. Evaluate licensee responses and take appropriate regulatory action to resolve vulnerabilities associated with updated site specific hazards.

NTTF RECOMMENDATION 2.3

The Task Force recommends that the NRC require licensees to reevaluate and upgrade as necessary the design-basis seismic and flooding protection of SSCs for each operating reactor.

2.3 Order licensees to perform seismic and flood protection walkdowns to identify and address plant-specific vulnerabilities and verify the adequacy of monitoring and maintenance for protection features such as watertight barriers and seals in the interim period until longer-term actions are completed to update the design basis for external events.

REGULATIONS AND GUIDANCE

1. GDC 2, "Design Bases for Protection Against Natural Phenomena," of Appendix A, "General Design Criteria for Nuclear Power Plants," to 10 CFR Part 50, "Domestic Licensing of Production and Utilization Facilities," requires, in part, that SSCs important to safety be designed to withstand the effects of natural phenomena such as floods, tsunami, and seiches without loss of capability to perform their safety functions.
2. 10 CFR Part 100, "Reactor Site Criteria," Appendix A, "Seismic and Geologic Siting Criteria for Nuclear Power Plants," was established to provide detailed criteria to evaluate the suitability of proposed sites and the suitability of the plant design basis established in consideration of the seismic and geologic characteristics of the proposed sites.
3. RG 1.29, "Seismic Design Classification," issued June 1972 and updated August 1973, February 1976, September 1978, and March 2007.
4. RG 1.59, "Design Basis Floods for Nuclear Power Plants," issued August 1973 and updated April 1976 and August 1977.
5. RG 1.60, "Design Response Spectra for Seismic Design of Nuclear Power Plants," issued October 1973 and updated December 1973.
6. RG 1.102, "Flood Protection for Nuclear Power Plants," issued October 1975 and updated September 1976.
7. RG 1.125, "Physical Models for Design and Operation of Hydraulic Structures and Systems for Nuclear Power Plants," issued March 1977 and updated October 1978 and March 2009.

STAFF ASSESSMENT OF NTTF RECOMMENDATION 2.3

The NRC should undertake regulatory activities to have licensees perform seismic and flood protection walkdowns to ensure that existing protection and mitigation measures are available, functional, and adequately maintained.

Seismic hazards. The staff's assessment of this recommendation indicates that some guidance for seismic protection walkdowns exists. Recent plant inspections by staff in accordance with Temporary Instruction 2515/183, "Followup to the Fukushima Daiichi Nuclear Station Fuel Damage Event," and licensees' plant inspections in response to the Fukushima Daiichi accidents will help inform the implementation of this recommendation. In addition, the staff noted that results of ongoing inspections and evaluations of SSCs at Fukushima Daiichi and Daini Nuclear Power Stations may provide some insights for this recommendation. To the extent practical, the new information on the events at Fukushima Daiichi and Daini should be incorporated into the reevaluations. Evaluations of the recent earthquake near the North Anna Power Station on August 23, 2011, may also provide valuable insights.

Flooding hazards. With regard to flooding hazards, the Task Force and the staff have noted some plants rely on operator actions and temporary flood mitigation measures such as sandbagging, temporary flood walls and barriers, and portable equipment to perform safety functions. Results of staff's inspections at nuclear power sites in accordance with Temporary Instruction 2515/183 identified potential issues and observations regarding mitigation measures. Recent flooding at the Fort Calhoun site showed the importance of temporary flood mitigation measures.

The staff noted that guidance should be developed for both the seismic and flooding walkdowns with external stakeholder involvement to ensure consistency.

STAFF RECOMMENDATIONS

The staff recommends that the NRC, as a near-term action, undertake regulatory activities to:

Develop and issue a request for information to licensees pursuant to 10 CFR 50.54(f) to (1) develop a methodology and acceptance criteria for seismic and flooding walkdowns to be endorsed by the staff following interaction with external stakeholders, (2) perform seismic and flood protection walkdowns to identify and address plant-specific vulnerabilities (through corrective action program) and verify the adequacy of monitoring and maintenance for protection features, and (3) inform the NRC of the results of the walkdowns and corrective actions taken or planned.

NTTF RECOMMENDATION 4.1

The Task Force recommends that the NRC strengthen SBO [station blackout] mitigation capability at all operating and new reactors for design-basis and beyond-design-basis external events.

4.1 Initiate rulemaking to revise 10 CFR 50.63 to require each operating and new reactor licensee to: (1) establish a minimum coping time of 8 hours for a loss of all ac [alternating current] power, (2) establish the equipment, procedures, and training necessary to implement an "extended loss of all ac" coping time of 72 hours for core and spent fuel pool cooling and for reactor coolant system and primary containment integrity as needed, and (3) preplan and prestage offsite resources to support uninterrupted core and spent fuel pool cooling, and reactor coolant system and containment integrity as needed, including the ability to deliver the equipment to the site in the time period allowed for extended coping, under conditions involving significant degradation of offsite transportation infrastructure associated with significant natural disasters.

REGULATIONS AND GUIDANCE

1. 10 CFR 50.63, "Loss of All Alternating Current Power" (known as the "Station Blackout Rule"), requires that each nuclear power plant must be able to cool the reactor core and maintain containment integrity for a specified duration of an SBO.
2. RG 1.155, "Station Blackout," issued August 1988, describes an acceptable means to comply with 10 CFR 50.63.

STAFF ASSESSMENT OF NTTF RECOMMENDATIONS

The NRC should undertake regulatory activities intended to strengthen SBO mitigation capability at all operating and new reactors to address prolonged SBO stemming from design-basis and beyond-design-basis external events to provide core and spent fuel pool cooling, reactor coolant system integrity, and containment integrity. This regulatory action would consider the need for SBO power source(s) and mitigating equipment to be diverse and protected from external events.

This regulatory action would also examine whether there is a need to expand SBO mitigation requirements to require power reactors to mitigate an SBO event at a plant (each unit for multi-unit site) until either the onsite or offsite power source is restored to bring the power reactor to a cold shutdown and to maintain spent fuel pool cooling. This rulemaking would primarily amend 10 CFR 50.63 and would impact both operating reactor licensees and new reactor applications.

STAFF RECOMMENDATION

The staff recommends that the NRC, as a near-term action:

Engage stakeholders in support of rulemaking activities to enhance the capability to maintain safety through a prolonged SBO. These activities will include the development of the regulatory basis, a proposed rule, and implementing guidance.

NTTF Recommendation 4.2

The Task Force recommends that the NRC strengthen SBO mitigation capability at all operating and new reactors for design-basis and beyond-design-basis external events.

4.2. Order licensees to provide reasonable protection for equipment currently provided pursuant to 10 CFR 50.54(hh)(2) from the effects of design-basis external events and to add equipment as needed to address multi-unit events while other requirements are being revised and implemented.

Regulations and Guidance

1. 10 CFR 50.54(hh)(2) requires licensees to develop and implement guidance and strategies intended to maintain or restore core cooling, containment, and spent fuel pool cooling capabilities under circumstances associated with the loss of large areas of the plant due to explosions or fire.
2. The required strategies include firefighting, operations to mitigate fuel damage, and actions to minimize radiological release.
3. Nuclear Energy Institute (NEI) 06-12, Revision 2, "B.5.b Phase 2 & 3 Submittal Guidance," issued December 2006, provides guidance supporting 10 CFR 50.54(hh)(2).
4. The equipment procured and used to implement the strategies of 10 CFR 50.54(hh)(2) is controlled through the licensee's commitment management process (which follows NEI 99-04, "Guidelines for Managing NRC Commitment Changes," issued July 1999).

Staff Assessment of NTTF Recommendation

The staff concludes that equipment procured pursuant to 10 CFR 50.54(hh)(2) will provide, as an interim measure, some of the coping capability that is recommended for addressing the NTTF recommendations associated with prolonged SBO events. However, the staff notes the NTTF finding that the current guidance only addresses single unit capacity and storage of the equipment for security-related initiating events.

Specifically, the guidance in the NRC-endorsed NEI 06-12, for equipment used to implement the strategies in 10 CFR 50.54(hh)(2) via the extensive damage mitigation guidelines (EDMGs), is silent on whether the equipment needs to be protected from the effects of external events.

The staff agrees that there will be a benefit to reasonably protecting the mitigation equipment while still meeting the intended purpose for security-related events. Any regulatory action to direct licensees to reasonably protect this equipment will need to address what constitutes "reasonably protect."

This will be framed to support licensees taking practical actions that increase the likelihood that the equipment will survive the effects of external events while not reducing the availability of the equipment to function for its intended purpose, which is to support implementation of the strategies to mitigate the loss of large areas of the plant due to explosions and fires. Accordingly, "reasonably protect" would not necessarily mean locating the equipment in seismic Category I structures (unless that action is practical and does not adversely impact the mitigation of large fires and explosions).

The staff also concludes that use of this 10 CFR 50.54(hh)(2) equipment, as envisioned by the NTTF, will likely require the equipment be supplemented to address a multi-unit condition.

In the near-term, the staff concludes early interaction with external stakeholders would be beneficial to explore the 10 CFR 50.54(hh)(2) mitigation strategies that might be useful for prolonged SBOs as an interim measure until regulatory actions associated with Recommendation 4.1 (SBO rulemaking) are completed. In addition, this interaction would include a discussion of how those strategies might be expanded to better address the SBO conditions and how equipment might best be supplemented to support those modified strategies.

The results of this interaction would inform the staff actions going forward on whether, and how, to amend 10 CFR 50.54(hh)(2) to address both loss of large areas due to explosions and fires and prolonged SBO.

The staff concludes that it would be appropriate to redefine what level of protection of public health and safety should be regarded as adequate for reasonable protection and capacity of the 10 CFR 50.54(hh)(2) equipment.

STAFF RECOMMENDATIONS

The staff recommends that the NRC, as a near-term action, undertake regulatory activities to:

Develop and issue Orders to licensees to provide reasonable protection of the equipment used to satisfy the requirements of 10 CFR 50.54(hh)(2) from the effects of external events, and to establish and maintain sufficient capacity to mitigate multi-unit events. This would include stakeholder interactions to define acceptance criteria for reasonable protection of 10 CFR 50.54(hh)(2) equipment from design basis external hazards.

NTTF RECOMMENDATION 5.1

The Task Force recommends requiring reliable hardened vent designs in BWR [boiling-water reactor] facilities with Mark I and Mark II containments.

5.1 Order licensees to include a reliable hardened vent in BWR Mark I and Mark II containments.
- This order should include performance objectives for the design of hardened vents to ensure reliable operation and ease of use (both opening and closing) during a prolonged SBO.

REGULATIONS AND GUIDANCE

1. GL 89-16, "Installation of a Hardened Wetwell Vent," was issued to licensees of nuclear plants with BWR Mark I primary containments requesting that they consider voluntary installation of hardened wetwell vents under the provisions of 10 CFR 50.59, "Changes, Tests and Experiments," to provide assurance of pressure relief through a path with significant scrubbing of fission products should normal and design basis containment cooling systems not be available. Hardened wetwell airspace vents of varying designs, but all alternating current (AC) dependent, were installed in the currently operating units with Mark I containments primarily to avoid exceeding the primary containment pressure limit.
2. 10 CFR 50.54(hh)(2) requires licensees to develop and implement guidance and strategies to maintain or restore containment capabilities under the circumstances associated with loss of a large area of the plant due to explosions or fire; expectation B.2.e of the B.5.b Phase 1 Guidance Document dated February 25, 2002 (designated Safeguards Information) and Section 3.4.8 of the NRC-endorsed Phase 3 guidance in NEI 06-12, Revision 2, both specify that an acceptable means of meeting the 10 CFR 50.54(hh)(2) requirements includes the development of a procedure or strategy to allow venting primary containment to secondary containment, without AC power, as an alternate method to remove heat from the primary containment for BWR licensees. All currently operating BWR licensees, including those with BWR Mark I, Mark II, and Mark III containment designs, adopted this approach to meeting the requirements of 10 CFR 50.54(hh)(2). There are neither current NRC regulations that require this capability for other severe (beyond design basis) accidents nor design criteria for the vent paths used in this strategy.

STAFF ASSESSMENT OF NTTF RECOMMENDATIONS

BWR Mark I primary containments should have a reliable hardened vent for mitigating beyond design basis events. The staff will further evaluate and address this recommendation with respect to BWR Mark II primary containments in the 45-day notation vote paper.

This portion of the NTTF recommendation is consistent with previous staff studies and evaluation of Mark I primary containment design capabilities to withstand beyond design basis accident scenarios. The Fukushima accident highlighted the importance of the wetwell vent function, the accessibility of the valves and the capability for operation independent of AC power.

The staff concludes that it would be appropriate to redefine what level of protection of public health and safety should be regarded as adequate for venting of BWR Mark I primary containments.

STAFF RECOMMENDATION

The staff recommends that the NRC, as a near-term action, undertake regulatory activities to:

Develop and issue Orders to licensees with BWR Mark I primary containment designs to take action to ensure reliable hardened wetwell vents. This will include interactions with stakeholders to develop the technical bases and acceptance criteria for suitable design expectations for reliable hardened vents.

NTTF RECOMMENDATION 8

The Task Force recommends strengthening and integrating onsite emergency response capabilities such as EOPs [emergency operating procedures], SAMGs [severe accident management guidelines], and EDMGs.

8.1 Order licensees to modify the EOP technical guidelines (required by Supplement 1, "Requirements for Emergency Response Capability," to NUREG-0737, issued January 1983 (GL 82-33), to (1) include EOPs, SAMGs, and EDMGs in an integrated manner, (2) specify clear command and control strategies for their implementation, and (3) stipulate appropriate qualification and training for those who make decisions during emergencies.
- The Task Force strongly advises that the NRC encourage plant owners groups to undertake this activity rather than have each licensee develop its own approach. In addition, the Task Force encourages the use of the established NRC practice of publishing RGs (rather than NUREGs, supplements to NUREGs, or GLs) for endorsing any acceptable approaches submitted by the industry.

8.2 Modify Section 5.0, "Administrative Controls," of the Standard Technical Specifications for each operating reactor design to reference the approved EOP technical guidelines for that plant design.

8.3 Order licensees to modify each plant's technical specifications to conform to the above changes.

8.4 Initiate rulemaking to require more realistic, hands-on training and exercises on SAMGs and EDMGs for all staff expected to implement the strategies and those licensee staff expected to make decisions during emergencies, including emergency coordinators and emergency directors.

REGULATIONS AND GUIDANCE

1. RG 1.33, Revision 2, "Quality Assurance Program Requirements (Operation)," Appendix A, issued February 1978, required EOPs as a subset of the applicable procedures recommended in Section 5.0, "Administrative Controls," of licensee technical specifications.
2. NUREG-0737, "Clarification of TMI [Three Mile Island] Action Plan Requirements," Supplement 1, "Requirements for Emergency Response Capability," issued January 1983 (GL 82-33), required the development and submittal for review and approval of EOP technical guidelines.

3. Licensees developed SAMGs as a voluntary program, and the SAMGs are documented as meeting regulatory commitments. There is neither a requirement for realistic, hands-on training or exercises on SAMGs, nor a requirement for integration of the SAMGs, EOPs, and EDMGs.
4. 10 CFR 50.54(hh)(2) requires that licensees develop guidance and strategies. "EDMG" is the generic term used by industry for the required guidance and strategies. Requirements for exercise of EDMGs are included in the final rulemaking described in SECY-11-0053, "Final Rule: Enhancements to Emergency Preparedness Regulations (10 CFR Part 50 and 10 CFR Part 52)," dated April 8, 2011. There is no specific requirement for training on these guidance and strategies; the endorsed guidance on the subject in NEI 06-12, Revision 2, specifies training for 10 CFR 50.54(hh)(2).

STAFF ASSESSMENT OF NTTF RECOMMENDATIONS

EOPs, SAMGs, and EDMGs, should be strengthened and integrated. Transition points, command and control, decisionmaking, and training should be clarified.

SAMGs should be required along with qualification and training for those licensee staff expected to make decisions during beyond design basis accident scenarios using either the SAMGs or EDMGs.

Finally, the staff concludes that early interaction with stakeholders would be useful in determining the optimal mechanism for implementing these recommendations as requirements.

STAFF RECOMMENDATIONS

The staff recommends that the NRC, as a near-term action, undertake regulatory action to resolve NTTF Recommendations 8.1, 8.2, 8.3 and 8.4:

Issue an advanced notice of proposed rulemaking to engage stakeholders in rulemaking activities associated with the methodology for integration of onsite emergency response processes, procedures, training and exercises. Interact with stakeholders to modify the EOP generic technical guidelines in order to include guidance for SAMGs and EDMGs in an integrated manner and to clarify command and control issues as appropriate.

NTTF RECOMMENDATIONS 9.3 AND 9.4

The Task Force recommends that the NRC require that facility emergency plans address prolonged SBO and multiunit events.

9.3 Order licensees to do the following until rulemaking is complete:
- Determine and implement the required staff to fill all necessary positions for response to a multi-unit event

- Provide a means to power communications equipment needed to communicate onsite (e.g., radios for response teams and between facilities) and offsite (e.g., cellular telephones and satellite telephones) during a prolonged SBO.

9.4. Order licensees to complete the ERDS [Emergency Response Data System] modernization initiative by June 2012 to ensure multi-unit site monitoring capability.

REGULATIONS AND GUIDANCE

1. 10 CFR 50.47, "Emergency Plans," includes the 16 planning standards of 10 CFR 50.47(b), and Appendix E, "Emergency Planning and Preparedness for Production and Utilization Facilities," to 10 CFR Part 50 describes information needed to demonstrate compliance with EP requirements.
2. NUREG-0654, "Criteria for Preparation and Evaluation of Radiological Emergency Response Plans and Preparedness in Support of Nuclear Power Plants," Revision 1, issued November 1980, describes guidance and an acceptable means for demonstrating compliance with the Commission's regulations.
3. SECY-11-0053, "Final Rule: Enhancement to Emergency Preparedness Regulations (10 CFR Part 50 and 10 CFR Part 52)," dated April 8, 2011, codifies hostile-action-based enhancements, among others.
4. 10 CFR 50.27(b)(5) and Section IV.D.3 of Appendix E to 10 CFR Part 50 require that "licensees provide notification and instruction to the public within the plume exposure pathway emergency planning zone (EPZ)."
5. Section IV of Appendix E to 10 CFR Part 50 codifies the requirements for the NRC's ERDS.
6. NUREG-0696, "Functional Criteria for Emergency Response Facilities," issued February 1981, describes the facilities and systems that licensees can use to improve emergency response to accidents, such as the technical support system, operational support center, and emergency offsite facility.

STAFF'S ASSESSMENT OF NTTF RECOMMENDATIONS 9.3 AND 9.4

The staff's assessment of Recommendation 9.3 indicates that regulatory action should be initiated to determine the required staffing to fill all necessary positions for responding to a multiunit event. This would require both the NRC staff and licensees to reevaluate the current staffing assumptions and analysis for effectively responding to multi-unit incidents, in addition to actions being taken to satisfy the requirements of the recently affirmed Emergency Preparedness Final Rule. The staff is focused on licensees completing the staffing analyses only so that they could be done along with the actions required by the impending rule. Any resulting needs identified by those analyses related to work space or equipment will be considered as part of the 45-day review.

The staff also concludes that there is a need to strengthen the requirements to "provide a means to power communications equipment needed to communicate onsite (e.g., radios for response teams and between facilities) and offsite (e.g., cellular telephones and satellite telephones) during a prolonged SBO." This would require additional guidance regarding "acceptable" communications equipment that does not rely on the availability of facility AC power.

The staff's assessment of Recommendation 9.4 indicates this initiative is currently being implemented and is achievable without delay. The ERDS modernization initiative is already scheduled to be completed by June 2012. The NRC has an implementation schedule for all licensees regarding their site-specific ERDS modernization initiative; however, the staff will use additional regulatory tools if commitments are not met (e.g., a Confirmatory Order).

The staff notes early interaction with stakeholders will be essential to determine the optimal mechanisms for implementing each of the above recommendations.

STAFF RECOMMENDATION

The staff recommends that the NRC, as a near-term action, undertake regulatory activities to:

1. Develop and issue a request for information to licensees pursuant to 10 CFR 50.54(f) to (1) perform a staffing study to determine the required staff to fill all necessary positions to respond to a multi-unit event, (2) evaluate what enhancements would be needed to provide a means to power communications equipment necessary for licensee onsite and offsite communications during a prolonged station blackout event, and (3) inform the NRC of the results of the staffing study and any actions taken or planned, along with their implementation schedules, to react to the staffing study results and to enhance the communications equipment.
2. Evaluate licensee responses and take appropriate regulatory action.

The request for information will include a schedule for interactions with stakeholders to inform the NRC as the technical bases and acceptance criteria are developed for (1) ensuring sufficient licensee staffing for responding to multi-unit events, and (2) ensuring reliable licensee onsite and offsite communications during a prolonged SBO.

The staff also recommends that the NRC more closely monitor the industry's completion of the ERDS modernization initiative. The ERDS modernization initiative is scheduled to be completed by June 2012; however, if licensees fail to meet their implementation schedules, the staff will use additional regulatory tools (e.g., an Order) to ensure that licensees meet all requirements associated with the ERDS capability.

Chapter 4

PRIORITIZATION OF RECOMMENDED ACTIONS TO BE TAKEN IN RESPONSE TO FUKUSHIMA LESSONS LEARNED[*]

R. W. Borchardt

PURPOSE

The purpose of this paper is to provide, for Commission consideration, the staff's proposed prioritization of the Fukushima Near-Term Task Force (NTTF) recommendations to (1) reflect regulatory actions to be taken by the staff in response to the Fukushima lessons learned; (2) identify implementation challenges; (3) include the technical and regulatory bases for the prioritization; (4) identify additional recommendations, if any; and (5) include a schedule and milestones with recommendations for appropriate stakeholder engagement and involvement of the Advisory Committee on Reactor Safeguards (ACRS). The enclosure provides detailed information to address these points.

BACKGROUND

The NTTF was established to complete the near-term review required by the Chairman's tasking memorandum of March 23, 2011 (COMGBJ-11-0002). In SECY-11-0093, "Near-Term Report and Recommendations for Agency Actions Following the Events in Japan," dated July 12, 2011, the NTTF provided its recommendations to the Commission. The staff requirements memorandum (SRM) for SECY-11-0093, dated August 19, 2011, directed the staff to recommend a prioritization of the Task Force recommendations by October 3, 2011.
CONTACT: David L. Skeen, NRR/DE
301-415-3298

---

[*] This is an edited, reformatted and augmented version of a Policy Issue Notation Vote publication, for the Commissioners from: R. W. Borchardt Executive Director for Operations, dated October 3, 2011.

DISCUSSION

As directed by SRM-SECY-11-0093, the staff reviewed the NTTF recommendations within the context of the NRC's existing regulatory framework and considered the various regulatory vehicles available to the NRC to implement the recommendations. This review was conducted by a team consisting of NRC senior management representatives and technical experts.

PRIORITIZATION AND ASSESSMENT

The staff initially prioritized the recommendations based on its judgment of the potential and relative safety enhancement which could be realized by each. First, the staff considered whether any of the NTTF findings identified an imminent hazard to public health and safety. As was previously discussed in SECY-11-0124, "Recommended Actions to be Taken Without Delay from the Near-Term Task Force Report," the staff agrees with the NTTF that none of the findings rise to this level. Additionally, in SECY-11-0124, the staff identified a subset of the NTTF recommendations which should be undertaken without unnecessary delay. These are the recommendations that the staff previously concluded have the greatest potential for safety improvement in the near term, recognizing that the staff does not have sufficient resources to initiate action on all recommendations at this time.

The staff then performed an assessment of each NTTF recommendation to determine the required regulatory activities, an estimated schedule, and associated resource impacts. An important element of this assessment was the objective of not unnecessarily diverting the NRC's or nuclear industry's focus from other important, ongoing safety-significant activities in the course of addressing the NTTF recommendations. This should not, however, be interpreted as a lack of urgency on the part of the staff in addressing those NTTF recommendations identified as being initiated without unnecessary delay.

To further inform this process, the staff conducted a public meeting with representatives of the nuclear industry on September 21, 2011, to better understand their current plans and actions to address the lessons learned from the Fukushima Daiichi event. The meeting minutes and transcript are available in the Agencywide Documents Access and Management System (ADAMS) at ML11271A122.

As a result of the staff's prioritization and assessment process, the NTTF recommendations were prioritized into three tiers:

Tier 1. The first tier consists of those NTTF recommendations which the staff determined should be started without unnecessary delay and for which sufficient resource flexibility, including availability of critical skill sets, exists. This tier includes all the actions identified in SECY-11-0124 and two additional items. The additional items are the following: (1) the inclusion of Mark II containments in the staff's recommendation for reliable hardened vents associated with NTTF Recommendation 5.1, and (2) the implementation of spent fuel pool (SFP) instrumentation proposed in Recommendation 7.1. After submitting SECY-11-0124, the staff continued its review of these recommendations. This review led the staff to conclude that resolution of the reliable hardened vents issues for Mark I and II containments should be undertaken concurrently. The staff also concluded that installation of SFP instrumentation should be initiated without delay. Hence, the Tier 1 recommendations are the following:

2.1 Seismic and flood hazard reevaluations
2.3 Seismic and flood walkdowns
4.1 Station blackout (SBO) regulatory actions
4.2 Equipment covered under Title 10 of the *Code of Federal Regulations* (10 CFR) 50.54(hh)(2)
5.1 Reliable hardened vents for Mark I and Mark II containments
7.1 SFP instrumentation
8 Strengthening and integration of emergency operating procedures, severe accident management guidelines (SAMGs), and extensive damage mitigation guidelines
9.3 Emergency preparedness regulatory actions (staffing and communications)

Tier 2. The second tier consists of those NTTF recommendations which could not be initiated in the near term due to factors that include the need for further technical assessment and alignment, dependence on Tier 1 issues, or availability of critical skill sets. These actions do not require long-term study and can be initiated when sufficient technical information and applicable resources become available. The Tier 2 recommendations are the following:

7 SFP makeup capability (7.2, 7.3, 7.4, and 7.5)
9.3 Emergency preparedness regulatory actions (the remaining portions of Recommendation 9.3, with the exception of Emergency Response Data System (ERDS) capability addressed in Tier 3)

Tier 3. The third tier consists of those NTTF recommendations that require further staff study to support a regulatory action, have an associated shorter-term action that needs to be completed to inform the longer-term action, are dependent on the availability of critical skill sets, or are dependent on the resolution of NTTF Recommendation 1. The staff has focused its initial efforts on developing the schedules, milestones, and resources associated with Tier 1 and Tier 2 activities. Hence, information regarding the Tier 3 recommendations is not included in the enclosure. Once the staff has completed its evaluation of the resource impacts of the Tier 1 and Tier 2 recommendations, it will be able to more accurately address the Tier 3 recommendations.

The Tier 3 recommendations include all of the items identified for long-term evaluation in the NTTF report. In addition, the staff prioritized NTTF Recommendations 2.2, 9.1, 9.2, 9.3 (ERDS capability), and 12 into Tier 3. The Tier 3 recommendations and associated prioritization logic are as follows:

2.2 Ten-year confirmation of seismic and flooding hazards (dependent on Recommendation 2.1)
3 Potential enhancements to the capability to prevent or mitigate seismically-induced fires and floods (long-term evaluation)
5.2 Reliable hardened vents for other containment designs (long-term evaluation)
6 Hydrogen control and mitigation inside containment or in other buildings (long-term evaluation)

9.1/9.2 Emergency preparedness (EP) enhancements for prolonged SBO and multiunit events (dependent on availability of critical skill sets)
9.3 ERDS capability (related to long-term evaluation Recommendation 10)
10 Additional EP topics for prolonged SBO and multiunit events (long-term evaluation)
11 EP topics for decision-making, radiation monitoring, and public education (long-term evaluation)
12.1 Reactor Oversight Process modifications to reflect the recommended defense-in-depth framework (dependent on Recommendation 1)
12.2 Staff training on severe accidents and resident inspector training on SAMGs (dependent on Recommendation 8)

Additional Issues under Consideration

As directed by SRM-SECY-11-0093, the staff has sought to identify additional recommendations related to lessons learned from the Fukushima Daiichi event beyond those identified in the NTTF report. Many additional recommendations have been received both from NRC staff and external stakeholders, including the Office of Science and Technology Policy, Congress, international counterparts, other Federal and State agencies, non-governmental organizations, the public, and the nuclear industry.

These issues have been raised in a variety of forums, including the staff's August 31, 2011, public meeting and the Commission's September 9, 2011, meeting. In the process of beginning to evaluate these additional recommendations, the staff has emphasized maintaining discipline with regard to which recommendations are associated with the staff's efforts to implement lessons learned from the Fukushima Daiichi event and which are more appropriately addressed through other existing NRC processes (e.g., 10 CFR 2.206, 10 CFR 2.802, etc.). Going forward, the staff will focus on ensuring that issues which may, or may not, have a direct, clear nexus with the Fukushima Daiichi event are addressed through the appropriate regulatory process.

At this time the staff has identified a number of additional issues with a clear nexus to the Fukushima Daiichi event that may warrant regulatory action but which were not included with the NTTF recommendations. Although the staff's assessment of these issues is incomplete at this time, several of these issues have already been judged to warrant further consideration and potential prioritization based on relative safety significance, nexus to NTTF recommendations, and other ongoing staff activities.

A determination of whether any regulatory action is necessary will be made after the completion of this consideration. If the consideration determines that regulatory action is required, the staff will prioritize these additional recommendations consistent with the approach taken with the NTTF recommendations. The additional recommendations warranting further consideration and potential prioritization are:

- Filtration of containment vents
- Instrumentation for seismic monitoring
- Basis of emergency planning zone size

- Prestaging of potassium iodide beyond 10 miles Transfer of spent fuel to dry cask storage
- Loss of ultimate heat sink

There are additional potential recommendations that have been raised, but for which there has been insufficient time to consider in significant depth. In addition, the staff expects the list of potential additional recommendations to continue to increase as we receive feedback from our external stakeholders, through our interactions with the international regulatory community, and through the mining of the Fukushima Daiichi event for additional lessons learned by the nuclear industry and NRC. There are also numerous reports, either already issued or in preparation, including the official Government of Japan report, which the staff will continue to review to enhance our understanding of the event at Fukushima Daiichi.

OVERVIEW OF IMPLEMENTATION, SCHEDULE, AND RESOURCE CHALLENGES

The overriding challenge the staff will face when implementing actions to address the NTTF recommendations will be redefining agency priorities while ensuring that this process does not displace ongoing work that has greater safety benefit, work that is necessary for continued safe operation, or other existing high priority work. The staff has identified some examples of work, including National Fire Protection Association 805 reviews; resolution of Generic Safety Issue 191, "Assessment of Debris Accumulation on PWR [pressurized water reactor] Sump Performance;" implementation of the recently updated emergency preparedness rule; materials, fuel facility, and reactor oversight program activities; and near-term combined license reviews, which the staff does not intend to delay to work on the NTTF recommendations. This will be a continuous process as new operating reactor issues emerge which, because of their potential impact on safety, may take priority over action on some lower priority NTTF recommendations.

The staff will make use of available risk information and experience when performing these periodic re-evaluations.

The enclosed assessments provide an initial evaluation of the critical skill sets necessary to develop and complete the regulatory actions associated with each NTTF recommendation. However, the staff has not had sufficient time to fully integrate the actions assessed in the enclosures with the balance of the staff's ongoing work. Consequently, the enclosed schedules and milestones qualitatively reflect nominal schedules and any known interdependencies with other efforts.

Additionally, the staff proposes to initiate actions on the NTTF recommendations under the premise of assuring or redefining the level of protection of public health and safety that should be regarded as adequate in accordance with the backfit rule. The staff will engage stakeholders to inform its development of technical and regulatory bases for the imposition of new requirements associated with each of the recommendations in support of Commission decision-making.

The staff also recognizes that there are resource and implementation challenges that licensees and federal and state agencies may experience particularly with regard to skill sets in high demand (e.g., probabilistic risk assessment, seismic, and flooding expertise). Ultimately these resource and skill set constraints may impact the rate at which the Fukushima Daiichi lessons learned can be implemented by licensees.

For new reactor designs currently under review, safety issues should be resolved at the design stage, to the extent practical. Consistent with the Commission policy encouraging standardization, it would be prudent to implement safety enhancements prior to certification or design certification renewal. As such, the staff intends to begin interactions with new reactor stakeholders in the near term to allow sufficient opportunity for design certification applicants and design certification renewal applicants to address recommended design-related safety enhancements prior to completion of the staff's review. It should be noted that imposition of new requirements as part of a design certification renewal is governed by 10 CFR 52.59. The staff will encourage reactor vendors to provide enhanced safety features and safety margins consistent with the Commission policy on advanced reactors. With regard to near-term combined license reviews, the staff discusses options in SECY-11-0110, "Staff Statement In Support of the Uncontested Hearing for Issuance of Combined Licenses and Limited Work Authorizations for Vogtle Electric Generating Plant, Units 3 and 4 (Docket Nos. 52-025 and 52-026), dated August 9, 2011, and SECY-11-0115, "Staff Statement in Support of the Uncontested Hearing for Issuance of Combined Licenses for the Virgil C. Summer Nuclear Station, Units 2 and 3 (Docket Nos. 52-027 and 52-028)," dated August 19, 2011.

ADDITIONAL ACTIONS RELATED TO THE CHAIRMAN'S TASKING MEMORANDUM COMGBJ-11-0002

In COMGBJ-11-0002, the Commission directed the staff to develop a sequence of events following the March 11, 2011, earthquake and tsunami at the Fukushima Daiichi and to consider the applicability of lessons learned from the event to licensed facilities other than power reactors.

In response to this direction, the NRC and the Department of Energy signed the "Addendum to the Memorandum of Understanding between U.S. Nuclear Regulatory Commission and U.S. Department of Energy on Cooperative Nuclear Safety Research Related to Fukushima Daiichi Accident Study," (ADAMS ML111930010) in June 2011. This Addendum describes a cooperative research program to conduct a study of the Fukushima Daiichi accident in order to develop a thorough understanding of the accident progression of each reactor and spent fuel pool. The purpose of the study is to reconstruct the sequence of events at Fukushima Daiichi in order to characterize and model events from the perspective of accident mitigation and response and validate severe accident modeling. In addition, the staff is working with Federal counterparts, industry, and the international community, including the Government of Japan, to establish cooperative efforts to share and integrate specific information into a common understanding of the sequence of events of the Fukushima Daiichi accident.

The staff is also considering the applicability of lessons learned to licensed facilities other than power reactors and taking appropriate actions. For example, the staff is issuing a temporary instruction (TI) to guide the staff's independent verification of fuel facility licensees' ability to prevent and/or mitigate the consequences of events which could challenge the safety or licensing bases of those facilities. The TI will also enable staff to evaluate the adequacy of licensee emergency preparedness programs for dealing with the consequences of events.

The staff will also take into account insights from Generic Issue 199, "Implications of Updated Probabilistic Seismic Hazard Estimates in Central and Eastern United States on Existing Plants," in the evaluation of the inspection results. The staff also plans to evaluate the applicability of lessons learned to research and test reactors, independent spent fuel storage installations, and reactors that have permanently ceased operations but still maintain fuel in a SFP.

COMMITMENTS

The staff will provide an evaluation of the schedule and milestones, resources and critical skill sets, and implementation challenges related to addressing the Tier 3 recommendations to the Commission within 9 months. At the same time, the staff will also provide its prioritization of the additional recommendations identified in this paper to the Commission. Should the staff prioritize any of the additional recommendations as Tier 1, the staff will promptly inform the Commission of its determination.

RECOMMENDATIONS

The staff recommends that the Commission approve the prioritization of the NTTF recommendations provided above and direct the staff to take action on the Tier 1 and Tier 2 recommendations as described in the enclosure.

RESOURCES

The NRC's fiscal year 2012 (FY12) budget under Congressional review does not include resources for activities discussed in this paper. For FY13, the NRC's proposed budget was submitted to the Office of Management and Budget prior to the issuance of the NTTF report and, as such, includes limited funding for activities discussed in this paper.

The staff now anticipates that resource needs will exceed the current requests, as indicated in the enclosure.

The staff's estimate to undertake the Tier 1 and Tier 2 activities described in this paper is 30 FTE in FY12 and 90 FTE in FY13. However, the staff notes that these FTE values may change if funding for the use of contractors is allocated for these activities.

The enclosure provides, for each recommendation, the staff's resource estimate and the supporting schedules and milestones, including stakeholder engagement and, when appropriate, involvement of the ACRS. Additionally, within the enclosure the staff has identified the critical skill sets and potentially impacted organizations.

Coordination

The Office of the General Counsel has reviewed this paper and has no legal objection. The Office of the Chief Financial Officer has reviewed this paper for resource implications and has concurred.

/RA/
R. W. Borchardt
Executive Director for Operations
Enclosure:
Staff Assessment and Prioritization of NTTF Recommendations

Staff Assessment and Prioritization of Near-Term Task Force (NTTF) Recommendations

As directed by SRM-SECY-11-0093, the staff reviewed the NTTF recommendations within the context of the NRC's existing framework and considered the various regulatory vehicles available to the NRC to implement the recommendations. This review was conducted by a team consisting of NRC senior management representatives and technical experts.

The staff's prioritization and assessment process prioritized the NTTF recommendations into three tiers:

Tier 1. The first tier consists of those NTTF recommendations which the staff determined should be started without unnecessary delay and for which sufficient resource flexibility, including availability of critical skill sets, exists. This tier includes all the actions identified in SECY-11-0124 and two additional items. The additional items are the following: (1) the inclusion of Mark II containments in the staff's recommendation for reliable hardened vents associated with NTTF Recommendation 5.1 and (2) the implementation of spent fuel pool (SFP) instrumentation proposed in Recommendation 7.1. After submitting SECY-11-0124, the staff continued its review of these recommendations. This review led the staff to conclude that resolution of the reliable hardened vents issues for Mark I and II containments should be undertaken concurrently. The staff also concluded that installation of SFP instrumentation should be initiated without delay. Hence, the Tier 1 recommendations are the following:

2.1 Seismic and flood hazard reevaluations
2.3 Seismic and flood walkdowns
4.1 Station blackout regulatory actions
4.2 Equipment covered under Title 10 of the *Code of Federal Regulations* (10 CFR) 50.54(hh)(2)
5.1 Reliable hardened vents for Mark I and Mark II containments
7.1 Spent fuel pool instrumentation
8   Strengthening and integration of emergency operating procedures, severe accident management guidelines (SAMGs), and extensive damage mitigation guidelines
9.3 Emergency preparedness regulatory actions (staffing and communications)

Tier 2. The second tier consists of those NTTF recommendations which could not be initiated in the near term due to factors that include the need for further technical assessment and alignment, dependence on Tier 1 issues, or availability of critical skill sets. These actions do not require long term study and can be initiated when sufficient technical information and applicable resources become available. The Tier 2 recommendations are the following:

7 Spent fuel pool makeup capability (7.2, 7.3, 7.4, and 7.5)
9.3 Emergency preparedness regulatory actions (the remaining portions of Recommendation 9.3, with the exception of Emergency Response Data System (ERDS) capability addressed in Tier 3)

Tier 3. The third tier consists of those NTTF recommendations that require further staff study to support a regulatory action, have an associated shorter term action that needs to be completed to inform the longer term action, are dependent on the availability of critical skill sets, or are dependent on the resolution of NTTF Recommendation 1. The staff has focused its initial efforts on developing the schedules, milestones, and resources associated with Tier 1 and Tier 2 activities. Hence, information regarding the Tier 3 recommendations is not included in this enclosure. Once the staff has completed its evaluation of the resource impacts of the Tier 1 and Tier 2 recommendations, it will be able to more accurately address the Tier 3 recommendations.

The Tier 3 recommendations include all of the items identified for long-term evaluation in the NTTF report. In addition, the staff prioritized NTTF Recommendations 2.2, 9.1, 9.2, 9.3 (ERDS capability), and 12 into Tier 3. The Tier 3 recommendations and associated prioritization logic are as follows:

2.2 Ten-year confirmation of seismic and flooding hazards (dependent on Recommendation 2.1)
3 Potential enhancements to the capability to prevent or mitigate seismically induced fires and floods (long-term evaluation)
5.2 Reliable hardened vents for other containment designs (long-term evaluation)
6 Hydrogen control and mitigation inside containment or in other buildings (long-term evaluation)
9.1/9.2 Emergency preparedness (EP) enhancements for prolonged station blackout (SBO) and multiunit events (dependent on availability of critical skill sets)
9.3 ERDS capability (related to long-term evaluation Recommendation 10)
10 Additional EP topics for prolonged SBO and multiunit events (long-term evaluation)
11 EP topics for decision-making, radiation monitoring, and public education (long-term evaluation)
12.1 Reactor Oversight Process modifications to reflect the recommended defense-in-depth framework (dependent on Recommendation 1)
12.2 Staff training on severe accidents, resident inspector training on SAMGs (dependent on Recommendation 8)

This enclosure contains the assessments of the Tier 1 and Tier 2 NTTF recommendations in the order listed above. The title for each assessment clearly delineates whether it is Tier 1 or Tier 2. For each specific NTTF recommendation, this enclosure provides the staff's assessment and prioritization of the recommendations, including any unique challenges. Also provided are the staff's resource estimates and supporting schedules and milestones including, where applicable, appropriate stakeholder engagement and involvement of the Advisory Committee for Reactor Safeguards (ACRS). The staff has not had sufficient time to fully integrate the actions assessed in this enclosure with the balance of the staff's ongoing work. Consequently, the enclosed schedules and milestones qualitatively reflect nominal schedules and any known interdependencies with other efforts. Finally, the assessments provide the identified critical skill sets and potentially impacted organizations.

TIER 1 - NTTF RECOMMENDATION 2.1

The Task Force recommends the NRC require licensees to reevaluate and upgrade as necessary the design-basis seismic and flooding protection of structures, systems, and components (SSCs) for each operating reactor.

2.1 Order licensees to reevaluate the seismic and flooding hazards at their sites against current NRC requirements and guidance, and if necessary, update the design basis and SSCs important to safety to protect against the updated hazards.

Regulations and Guidance

1. General Design Criterion (GDC) 2, "Design Bases for Protection Against Natural Phenomena," of Appendix A, "General Design Criteria for Nuclear Power Plants," to Title10 of the *Code of Federal Regulations* (10 CFR) Part 50, "Domestic Licensing of Production and Utilization Facilities," requires, in part, that SSCs important to safety be designed to withstand the effects of natural phenomena such as floods, tsunami, and seiches without loss of capability to perform their safety functions. Plants that received construction permits before issuance of GDC 2 in 1971 meet the intent of the GDC.
2. 10 CFR Part 100, "Reactor Site Criteria," Appendix A, "Seismic and Geologic Siting Criteria for Nuclear Power Plants," was established to provide detailed criteria to evaluate the suitability of proposed sites and the suitability of the plant design basis established in consideration of the seismic and geologic characteristics of the proposed sites. Appendix A, which applies to stationary reactor site applications before January 11, 1997, provides a deterministic approach for developing the seismic plant design basis. In contrast, 10 CFR 100.23, which applies to applications on or after January 11, 1997, provides a detailed characterization of uncertainties and is being used by new reactor applicants to develop seismic design bases.
3. NUREG-0800, "Standard Review Plan for the Review of Safety Analysis Reports for Nuclear Power Plants: LWR [Light-Water Reactor] Edition," Section 2.4.6, "Probable Maximum Tsunami Hazards," issued November 1975 and updated June 1978, July 1981, and March 2007.

4. Regulatory Guide (RG) 1.29, "Seismic Design Classification," issued June 1972 and updated August 1973, February 1976, September 1978, and March 2007.
5. RG 1.59, "Design Basis Floods for Nuclear Power Plants," issued August 1973 and updated April 1976 and August 1977.
6. RG 1.60, "Design Response Spectra for Seismic Design of Nuclear Power Plants," issued October 1973 and updated December 1973.
7. RG 1.102, "Flood Protection for Nuclear Power Plants," issued October 1975 and updated September 1976.
8. RG 1.125, "Physical Models for Design and Operation of Hydraulic Structures and Systems for Nuclear Power Plants," issued March 1977 and updated October 1978 and March 2009.
9. RG 1.208, "A Performance-Based Approach To Define the Site-Specific Earthquake Ground Motion," issued March 2007.

Staff Assessment and Basis for Prioritization

The staff's assessment of this recommendation indicates that plants may differ in the way they ensure safety against natural phenomena. The staff concluded that sufficient regulatory guidance currently exists to permit licensee reevaluations. However, the staff noted that results of inspections of SSCs at Fukushima Daiichi and Daini Nuclear Power Stations may help inform the implementation of this recommendation. To the extent practical, the new information on the events at Fukushima Daiichi and Daini should be incorporated into the reevaluations. The staff also noted that the implementation of this recommendation would require significant resources for both licensees and NRC, as well as specialized expertise to review licensee reevaluations and to document results of staff evaluations.

Seismic hazards. The state of knowledge of seismic hazards within the United States has evolved to the point that it would be appropriate for licensees to reevaluate the designs of existing nuclear power reactors to ensure that SSCs important to safety will withstand a seismic event without loss of capability to perform their intended safety function. The staff notes that ongoing activities to resolve Generic Issue (GI) 199, "Implications of Updated Probabilistic Seismic Estimates in Central and Eastern United States on Existing Plants," are directly related to this issue and will be considered in the resolution of Recommendation 2.1. Draft Generic Letter (GL) 2011-XX, "Seismic Risk Evaluations for Operating Reactors," issued for public comment on September 1, 2011, (Agencywide Documents Access and Management System (ADAMS) Accession No. ML111710783) provides detailed guidance for developing appropriate seismic hazards using the most recent models and methods and also for quantifying seismic risk to resolve GI-199. Currently, the draft generic letter allows for either seismic margin or probabilistic risk analyses for sites where the current seismic hazard exceeds the plant's design basis. However, as part of the resolution of Recommendation 2.1, the staff is considering whether a probabilistic risk or a seismic margins analysis is more appropriate.

Flooding hazards. The assumptions and factors that were considered in flood protection at operating plants vary. In some cases, the design bases did not consider the effects from the local intense precipitation and related site drainage. In other cases, the probable maximum flood is calculated differently at units co-located at the same site, depending on the time of licensing, resulting in different design-basis flood protection. The NTTF and the staff noted that some plants rely on operator actions and temporary flood mitigation measures such as sandbagging, temporary flood walls and barriers, and portable equipment to perform safety functions. For several sites, the staff noted that all appropriate flooding hazards are not documented in the Updated Final Safety Analysis Report (UFSAR). The NTTF and the staff also noted that flooding risks are of concern because of a "cliff-edge" effect, in that the safety consequences of a flooding event may increase sharply with a small increase in the flooding level. Therefore, all licensees should confirm that SSCs important to safety are adequately protected from floods.

The staff concludes that this recommendation would improve safety. Since sufficient resource flexibility, including availability of critical skill sets, exists, the staff prioritized this action as a Tier 1 recommendation.

Staff Recommendations

The staff recommends that the NRC, as a near-term action, undertake regulatory activities to:

1. Continue stakeholder interactions to discuss the technical basis and acceptance criteria for conducting a reevaluation of site specific seismic hazards. This would include implementation considerations of the hazard and risk methodologies described in draft Generic Letter (GL) 2011-XX, "Seismic Risk Evaluations for Operating Reactors."
2. Interact with stakeholders to inform NRC's process for defining guidelines for the application of present-day regulatory guidance and methodologies being used for early site permit and combined license reviews to the reevaluation of flooding hazards at operating reactors.
3. Develop and issue a request for information to licensees pursuant to 10 CFR 50.54(f) to (1) reevaluate site-specific seismic hazards using the methodology discussed in item 1 above, and (2) identify actions that have been taken, or are planned, to address plant-specific issues associated with the updated seismic hazards (including potential changes to the licensing or design basis of a plant).
4. Develop and issue a request for information to licensees pursuant to 10 CFR 50.54(f) to (1) reevaluate site-specific flooding hazards using the methodology discussed in item 2 above, and (2) identify actions that have been taken or are planned to address plant-specific issues associated with the updated flooding hazards (including potential changes to the licensing or design basis of a plant).
5. Evaluate licensee responses and take appropriate regulatory action to resolve issues associated with updated site-specific hazards.

Unique Implementation Challenges

The staff recognizes that the NRC and industry have limited, specialized expertise (e.g., seismologist, hydrologists) to complete the actions associated with this recommendation.

Schedules and Milestones

Reevaluation of Seismic Hazards:

I. Issue 10 CFR 50.54(f) letter – 6 months
   a) Stakeholder interaction and technical development (e.g., methods, technical basis, acceptance criteria, etc.)
   b) Develop 10 CFR 50.54(f) letter
   c) Issue 10 CFR 50.54(f) letter

II. Evaluate licensee responses to 10 CFR 50.54(f) letter – Based on a timeline to be developed during the stakeholder interaction taking into account available resources.
   a) Write safety evaluation or NUREG to document staff conclusions

III. Issue orders to licensees (if needed) – 3 months following decision to issue orders
   a) Develop regulatory basis and draft orders
   b) Issue orders

IV. Inspection Activities – Schedule to be determined
   a) Develop Temporary Instruction
   b) Conduct inspections and document results
   c) Update Standardized Plant Analysis Risk (SPAR) models

V. Issue letters to close out 10 CFR 50.54(f) letter and/or orders – 1 month after last inspection

Reevaluation of Flooding Hazards:

I. Develop 10 CFR 50.54(f) letter – 8 months
   a) Stakeholder interaction and technical development (e.g., methods, technical basis, acceptance criteria, etc.)
   b) Develop 10 CFR 50.54(f) letter
   c) Issue 10 CFR 50.54(f) letter

II. Evaluate licensee responses to 10 CFR 50.54(f) letter – Based on a timeline to be developed during the stakeholder interaction taking into account available resources.
   a) Write safety evaluation or NUREG to document staff conclusions

III. Issue orders to licensees (if needed) – 3 months following decision to issue orders
   a) Develop regulatory basis and draft orders
   b) Issue orders

IV. Inspection Activities – Schedule to be determined
   a) Develop Temporary Instruction
   b) Conduct inspections and document results
   c) Update SPAR models

V. Issue letters to close out 10 CFR 50.54(f) letter and/or orders – 1 month after last inspection

TIER 1 - NTTF RECOMMENDATION 2.1 SCHEDULE FOR SEISMIC REEVALUATIONS

I. Develop 10 CFR 50.54(f) letter – 6 months
II. Evaluate licensee responses to 10 CFR 50.54(f) letter – Schedule to be determined
III. Issue orders to licensees (if needed) – 3 months following decision to issue orders
IV. Conduct inspection activities – Schedule to be determined
V. Issue letters to close out 10 CFR 50.54(f) letter and/or orders – 1 month after last inspection

Resources for Seismic Reevaluations

Activity	Resource Category	Specific Expertise Needed	Estimated FTE	Locations of Most Applicable Expertise within NRC
Develop 50.54(f) letter	Project/Program Management	Plant Licensing	0.25	NRR
	Technical	Seismology	0.5	NRO, RES, NMSS
		Structural Engineering	0.25	NRR, NRO, RES, NMSS
		Probabilistic Risk Assessment	0.25	NRR, NRO, RES
	Legal	Plant Licensing	0.25	OGC
Evaluate licensee responses to 50.54(f) letter	Project/Program Management	Plant Licensing	0.25	NRR
	Technical	Seismology	3.25	NRO, RES, NMSS
		Geotechnical Engineering	3.25	NRO, RES
		Probabilistic Risk Assessment	10.0	NRR, NRO, RES
		Structural Engineering	4.5	NRR, NRO, RES, NMSS
	Legal	Plant Licensing	0.25	OGC
Issue orders to licensees (if needed)	Project/Program Management	Plant Licensing	0.25	NRR
	Legal	Plant Licensing	0.25	OGC
	Technical	Seismology	0.3	NRO, RES, NMSS
		Structural Engineering	0.2	NRR, NRO, RES, NMSS
		Probabilistic Risk Assessment	0.1	NRR, NRO, RES
IV. Conduct inspection activities	Regional Inspection	Inspection	3.3	All Regions
	Project/Program Management	Inspection Program Management	0.25	NRR
	Technical	Seismology	0.1	NRO, RES, NMSS
		Structural Engineering	0.1	NRR, NRO, RES, NMSS
		Probabilistic Risk Assessment	2.0	NRR, NRO, RES
V. Issue letters to close out 50.54(f) letter and/or orders	Project/Program Management	Project Management	0.25	NRR
	Legal	Plant Licensing	0.25	OGC
Total FTE			30.35	

Notes:
1) Where appropriate and available, technical assistance dollars will be used to resolve this recommendation. 2) The timing and necessary resources for the activities associated with this

NTTF recommendation will likely overlap with those needed for Recommendations 2.3. The implications of the competition for resources between these NTTF recommendations have not been fully investigated at this time.

SCHEDULE FOR FLOODING REEVALUATIONS

I. Develop 10 CFR 50.54(f) letter – 8 months
II. Evaluate licensee responses to 10 CFR 50.54(f) letter – Schedule to be determined
III. Issue orders to licensees (if needed) – 3 months following decision to issue orders
IV. Conduct inspection activities – Schedule to be determined
V. Issue letters to close out 10 CFR 50.54(f) letter and/or orders – 1 month after last inspection

Resources for Flooding Reevaluations

Activity	Resource Category	Specific Expertise Needed	Estimated FTE	Locations of Most Applicable Expertise within NRC
Develop 50.54(f) letter	Project/Program Management	Plant Licensing	0.25	NRR
	Technical	Surface Water Hydrology	0.9	NRO, RES, NMSS, FSME
		Probabilistic Risk Assessment	0.1	NRR, NRO, RES
	Legal	Plant Licensing	0.25	OGC
Evaluate licensee responses to 50.54(f) letter	Project/Program Management	Plant Licensing	0.25	NRR
	Technical	Surface Water Hydrology	10.5	NRO, RES, NMSS, FSME
		Probabilistic Risk Assessment	0.5	NRR, NRO, RES
	Legal	Plant Licensing	0.25	OGC
Issue orders to licensees (if needed)	Project/Program Management	Plant Licensing	0.1	NRR
	Legal	Plant Licensing	0.25	OGC
	Technical	Surface Water Hydrology	0.4	NRO, RES, NMSS, FSME
		Probabilistic Risk Assessment	0.1	NRR, NRO, RES
Conduct inspection activities	Regional inspection	Inspection	3.3	All Regions
	Project/Program Management	Inspection Program Management	0.25	NRR
	Technical	Surface Water Hydrology	0.1	NRO, RES, NMSS, FSME
		Probabilistic Risk Assessment	2.0	NRR, NRO, RES
Issue letters to close out 50.54(f) letter and/or orders	Project/Program Management	Plant Licensing	0.25	NRR
	Legal	Plant Licensing	0.25	OGC
Total FTE			20.0	

Notes:
1) Where appropriate and available, technical assistance dollars will be used to resolve this recommendation. 2) The timing and necessary resources for the activities associated with this NTTF recommendation will likely overlap with those needed for Recommendations 2.3. The implications of the competition for resources between these NTTF recommendations have not been fully investigated at this time.

TIER 1 - NTTF RECOMMENDATION 2.3

The Task Force recommends that the NRC require licensees to reevaluate and upgrade as necessary the design-basis seismic and flooding protection of SSCs for each operating reactor.

> 2.3 Order licensees to perform seismic and flood protection walkdowns to identify and address plant-specific vulnerabilities and verify the adequacy of monitoring and maintenance for protection features such as watertight barriers and seals in the interim period until longer-term actions are completed to update the design basis for external events.

Regulations and Guidance

1) GDC 2, "Design Bases for Protection Against Natural Phenomena," of Appendix A, "General Design Criteria for Nuclear Power Plants," to 10 CFR Part 50, "Domestic Licensing of Production and Utilization Facilities," requires, in part, that SSCs important to safety be designed to withstand the effects of natural phenomena such as floods, tsunami, and seiches without loss of capability to perform their safety functions.
2) 10 CFR Part 100, "Reactor Site Criteria," Appendix A, "Seismic and Geologic Siting Criteria for Nuclear Power Plants," was established to provide detailed criteria to evaluate the suitability of proposed sites and the suitability of the plant design basis established in consideration of the seismic and geologic characteristics of the proposed sites. Appendix A, which applies to stationary reactor site applications before January 11, 1997, provides a deterministic approach for developing the seismic plant design basis. In contrast, 10 CFR 100.23, which applies to applications on or after January 11, 1997, provides a detailed characterization of uncertainties and is being used by new reactor applicants to develop seismic design bases.
3) NUREG-0800, "Standard Review Plan for the Review of Safety Analysis Reports for Nuclear Power Plants: LWR Edition," Section 2.4.6, "Probable Maximum Tsunami Hazards," issued November 1975 and updated June 1978, July 1981, and March 2007.
4) RG 1.29, "Seismic Design Classification," issued June 1972 and updated August 1973, February 1976, September 1978, and March 2007.
5) RG 1.59, "Design Basis Floods for Nuclear Power Plants," issued August 1973 and updated April 1976 and August 1977.
6) RG 1.60, "Design Response Spectra for Seismic Design of Nuclear Power Plants," issued October 1973 and updated December 1973.
7) RG 1.102, "Flood Protection for Nuclear Power Plants," issued October 1975 and updated September 1976.
8) RG 1.125, "Physical Models for Design and Operation of Hydraulic Structures and Systems for Nuclear Power Plants," issued March 1977 and updated October 1978 and March 2009.

Staff Assessment and Basis for Prioritization

The NRC should undertake regulatory activities to have licensees perform seismic and flood protection walkdowns to ensure that existing protection and mitigation measures are available, functional, and adequately maintained.

Seismic hazards. The staff's assessment of this recommendation indicates that some guidance for seismic protection walkdowns exists, such as Electric Power Research Institute (EPRI) report NP-6041-SL Revision 1, "A Methodology for Assessment of Nuclear Power Plant Seismic Margin", Seismic Qualification Utility Group procedure, "Generic Implementation Procedure (GIP) for Seismic Verification of Nuclear Plant Equipment," and International Atomic Energy Agency (IAEA) NS-G-2.13, "Evaluation of Seismic Safety for Existing Nuclear Installations." Recent plant inspections by staff in accordance with TI 2515/183, "Followup to the Fukushima Daiichi Nuclear Station Fuel Damage Event," and licensees' plant inspections in response to the Fukushima Daiichi accidents will help inform the implementation of this recommendation. In addition, the staff noted that results of ongoing inspections and evaluations of SSCs at Fukushima Daiichi and Daini Nuclear Power Stations may provide some insights for this recommendation. To the extent practical, the new information on the events at Fukushima Daiichi and Daini should be incorporated into the reevaluations. Evaluations of the recent earthquake near the North Anna Power Station on August 23, 2011, may also provide valuable insights.

Flooding hazards. With regard to flooding hazards, the Task Force and the staff have noted some plants rely on operator actions and temporary flood mitigation measures such as sandbagging, temporary flood walls and barriers, and portable equipment to perform safety functions. Results of staff's inspections at nuclear power sites in accordance with TI 2515/183 identified potential issues and observations regarding mitigation measures. Recent flooding at the Fort Calhoun site showed the importance of temporary flood mitigation measures.

The staff noted that guidance should be developed for both the seismic and flooding walkdowns with external stakeholder involvement to ensure consistency.

The staff concludes that this recommendation would improve safety. Since sufficient resource flexibility, including availability of critical skill sets, exists, the staff prioritized this action as a Tier 1 recommendation.

Staff Recommendations

The staff recommends that the NRC, as a near-term action, undertake regulatory activities to:

1. Engage stakeholders to inform development of a methodology and acceptance criteria for seismic and flooding walkdowns; and
2. Develop and issue a request for information to licensees pursuant to 10 CFR 50.54(f) to (1) perform seismic and flood protection walkdowns to identify and address plant-specific issues (through corrective action program) and verify the adequacy of monitoring and maintenance for protection features and (2) inform the NRC of the results of the walkdowns and corrective actions taken or planned.

Unique Implementation Challenges

The staff did not identify any unique challenges which would preclude moving forward in a timely manner.

Schedules and Milestones
Seismic Walkdowns:

I. Issue 10 CFR 50.54(f) letter – 6 months
    a) Stakeholder interaction and technical development (e.g., methods, technical basis, acceptance criteria, etc.)
    b) Develop 10 CFR 50.54(f) letter
    c) Issue 10 CFR 50.54(f) letter

II. Evaluate licensee responses to 10 CFR 50.54(f) letter – Based on a timeline to be developed during the stakeholder interaction taking into account available resources
    a) Write safety evaluation or NUREG to document staff conclusions

III. Issue orders to licensees (if needed) – 3 months following decision to issue orders
     Develop regulatory basis and draft orders
    a) Issue orders

IV. Conduct inspection activities – Schedule to be determined
    b) Develop Temporary Instruction
    c) Conduct inspections and document results
    d) Update SPAR models

V. Issue letters to close out 10 CFR 50.54(f) letter and/or orders – 1 month after last inspection

Flooding Walkdowns:

I. Issue 10 CFR 50.54(f) letter – 8 months
    a) Stakeholder interaction and technical development (e.g., methods, technical basis, acceptance criteria, etc.)
    b) Develop 10 CFR 50.54(f) letter
    c) Issue 10 CFR 50.54(f) letter

II. Evaluate licensee responses to 10 CFR 50.54(f) letter – Based on a timeline to be developed during the stakeholder interaction taking into account available resources.
    a) Write safety evaluation or NUREG to document staff conclusions

III. Issue orders to licensees (if needed) – 3 months following decision to issue orders
    a) Develop regulatory basis and draft orders
    b) Issue orders

IV. Conduct inspection activities – Schedule to be determined
   a) Develop Temporary Instruction
   b) Conduct inspections and document results
   c) Update SPAR models

V. Issue letters to close out 10 CFR 50.54(f) letter and/or orders – 1 month after last inspection.

TIER 1 - NTTF RECOMMENDATION 2.3

Schedule Related to Seismic Walkdowns

I. Develop 10 CFR 50.54(f) letter – 6 months
II. Evaluate licensee responses to 10 CFR 50.54(f) letter – Schedule to be determined
III. Issue orders to licensees (if needed) – 3 months following decision to issue orders
IV. Conduct inspection activities – Schedule to be determined
V. Issue letters to close out 10 CFR 50.54(f) letter and/or orders – 1 month after last inspection

Resources Related to Seismic Walkdowns

Activity	Resource Category	Specific Expertise Needed	Estimated FTE	Locations of Most Applicable Expertise within NRC
I Develop 10 CFR 50.54(f) letter	Project/Program Management	Plant Licensing	0.25	NRR
	Technical	Seismology	0.5	NRO, RES, NMSS
		Structural Engineering	0.1	NRR, NRO, RES, NMSS
		Mechanical Engineering	0.1	NRR, NRO, RES
		Instrumentation and Control/ Electrical Engineering	0.1	NRR, NRO, RES
		Probabilistic Risk Assessment	0.1	NRR, NRO, RES
	Legal	Plant Licensing	0.25	OGC
II Evaluate licensee responses to 10 CFR 50.54(f) letter	Project/Program Management	Plant Licensing	0.25	NRR
	Technical	Seismology	1.0	NRO, RES, NMSS
		Structural Engineering	1.5	NRR, NRO, RES, NMSS
		Mechanical Engineering	1.5	NRR, NRO, RES
		Instrumentation and Control/ Electrical Engineering	1.5	NRR, NRO, RES
		Probabilistic Risk Assessment	0.5	NRR, NRO, RES
	Legal	Plant Licensing	0.25	OGC
III Issue orders to licensees (if needed)	Project/Program Management	Plant Licensing	0.8	NRR
	Technical	Seismology	0.25	NRO, RES, NMSS
		Structural Engineering	0.25	NRR, NRO, RES, NMSS

Table (Continued)

Activity	Resource Category	Specific Expertise Needed	Estimated FTE	Locations of Most Applicable Expertise within NRC
		Mechanical Engineering	0.25	NRR, NRO, RES
		Instrumentation and Control/Electrical Engineering	0.25	NRR, NRO, RES
		Probabilistic Risk Assessment	0.25	NRR, NRO, RES
	Legal	Plant Licensing	0.25	OGC
IV Conduct inspection activities	Project/Program Management	Inspection Program Management	0.25	NRR
	Technical	Seismology	0.1	NRO, RES, NMSS
		Structural Engineering	0.1	NRR, NRO, RES, NMSS
		Mechanical Engineering	0.1	NRR, NRO, RES
		Instrumentation and Control/Electrical Engineering	0.1	NRR, NRO, RES
		Probabilistic Risk Assessment	2.0	NRR, NRO, RES
	Regional Inspection	Inspection	3.3	All Regions
V Issue letters to close out 10 CFR 50.54(f) letter and/or orders	Project/Program Management	Plant Licensing	0.25	NRR
	Legal	Plant Licensing	0.25	OGC
Total FTE			*16.65*	

Notes:
1) Where appropriate and available, technical assistance dollars will be used to resolve this recommendation.
2) The timing and necessary resources for the activities associated with this NTTF recommendation will likely overlap with those needed for Recommendations 2.1. The implications of the competition for resources between these NTTF recommendations have not been fully investigated at this time.

SCHEDULE RELATED TO FLOODING WALKDOWNS

I. Develop 10 CFR 50.54(f) letter – 8 months
II. Evaluate licensee responses to 10 CFR 50.54(f) letter – Schedule to be determined
III. Issue orders to licensees (if needed) – 3 months following decision to issue orders
IV. Conduct inspection activities – Schedule to be determined
V. Issue letters to close out 10 CFR 50.54(f) letter and/or orders – 1 month after last inspection

Resources Related to Flooding Walkdowns

Activity	Resource Category	Specific Expertise Needed	Estimated FTE	Locations of Most Applicable Expertise within NRC
I Develop 10 CFR 50.54(f) letter	Project/Program Management	Plant Licensing	0.25	NRR
	Technical	Surface Water Hydrology	0.2	NRO, RES, NMSS, FSME
		Mechanical Engineering	0.3	NRR, NRO, RES
		Structural Engineering	0.3	NRR, NRO, RES
		Probabilistic Risk Assessment	0.1	NRR, NRO, RES
		Instrumentation and Control/Electrical Engineering	0.3	NRR, NRO, RES
	Legal	Plant Licensing	0.25	OGC
II Evaluate licensee responses to 10 CFR 50.54(f) letter	Project/Program Management	Plant Licensing	0.25	NRR
	Technical	Surface Water Hydrology	0.5	NRO, RES, NMSS, FSME
		Mechanical Engineering	1.5	NRR, NRO, RES
		Structural Engineering	1.5	NRR, NRO, RES
		Probabilistic Risk Assessment	0.5	NRR, NRO, RES
		Instrumentation and Control/Electrical Engineering	1.5	NRR, NRO, RES
	Legal	Plant Licensing	0.25	OGC
III Issue orders to licensees (if needed)	Project/Program Management	Plant Licensing	0.8	NRR
	Technical	Surface Water Hydrology	0.25	NRO, RES
		Structural Engineering	0.25	NRR, NRO, RES
		Mechanical Engineering	0.25	NRR, NRO, RES
		Instrumentation and Control/Electrical Engineering	0.25	NRR, NRO, RES
		Probabilistic Risk Assessment	0.25	NRR, NRO, RES
	Legal	Plant Licensing	0.25	OGC
IV Conduct inspection activities	Regional inspection	Inspection	3.3	All Regions
	Project/Program Management	Program Management	0.25	NRR
	Technical	Mechanical Engineering	0.1	NRR, NRO, RES
		Structural Engineering	0.1	NRR, NRO, RES
		Instrumentation and Control/Electrical Engineering	0.1	NRR, NRO, RES
		Probabilistic Risk Assessment	2.0	NRR, NRO, RES
V Issue letters to close out 10 CFR 50.54(f) letter and/or orders	Project/Program Management	Plant Licensing	0.25	NRR
	Legal	Plant Licensing	0.25	OGC
Total FTE			16.35	

Notes:
1) Where appropriate and available, technical assistance dollars will be used to resolve this recommendation.
2) The timing and necessary resources for the activities associated with this NTTF recommendation will likely overlap with those needed for Recommendations 2.1. The implications of the competition for resources between these NTTF recommendations have not been fully investigated at this time.

The Task Force recommends that the NRC strengthen station blackout (SBO) mitigation capability at all operating and new reactors for design-basis and beyond-design-basis external events.

4.1 Initiate rulemaking to revise 10 CFR 50.63 to require each operating and new reactor licensee to: (1) establish a minimum coping time of 8 hours for a loss of all alternating current (ac) power, (2) establish the equipment, procedures, and training necessary to implement an "extended loss of all ac" coping time of 72 hours for core and spent fuel pool cooling and for reactor coolant system and primary containment integrity as needed, and (3) preplan and prestage offsite resources to support uninterrupted core and spent fuel pool cooling, and reactor coolant system and containment integrity as needed, including the ability to deliver the equipment to the site in the time period allowed for extended coping, under conditions involving significant degradation of offsite transportation infrastructure associated with significant natural disasters.

Regulations and Guidance

1) 10 CFR 50.63, "Loss of All Alternating Current Power" (known as the "Station Blackout Rule"), requires that each nuclear power plant must be able to cool the reactor core and maintain containment integrity for a specified duration of an SBO.
2) RG 1.155, "Station Blackout," issued August 1988, describes an acceptable means to comply with 10 CFR 50.63.

Staff Assessment and Basis for Prioritization

The staff concludes that the regulatory solution for SBO mitigation is implementation of new requirements intended to strengthen SBO mitigation capability at all operating and new reactors to address prolonged SBO stemming from design-basis and beyond-design-basis external events to provide core and spent fuel pool cooling, reactor coolant system integrity, and containment integrity. This regulatory action would consider the need for SBO power source(s) and mitigating equipment to be diverse and protected from external events. This regulatory action would also examine whether there is a need to expand SBO mitigation requirements to require power reactors to mitigate an SBO event at a plant (each unit for multiunit site) until either the onsite or offsite power source is restored to bring the power reactor to a cold shutdown and to maintain spent fuel pool cooling. This rulemaking would primarily amend 10 CFR 50.63 and would impact both operating reactor licensees and new reactor applications.

The staff concludes that this recommendation would improve safety. Since sufficient resource flexibility, including availability of critical skill sets, exists, the staff prioritized this action as a Tier 1 recommendation. However, since the staff is proposing action on Recommendation 4.2 as an interim measure and no imminent hazard was identified, the staff recommends following its standard rulemaking process, which allows for appropriate stakeholder involvement consistent with the rulemaking process and schedule established in

SECY-11-0032, "Consideration of Cumulative Effects of Regulation in the Rulemaking Process."

Staff Recommendation

The staff recommends that the NRC, as a near-term action, undertake regulatory activities to:

Engage stakeholders in support of rulemaking activities to enhance the capability to maintain safety through a prolonged SBO. These activities will include the development of the regulatory basis, a proposed rule, and implementing guidance consistent with the rulemaking process and schedule established in SECY-11-0032, "Consideration of Cumulative Effects of Regulation in the Rulemaking Process."

Unique Implementation Challenges

While the staff determined that this is a highly complex rulemaking, it did not identify any unique challenges which would preclude moving forward in a timely manner.

Schedule and Milestones

I. Dvelop and issue final rule - 4.25 years
   a) Develop regulatory basis incorporating stakeholder feedback - nominally 13 months following initiation of the action
   b) Issue proposed rule and supporting guidance for comment - nominally additional 16 months following completion and acceptance of the regulatory basis (incorporates 4 months for Commission review and staff response to SRM)
   c) Meet with ACRS during the proposed rule stage (if requested by ACRS)
   d) Issue final rule and supporting guidance- nominally additional 22 months (accounts for 75 day public comment period, 4 months of Commission review and staff response to final rule SRM, 3 months for Office of Management and Budget (OMB) approval for final rule, and meet with ACRS)
II. Licensing activities – Schedule to be determined, dependent on rule requirements
   a) Licensee submittals
   b) Staff review and safety evaluation issuance
III. Inspection activities – Schedule to be determined, dependent on licensee modifications
   a) Incorporate inspection into Reactor Oversight Process (ROP), including updating Standardized Plant Analysis Risk (SPAR) models to support significance determination
   b) Conduct inspections and document results
   c) Update SPAR models

Tier 1 - NTTF Recommendation 4.1

Schedule

I.   Develop and issue final rule - 4.25 years
II. Licensing activities – Schedule to be determined
III. Inspection activities – Schedule to be determined

Resources

Activity	Resource Category	Specific Expertise Needed	Estimated FTE	Locations of Most Applicable Expertise within NRC
Develop and issue final rule	Project/Program Management	Rulemaking	1.5	NRR, NRO, FSME
	Technical	Electrical Engineering	2.5	NRR, NRO, RES
		Mechanical Engineering	1.5	NRR, NRO, RES
		Probabilistic Risk Assessment	0.5	NRR, NRO, RES
	Legal	Rulemaking	0.5	OGC
Licensing activities	Project/Program Management	Plant Licensing	2.0	NRR
	Technical	Electrical Engineering	6.0	NRR, NRO, RES
		Mechanical Engineering	1.0	NRR, NRO, RES
		Probabilistic Risk Assessment	1.0	NRR, NRO, RES
	Legal	Plant Licensing	0.25	OGC
Inspection activities	Regional Inspection	Inspection	4.0	All Regions
	Project/Program Management	Inspection Program Management	0.5	NRR
	Technical	Probabilistic Risk Assessment	1.1	NRR, NRO, RES
Total FTE			22.35	

Notes:
1) Where appropriate and available, technical assistance dollars will be used to resolve this recommendation.
2) The timing and necessary resources for the activities associated with this NTTF recommendation will likely overlap with those needed for Recommendation 4.2. The implications of the competition for resources between these NTTF recommendations have not been fully investigated at this time. If resource limitations require prioritization between Recommendations 4.1 and 4.2, the staff will place a higher priority on completing 4.2 first.

Tier 1- NTTF Recommendation 4.2

The Task Force recommends that the NRC strengthen SBO mitigation capability at all operating and new reactors for design-basis and beyond-design-basis external events.

4.2 Order licensees to provide reasonable protection for equipment currently provided pursuant to 10 CFR 50.54(hh)(2) from the effects of design-basis external events and to add equipment as needed to address multiunit events while other requirements are being revised and implemented.

Regulations and Guidance

1. 10 CFR 50.54(hh)(2) requires licensees to develop and implement guidance and strategies intended to maintain or restore core cooling, containment, and spent fuel pool cooling capabilities under circumstances associated with the loss of large areas of the plant due to explosions or fire.
2. The required strategies include firefighting, operations to mitigate fuel damage, and actions to minimize radiological release.
3. Nuclear Energy Institute (NEI) 06-12, Revision 2, "B.5.b Phase 2 & 3 Submittal Guidance," issued December 2006, provides guidance supporting 10 CFR 50.54(hh)(2).
4. The equipment procured and used to implement the strategies of 10 CFR 50.54(hh)(2) is controlled through the licensee's commitment management process (which follows NEI 99-04, "Guidelines for Managing NRC Commitment Changes," issued July 1999).

Staff Assessment and Basis for Prioritization

The staff concludes that equipment procured pursuant to 10 CFR 50.54(hh)(2) will provide, as an interim measure, some of the coping capability that is recommended for addressing the NTTF recommendations associated with prolonged SBO events. However, the staff notes the NTTF finding that the current guidance only addresses single unit capacity and storage of the equipment for security-related initiating events. Specifically, the guidance in the NRC-endorsed NEI 06-12, for equipment used to implement the strategies in 10 CFR 50.54(hh)(2) via the extensive damage mitigation guidelines (EDMGs), is silent on whether the equipment needs to be protected from the effects of external events. The staff agrees that there will be a benefit to reasonably protecting the mitigation equipment while still meeting the intended purpose for security-related events

The staff also concludes that use of this 10 CFR 50.54(hh)(2) equipment, as envisioned by the NTTF, will likely require the equipment be supplemented to address a multiunit condition.

In addition, consistent with the discussion in Regulatory Issue Summary (RIS) 2008-15, "NRC Staff Position on Crediting Mitigating Strategies Implemented in Response to Security Orders in Risk-Informed Licensing Actions and in the Significance Determination Process," to capture the potential safety benefit and credit the manual actions associated with using this equipment for mitigating a prolonged SBO, the actions must be proceduralized and training implemented in addition to the assessment of staffing needs under Recommendation 9.3.

Any regulatory action to direct licensees to reasonably protect this equipment will need to address what constitutes "reasonably protect." This will be framed to support licensees taking practical actions that increase the likelihood that the equipment will survive the effects of external events while not reducing the availability of the equipment to function for its intended purpose, which is to support implementation of the strategies to mitigate the loss of large areas of the plant due to explosions and fires. Accordingly, "reasonably protect" would not necessarily mean locating the equipment in seismic Category I structures (unless that action is practical and does not adversely impact the mitigation of large fires and explosions). These issues need to be explored with stakeholders. The staff concludes that this recommendation would improve safety. Since sufficient resource flexibility, including availability of critical skill sets, exists, the staff prioritized this action as a Tier 1 recommendation.

In addition, action on this recommendation enhances defense-in-depth and supports following a standard rulemaking process for Recommendation 4.1.

Staff Recommendations

The staff recommends that the NRC, as a near-term action, undertake regulatory activities to:

1. Interact with stakeholders to do the following: (1) inform development of acceptance criteria for reasonable protection of 10 CFR 50.54(hh)(2) equipment from design-basis external hazards, (2) assess the need to supplement equipment to support multiunit event mitigation, and (3) discuss the need to develop and train on supporting strategies.
2. Order licensees to do the following: (1) provide reasonable protection of the equipment used to satisfy the requirements of 10 CFR 50.54(hh)(2) from the effects of external events, (2) establish and maintain sufficient capacity to mitigate multiunit events, and (3) develop, implement, and maintain strategies and associated training.

Unique Implementation Challenges

The staff did not identify any unique challenges which would preclude moving forward in a timely manner.

Schedule and Milestones

I. Develop and issue order – 6 months
   a) Interact with stakeholders to inform development of the regulatory basis and acceptance criteria for reasonable protection and capacity of equipment
   b) Issue order
II. Licensing activities – 4 months
   a) Licensee responses
   b) Staff review of licensee responses and staff safety evaluation
III. Inspection activities – Schedule to be determined, dependent on order implementation

a) Develop Temporary Instruction
b) Conduct inspections and document results
c) Update SPAR models

IV. Issue letters to close out order – 1 month after last inspection

TIER 1 - NTTF RECOMMENDATION 4.2

Schedule

I. Develop and issue order – 6 months
II. Licensing activities – 4 months
III. Inspection activities – Schedule to be determined
IV. Issue letters to close out order – 1 month after last inspection

Resources

Activity	Resource Category	Specific Expertise Needed	Estimated FTE	Locations of Most Applicable Expertise within NRC
I. Develop and issue order	Project/Program Management	Plant Licensing	0.25	NRR
	Technical	Fire Protection	1.0	NRR, NRO, RES
		Mechanical/Structural Engineering	1.0	NRR, NRO, RES, NMSS
	Legal	Plant Licensing	0.25	OGC
Licensing activities	Project/Program Management	Plant Licensing	0.75	NRR
	Technical	Fire Protection	0.5	NRR, NRO, RES
		Mechanical/Structural Engineering	0.75	NRR, NRO, RES, NMSS
	Legal	Plant Licensing	0.25	OGC
Inspection activities	Regional inspection	Inspection	10.3	All Regions
	Project/Program Management	Inspection Program Management	0.5	NRR
	Technical	Fire Protection	0.1	NRR, NRO, RES
		Mechanical/Structural Engineering	0.1	NRR, NRO, RES, NMSS
		Probabilistic Risk Assessment	2.5	NRR, NRO, RES
Issue letters to close out order	Project/Program Management	Plant Licensing	0.25	NRR
	Legal	Plant Licensing	0.25	OGC
Total FTE			18.75	

Notes:
1) Where appropriate and available, technical assistance dollars will be used to resolve this recommendation
2) The timing and necessary resources for the activities associated with this NTTF recommendation will likely overlap with those needed for Recommendation 4.1. The implications of the competition for resources between these NTTF recommendations have not been fully investigated at this time. If resource limitations require prioritization between Recommendations 4.1 and 4.2, the staff will place a higher priority on completing 4.2 first

TIER 1 - NTTF RECOMMENDATION 5.1

The Task Force recommends requiring reliable hardened vent designs in Boiling Water Reactor (BWR) reactor facilities with Mark I and Mark II containments.

5.1 Order licensees to include a reliable hardened vent in BWR Mark I and Mark II containments.

- This order should include performance objectives for the design of hardened vents to ensure reliable operation and ease of use (both opening and closing) during a prolonged SBO.

Regulations and Guidance

1. GDC 16 – Containment design. Reactor containment and associated systems shall be provided to establish an essentially leak-tight barrier against the uncontrolled release of radioactivity to the environment and to assure that the containment design conditions important to safety are not exceeded for as long as postulated accident conditions require.
2. GL 89-16, "Installation of a Hardened Wetwell Vent," was issued to licensees of nuclear plants with BWR Mark I primary containments requesting that they consider voluntary installation of hardened wetwell vents under the provisions of 10 CFR 50.59, "Changes, Tests and Experiments," to provide assurance of pressure relief through a path with significant scrubbing of fission products should normal and design basis containment cooling systems not be available. Hardened wetwell airspace vents of varying designs, but all AC dependent, were installed in the currently operating units with Mark I containments primarily to avoid exceeding the primary containment pressure limit.
3. 10 CFR 50.54(hh)(2) requires licensees to develop and implement guidance and strategies to maintain or restore containment capabilities under the circumstances associated with loss of a large area of the plant due to explosions or fire; expectation B.2.e of the B.5.b Phase 1 Guidance Document dated February 25, 2002 (designated Safeguards Information) and Section 3.4.8 of the NRC-endorsed Phase 3 guidance in NEI 06-12, Revision 2, "B.5.b Phase 2 & 3 Submittal Guidance," both specify that an acceptable means of meeting the 10 CFR 50.54(hh)(2) requirements includes the development of a procedure or strategy to allow venting primary containment to secondary containment, without AC power, as an alternate method to remove heat from the primary containment for BWR licensees. All currently operating BWR licensees, including those with BWR Mark I, Mark II, and Mark III containment designs, adopted this approach to meeting the requirements of 10 CFR 50.54(hh)(2). There are neither current NRC regulations that require this capability for other severe (beyond-designbasis) accidents, nor design criteria for the vent paths used in this strategy.

Staff Assessment and Basis for Prioritization

BWR Mark I primary containments should have a reliable hardened vent for mitigating beyonddesign-basis events. The NTTF recommendation aligns with long-standing staff recommendations for the Mark I as documented in SECY 89-17, "Mark I Containment Performance Improvement Program," and GL 89-16.

The Fukushima Daiichi accident highlighted the importance of the wetwell vent function, the accessibility of the valves and the capability for operation independent of AC power. All Mark I plants have installed a hardened vent. The degree to which the vent can be used during an extended SBO relies on actions taken to comply with 10 CFR 50.54(hh)(2). Further, these vents have not been designed to any standard governing "ease of use," comprising accessibility and operability under a range of conditions including SBO and high radiation fields.

The staff has also performed extensive studies of the safety benefits of containment venting for the Mark II containment design, which like the Mark I is an inerted pressure suppression design, although of larger volume. The Mark II was not included in the scope of GL 89-16 at the time it was written in part because the wetwell scrubbing of a fission product release from containment resulting from a beyond-design-basis accident was felt to be less certain than for the Mark I.

In light of Fukushima Daiichi and the benefits of preserving the integrity of the containment in beyond-design-basis accidents, Mark II plants should have a reliable hardened vent either on the basis of either (1) more recent analysis that acceptably reduces the uncertainty of a scrubbed release, or (2) a design that reduces the uncertainty.

The staff concludes that it would be appropriate to redefine what level of protection of public health and safety should be regarded as adequate for venting of BWR Mark I and Mark II primary containments.

In addition, the issue of containment vent filtration has been raised as an additional recommendation which is undergoing further staff review. The staff will need to develop a regulatory basis and acceptance criteria for the reliable hardened vent that encompasses prolonged SBO operation, vent capacity, accessibility, and safe hydrogen and fission product processing for both Mark I and Mark II containments.

The staff concludes that this recommendation would improve safety. Since sufficient resource flexibility, including availability of critical skill sets, exists, the staff prioritized this action as a Tier 1 recommendation.

Staff Recommendations

The staff recommends that the NRC, as a near-term action, undertake regulatory activities to:

1) Interact with stakeholders to inform development of the technical bases and acceptance criteria for suitable design expectations for reliable hardened vents.
2) Develop and issue orders to licensees with BWR Mark I and Mark II primary containment designs to take action to ensure reliable hardened wetwell vents.

Unique Implementation Challenges

The staff did not identify any unique challenges which would preclude moving forward in a timely manner.

Schedule and Milestones

I. Develop and issue order – 6 months
    a) Interact with stakeholders to inform the development of the regulatory basis and acceptance criteria for reliable hardened wetwell vents
    b) Issue order
II. Licensing activities – Schedule to be determined, dependent on design considerations Licensee responses Staff review of licensee responses and issue staff safety evaluation
III. Inspection activities – Schedule to be determined, dependent on order implementation Develop Temporary Instruction Conduct inspections and document inspection results
IV. Issue letters to close out order – 1 month after last inspection

TIER 1 - NTTF RECOMMENDATION 7.1

Schedule

I. Develop and issue order – 6 months
II. Licensing activities – 4 months
III. Inspection activities – Schedule to be determined
IV. Issue letters to close out order – 1 month after last inspection

Resources

Activity	Resource Category	Specific Expertise Needed	Estimated FTE	Locations of Most Applicable Expertise within NRC
I. Develop and issue order	Project/Program Management	Plant Licensing	0.25	NRR
	Technical	Nuclear Engineering	0.2	NRR, NRO, RES
		Mechanical Engineering	0.2	NRR, NRO, RES
		Instrumentation and Control/Electrical Engineering	0.1	NRR, NRO, RES
		Probabilistic Risk Assessment	0.1	NRR, NRO, RES
	Legal	Plant Licensing	0.25	OGC
Licensing activities	Project/Program Management	Plant Licensing	0.75	NRR
	Technical	Nuclear Engineering	0.2	NRR, NRO, RES
		Mechanical Engineering	0.75	NRR, NRO, RES

Resources (Continued)

Activity	Resource Category	Specific Expertise Needed	Estimated FTE	Locations of Most Applicable Expertise within NRC
		Instrumentation and Control/Electrical Engineering	0.2	NRR, NRO, RES
		Probabilistic Risk Assessment	0.2	NRR, NRO, RES
	Legal	Plant Licensing	0.25	OGC
Inspection activities	Project/Program Management	Program Management	0.5	NRR
	Regional inspection	Inspection	3.7	All Regions
	Technical	Mechanical Engineering	0.1	NRR, NRO, RES
		Instrumentation and Control/Electrical Engineering	0.1	NRR, NRO, RES
IV. Issue letters to close out order	Project/Program Management	Plant Licensing	0.25	NRR
	Legal	Plant Licensing	0.25	OGC
Total FTE			8.35	

Note: 1) Where appropriate and available, technical assistance dollars will be used to resolve this recommendation.

TIER 1 - NTTF RECOMMENDATION 7.1

The Task Force recommends enhancing instrumentation for the spent fuel pool (SFP).

7.1 Order licensees to provide sufficient safety-related instrumentation, able to withstand design-basis natural phenomena, to monitor key SFP parameters (i.e., water level, temperature, and area radiation levels) from the control room.

Regulations and Guidance

1) General Design Criterion (GDC) 61, "Fuel storage and handling and radioactivity control," of Appendix A to 10 CFR Part 50 specifies that the SFP be designed to prevent a significant reduction in SFP coolant inventory under accident conditions.
2) GDC 63, "Monitoring fuel and waste storage," of Appendix A to 10 CFR Part 50 specifies that appropriate instrumentation be provided to (1) detect conditions that may result in a loss of residual heat removal capability and (2) initiate appropriate safety actions

Staff Assessment and Basis for Prioritization

The staff concludes that the existing SFP instrumentation requirements should be redefined. The staff recommends the enhancement of existing SFP instrumentation to reliably indicate SFP water level under conditions consistent with loss of forced cooling.

Current SFP instrumentation often is not designed to remain functional under accident conditions. Instrumentation with improved reliability and operating range would provide information to operators on SFP conditions during extended loss of forced cooling and loss of coolant inventory events. For the instrumentation to provide information necessary to support operator event response, the instrumentation must operate reliably in a harsh environment (SFP water at saturation conditions) and be provided with a reliable, potentially safety-related, supply of power. The staff concludes that this recommendation would improve safety. Since sufficient resource flexibility, including availability of critical skill sets, exists, the staff prioritized this action as a Tier 1 recommendation. In addition, action on this recommendation enhances operator event response and supports following a standard rulemaking process for Recommendations 7.2, 7.3, 7.4, and 7.5.

Staff Recommendations

The staff recommends that the NRC, as a near-term action, undertake regulatory activities to:

1. Engage stakeholders to inform the determination of (1) what constitutes reliable (potentially safety-related) SFP instrumentation, (2) what conditions the instrumentation must withstand to fulfill its intended function, (3) which SFP parameters should be monitored (e.g., water level, temperature, and area radiation levels), (4) what makeup strategies could be implemented, and (5) where indications are needed (e.g., control room and/or remote location).
2. Develop and issue order to licensees to provide reliable SFP instrumentation.

Unique Implementation Challenges

The staff did not identify any unique challenges which would preclude moving forward in a timely manner.

Schedule and Milestones

I. Develop and issue order – 6 months
   a) Interact with stakeholders to determine instrumentation requirements
   b) Issue order
II. Licensing activities – 4 months
   a) Licensee responses

b) Staff review of licensee responses and staff safety evaluation
III. Inspection activities – Schedule to be determined, dependent on order implementation
   a) Develop Temporary Instruction
   b) Conduct inspections and document results
IV. Issue letters to close out order – 1 month after last inspection

TIER 1 - NTTF RECOMMENDATION 7.1

Schedule

I. Develop and issue order – 6 months
II. Licensing activities – 4 months
III. Inspection activities – Schedule to be determined
IV. Issue letters to close out order – 1 month after last inspection

Resources

Activity	Resource Category	Specific Expertise Needed	Estimated FTE	Locations of Most Applicable Expertise within NRC
I. Develop and issue order	Project/Program Management	Plant Licensing	0.25	NRR
	Technical	Electrical Engineering/Instrumentation and Control	0.75	NRR, NRO, RES, NMSS
		Mechanical Engineering	0.75	NRR, NRO, RES, NMSS
	Legal	Plant Licensing	0.25	OGC
Licensing activities	Project/Program Management	Plant Licensing	0.25	NRR
	Technical	Electrical Engineering/Instrumentation and Control	0.5	NRR, NRO, NMSS
		Mechanical Engineering	0.5	NRR, NRO, NMSS
	Legal	Plant Licensing	0.25	OGC
Inspection activities	Regional Inspection	Inspection	4.2	All Regions
	Project/Program Management	Inspection Program Management	0.5	NRR
	Technical	Electrical Engineering/Instrumentation and Control	0.1	NRR, NRO, NMSS
		Mechanical Engineering	0.1	NRR, NRO, NMSS
Issue letters to close out of order	Project/Program Management	Plant Licensing	0.1	NRR
	Legal	Plant Licensing	0.25	OGC
Total FTE			8.75	

Note:
1) Where appropriate and available, technical assistance dollars will be used to resolve this recommendation

TIER 1 - NTTF RECOMMENDATION 8

The Task Force recommends strengthening and integrating onsite emergency response capabilities such as emergency operating procedures (EOPs), severe accident management guidelines (SAMGs), and extensive damage mitigation guidelines (EDMGs).

8.1. Order licensees to modify the EOP technical guidelines (required by Supplement 1, "Requirements for Emergency Response Capability," to NUREG-0737, issued January 1983 (GL 82-33), to (1) include EOPs, SAMGs, and EDMGs in an integrated manner, (2) specify clear command and control strategies for their implementation, and (3) stipulate appropriate qualification and training for those who make decisions during emergencies.

- The Task Force strongly advises that the NRC encourage plant owners groups to undertake this activity rather than have each licensee develop its own approach. In addition, the Task Force encourages the use of the established NRC practice of publishing RGs (rather than NUREGs, supplements to NUREGs, or GLs) for endorsing any acceptable approaches submitted by the industry.

8.2 Modify Section 5.0, "Administrative Controls," of the Standard Technical Specifications for each operating reactor design to reference the approved EOP technical guidelines for that plant design.

8.3 Order licensees to modify each plant's technical specifications to conform to the above changes.

8.4 Initiate rulemaking to require more realistic, hands-on training and exercises on SAMGs and EDMGs for all staff expected to implement the strategies and those licensee staff expected to make decisions during emergencies, including emergency coordinators and emergency directors.

Regulations and Guidance

1. RG 1.33, Revision 2, "Quality Assurance Program Requirements (Operation)," Appendix A, issued February 1978, required EOPs as a subset of the applicable procedures recommended in Section 5.0, "Administrative Controls," of licensee technical specifications.
2. NUREG-0737, "Clarification of TMI [Three Mile Island] Action Plan Requirements," Supplement 1, "Requirements for Emergency Response Capability," issued January 1983 (GL 82-33), required the development and submittal for review and approval of EOP technical guidelines.
3. Licensees developed SAMGs as a voluntary program, and the SAMGs are documented as meeting regulatory commitments. There is neither a requirement for realistic, hands-on training or exercises on SAMGs, nor a requirement for integration of the SAMGs, EOPs, and EDMGs.

4. 10 CFR 50.54(hh)(2) requires that licensees develop guidance and strategies. "EDMG" is the generic term used by industry for the required guidance and strategies. Requirements for exercise of EDMGs are included in the final rulemaking described in SECY-11-0053, "Final Rule: Enhancements to Emergency Preparedness Regulations (10 CFR Part 50 and 10 CFR Part 52)," dated April 8, 2011. There is no specific requirement for training on these guidance and strategies; the endorsed guidance on the subject in NEI 06-12, Revision 2, specifies training for 10 CFR 50.54(hh)(2).

Staff Assessment and Basis for Prioritization

EOPs, SAMGs, and EDMGs should be strengthened and integrated. Transition points, command and control, decision-making, and training should be clarified.

SAMGs should be required along with qualification and training for those licensee staff expected to make decisions during beyond-design-basis accident scenarios using either the SAMGs or EDMGs.

Finally the staff concludes that early interactions with stakeholders would be useful in determining the optimal mechanism for implementing these recommendations as requirements.

The staff concludes that this recommendation would improve safety. Since sufficient resource flexibility, including availability of critical skill sets, exists, the staff prioritized this action as a Tier 1 recommendation. However, since these procedures and guidelines already exist and are available for operator use and no imminent hazard was identified, the staff recommends following its standard rulemaking process, which allows for appropriate stakeholder involvement consistent with the rulemaking process and schedule established in SECY-11-0032.

Staff Recommendations

The staff recommends that the NRC, as a near-term action, undertake regulatory action to resolve NTTF Recommendations 8.1, 8.2, 8.3 and 8.4:

1. Issue an advanced notice of proposed rulemaking (ANPR) to engage stakeholders in rulemaking activities associated with the methodology for integration of onsite emergency response processes, procedures, training and exercises.
2. Interact with stakeholders to inform the modification of EOP generic technical guidelines to include guidance for SAMGs and EDMGs in an integrated manner and to clarify command and control issues as appropriate.

Unique Implementation Challenges

While the staff determined that this is a highly complex rulemaking, it did not identify any unique challenges which would preclude moving forward in a timely manner. An important consideration as the staff implements this recommendation will be to ensure that operator training requirements remain appropriately focused on the most risk-significant scenarios.

Schedule and Milestones

I. Develop and issue final rule - 4.25 years
   a) Develop and issue an ANPR to obtain stakeholder input – 4 months
   b) Develop regulatory basis incorporating stakeholder feedback - nominally 13 months following initiation of the action
   c) Issue proposed rule and supporting guidance for comment - nominally additional 16 months following completion and acceptance of the regulatory basis (incorporates 4 months for Commission review and staff response to SRM)
   d) Meet with ACRS during the proposed rule stage (if requested by ACRS)
   e) Issue final rule and supporting guidance - nominally additional 22 months (accounts for 75 day public comment period, 4 months of Commission review and staff response to final rule SRM, 3 months for OMB approval for final rule, and meet with ACRS)

II. Licensing activities – Schedule to be determined, dependent on rule requirements
   a) Licensee submittals
   b) Staff review and safety evaluation issuance

III. Inspection activities – Schedule to be determined, dependent on licensee implementation timeframe
   a) Incorporate inspection into ROP
   b) Conduct inspections and document results

TIER 1 - NTTF RECOMMENDATION 8

Schedule

I. Develop and issue final rule - 4.25 years
II. Licensing activities – Schedule to be determined
III. Inspection activities – Schedule to be determined

Resources

Activity	Resource Category	Specific Expertise Needed	Estimated FTE	Locations of Most Applicable Expertise within NRC
I. Develop and issue final rule	Project/Program Management	Rulemaking	1.5	NRR, NRO, FSME
	Technical	Human Factors	1.5	NRR, NRO, RES
		Operator Licensing	1.5	NRR

Resources (Continued)

Activity	Resource Category	Specific Expertise Needed	Estimated FTE	Locations of Most Applicable Expertise within NRC
Licensing activities		Incident Response/ Emergency Preparedness	1.5	NSIR
		Nuclear Engineering	0.5	NRR, NRO, RES
	Legal	Rulemaking	0.5	OGC
	Project/Program Management	Plant Licensing	0.25	NRR
	Technical	Human Factors	1.0	NRR, NRO, RES
		Operator Licensing	1.0	NRR
		Incident Response/ Emergency Preparedness	1.0	NSIR
		Nuclear Engineering	0.5	NRR, NRO, RES
	Legal	Plant Licensing	0.25	OGC
Inspection activities	Regional Inspection	Inspection	10.8	All Regions
	Project/Program Management	Inspection Program Management	2.0	NRR
Total FTE			23.8	

Notes:
1) Where appropriate and available, technical assistance dollars will be used to resolve this recommendation.
2) Inspection resources include an estimate for staff training, including headquarters staff, that would cover Recommendation 12.2.

TIER 1 - NTTF RECOMMENDATION 9.3
(STAFFING AND COMMUNICATIONS)

The Task Force recommends that the NRC require that facility emergency plans address prolonged SBO and multiunit events.

9.3 Order licensees to do the following until rulemaking is complete:

- Determine and implement the required staff to fill all necessary positions for response to a multi-unit event
- Provide a means to power communications equipment needed to communicate onsite (e.g., radios for response teams and between facilities) and offsite (e.g., cellular telephones and satellite telephones) during a prolonged SBO.

Regulations and Guidance

1) 10 CFR 50.47, "Emergency Plans," includes the 16 planning standards of 10 CFR 50.47(b), and Appendix E, "Emergency Planning and Preparedness for Production and Utilization Facilities," to 10 CFR Part 50 describes information needed to demonstrate compliance with EP requirements.
2) NUREG-0654, "Criteria for Preparation and Evaluation of Radiological Emergency Response Plans and Preparedness in Support of Nuclear Power Plants," Revision 1,

issued November 1980, describes guidance and an acceptable means for demonstrating compliance with the Commission's regulations.
3) SECY-11-0053, "Final Rule: Enhancement to Emergency Preparedness Regulations (10 CFR Part 50 and 10 CFR Part 52)," dated April 8, 2011, codifies hostile-action-based enhancements, among others.
4) NUREG-0696, "Functional Criteria for Emergency Response Facilities," issued February 1981, describes the facilities and systems that licensees can use to improve emergency response to accidents, such as the technical support system, operational support center, and emergency offsite facility.

Staff Assessment and Basis for Prioritization

The staff's assessment of Recommendation 9.3 indicates that regulatory action should be initiated to determine the required staffing to fill all necessary positions for responding to a multiunit event. This would require both the NRC staff and licensees to reevaluate the current staffing assumptions and analysis for effectively responding to multiunit incidents, in addition to actions being taken to satisfy the requirements of the recently affirmed Emergency Preparedness Final Rule. The staff is focused on licensees completing the staffing analyses only so that they could be done along with the actions required by the impending rule.

The staff also concludes that there is a need to strengthen the requirements to provide a means to power communications equipment needed to communicate onsite (e.g., radios for response teams and between facilities) and offsite (e.g., cellular telephones and satellite telephones) during a prolonged SBO. This would require additional guidance regarding what constitutes acceptable communications equipment that does not rely on the availability of facility AC power.

The staff concludes that this recommendation would improve safety. Since sufficient resource flexibility, including availability of critical skill sets, exists, the staff prioritized this action as a Tier 1 recommendation.

Staff Recommendations

The staff recommends that the NRC, as a near-term action, undertake regulatory activities to:

1. Engage stakeholders to (1) inform development of a methodology to perform a staffing study to determine the required staff to fill all necessary positions to respond to a multiunit event, and (2) discuss potential enhancements that could provide a means to power communications equipment necessary for licensee onsite and offsite communications during a prolonged SBO event,
2. Develop and issue a request for information to licensees pursuant to 10 CFR 50.54(f) to (1) perform a staffing study to determine the required staff to fill all necessary positions to respond to a multiunit event, (2) evaluate what enhancements would be needed to provide a means to power communications equipment necessary for licensee onsite and offsite communications during a prolonged SBO event, and (3)

inform the NRC of the results of the staffing study and any actions taken or planned, along with their implementation schedules, to react to the staffing study results and to enhance the communications equipment, and

3. Evaluate licensee responses and take regulatory action to require implementation, as appropriate.

Unique Implementation Challenges

The staff is currently engaged in the implementation of the recently approved revision to the EP regulations. This is the most extensive revision since the EP regulations were promulgated in 1980 in response to the TMI accident. The staff has committed to a significant outreach effort to help ensure consistent licensee implementation and in response to requests from offsite response organizations. The development of technical information in support of Recommendation 9.3 will require significant effort from the staff and licensees and must be coordinated with the ongoing EP Rule implementation.

Schedule and Milestones

I. Issue 10 CFR 50.54(f) letter – 6 months following initiation of action
   a) Stakeholder interaction and technical development (e.g., methods, technical basis, acceptance criteria, etc.)
   b) Develop 10 CFR 50.54(f) letter
   c) Issue 10 CFR 50.54(f) letter

II. Evaluate licensee responses to 10 CFR 50.54(f) letter – Based on a timeline to be developed during the stakeholder interaction taking into account available resources.
   a) Write safety evaluation or NUREG to document staff conclusions

III. Issue orders to licensees (if needed) – 3 months following decision to issue orders
   a) Develop regulatory basis and draft orders
   b) Issue orders

IV. Conduct inspection activities – Schedule to be determined
   a) Develop Temporary Instruction
   b) Conduct inspections and document results

V. Issue letters to close out 10 CFR 50.54(f) letter and/or orders – 1 month after last inspection

TIER 1 - NTTF RECOMMENDATION 9.3
(STAFFING AND COMMUNICATIONS)

Schedule

I. Develop 10 CFR 50.54(f) letter – 6 months
II. Evaluate licensee responses to 10 CFR 50.54(f) letter – Schedule to be determined
III. Issue orders to licensees (if needed) – 3 months following decision to issue orders
IV. Conduct inspection activities – Schedule to be determined
V. Issue letters to close out 10 CFR 50.54(f) letter and/or orders – 1 month after last inspection

Resources

Activity	Resource Category	Specific Expertise Needed	Estimated FTE	Locations of Most Applicable Expertise within NRC
Develop 50.54(f) letter	Project/Program Management	Plant Licensing	0.25	NRR
	Technical	Emergency Preparedness	0.5	NSIR
	Legal	Plant Licensing	0.25	OGC
Evaluate licensee responses to 50.54(f) letter	Project/Program Management	Plant Licensing	0.25	NRR
	Technical	Emergency Preparedness	0.75	NSIR
	Legal	Plant Licensing	0.25	OGC
Issue orders to licensees (if needed)	Project/Program Management	Plant Licensing	0.25	NRR
	Technical	Emergency Preparedness	0.5	NSIR
	Legal	Plant Licensing	0.25	OGC
Conduct inspection activities	Regional Inspection	Inspection	4.2	All Regions
	Project/Program Management	Inspection Program Management	0.5	NRR
	Technical	Emergency Preparedness	0.25	NSIR
Issue letters to close out 50.54(f) letter and/or orders	Project/Program Management	Project Management	0.25	NRR
	Legal	Plant Licensing	0.25	OGC
Total FTE			8.7	

Note:
1) Where appropriate and available, technical assistance dollars will be used to resolve this recommendation.

TIER 2 - NTTF RECOMMENDATIONS 7.2, 7.3, 7.4, AND 7.5

The Task Force recommends enhancing SFP makeup capability and instrumentation.

7.2 Order licensees to provide safety-related AC electrical power for the SFP makeup system.

7.3 Order licensees to revise their technical specifications to address requirements to have one train of onsite emergency electrical power operable for SFP makeup and spent fuel pool instrumentation when there is irradiated fuel in the SFP, regardless of the operational mode of the reactor.

7.4 Order licensees to have an installed seismically qualified means to spray water into the spent fuel pools, including an easily accessible connection to supply the water (e.g., using a portable pump or pumper truck) at grade outside the building.

7.5 Initiate rulemaking or licensing activities or both to require the actions related to the SFP described in Recommendations 7.1-7.4.

Regulations and Guidance

1) General Design Criterion (GDC) 61, "Fuel storage and handling and radioactivity control," of Appendix A to 10 CFR Part 50 specifies that the SFP be designed to prevent a significant reduction in SFP coolant inventory under accident conditions.

2) GDC 63, "Monitoring fuel and waste storage," of Appendix A to 10 CFR Part 50 specifies that appropriate instrumentation be provided to (1) detect conditions that may result in a loss of residual heat removal capability and (2) initiate appropriate safety actions

3) 10 CFR 50.54(hh)(2) requires licensees to develop and implement guidance and strategies intended to maintain or restore core cooling, containment, and spent fuel pool cooling capabilities under circumstances associated with the loss of large areas of the plant due to explosions or fire.

4) Nuclear Energy Institute (NEI) 06-12, Revision 2, "B.5.b Phase 2 & 3 Submittal Guidance," issued December 2006, provides guidance supporting 10 CFR 50.54(hh)(2).

Staff Assessment and Basis for Prioritization

As a follow-on activity to the completion of Recommendation 7.1, the staff concludes that the existing SFP instrumentation and makeup requirements should be enhanced through rulemaking. The staff recommends the enhancement of existing SFP instrumentation to reliably indicate SFP conditions consistent with loss of forced cooling. The staff recognizes that the equipment procured pursuant to 10 CFR 50.54(hh)(2) has enhanced SFP makeup capability, but the associated guidance does not address reliability of the makeup function with respect to access and equipment availability.

The enhanced capabilities should consider risk insights for the SFP. Risk is higher during and immediately after refueling due to the following: (1) increased heat load from recently discharged fuel; (2) increased number of potential drain paths (more connected non-seismic structures and systems); (3) increased potential to drain to a lower elevation (the fuel transfer path typically is the lowest SFP penetration); and, (4) fewer controls on the availability of makeup water systems (e.g., essential service water provides safety-related makeup at many sites, but all trains may be removed from service for maintenance when all irradiated fuel has been transferred to the SFP).

Recommendations 7.2, 7.3, and 7.4 all relate to the reliability of SFP makeup.

Recommendations 7.2 and 7.3 relate to makeup capability using permanently installed makeup systems and address the quality and availability of onsite AC power to support that function. Makeup capability at all operating reactors currently requires manual operator actions outside the control room. Recommendation 7.4 would require a method of supplying makeup or spray via a seismically qualified flow path, where the system's reliability would be based upon the reliability of the pumping system and water source employed. Recommendation 7.4 would allow initiation of makeup from outside the structure housing the SFP, for scenarios when the SFP deck is inaccessible, and enhances defense-in-depth by incorporating a spray capability for mitigation of beyond-design-basis events.

The staff concludes that this recommendation would improve safety. Since the staff is proposing to initiate action on Recommendations 4.2 and 7.1 to enhance defense-in-depth and operator event response, the staff has concluded that it is appropriate to initiate this rulemaking after consideration of insights from Tier 1 Recommendations 2.1, 4.1, and 4.2. As such, the staff has prioritized this action as a Tier 2 recommendation. This rulemaking can be initiated when sufficient technical information becomes available.

Staff Recommendation

Once sufficient technical information is available, the staff recommends that the NRC undertake regulatory activities to:

> Engage stakeholders in support of rulemaking activities to provide reliable SFP instrumentation and makeup capabilities. These activities will include the development of the regulatory basis, a proposed rule, and implementing guidance consistent with the rulemaking process and schedule established in SECY-11-0032.

Unique Implementation Challenges

The staff did not identify any unique challenges with this rulemaking.

Schedule and Milestones

I. Develop and issue final rule - 4.25 years following initiation of action
   a) Develop regulatory basis incorporating stakeholder feedback - nominally 13 months following initiation of the action
   b) Issue proposed rule and supporting guidance for comment - nominally additional 16 months following completion and acceptance of the regulatory basis (incorporates 4 months for Commission review and staff response to SRM)
   c) Meet with ACRS during the proposed rule stage (if requested by ACRS)
   d) Issue final SFP rule and supporting guidance - nominally additional 22 months (accounts for 75 day public comment period, 4 months of Commission review and staff response to final rule SRM, 3 months for OMB approval for final rule, and meet with ACRS).
II. Licensing activities – Schedule to be determined, dependent on rule requirements

a) Licensee submittals
   b) Staff review and safety evaluation issuance
III. Inspection activities – Schedule to be determined, dependent on licensee modifications
   a) Incorporate inspection into the ROP
   b) Conduct inspections and document results

TIER 2 - NTTF RECOMMENDATIONS 7.2, 7.3. 7.4, AND 7.5

Schedule

I. Develop and issue final rule - 4.25 years following initiation of action
II. Licensing activities – Schedule to be determined
III. Inspection activities – Schedule to be determined

Resources

Activity	Resource Category	Specific Expertise Needed	Estimated FTE	Locations of Most Applicable Expertise within NRC
I. Develop and issue final rule	Project/Program Management	Rulemaking	1.5	NRR, NRO, FSME
	Technical	Electrical Engineering/Instrumentation and Control	1.5	NRR, NRO, RES, NMSS
		Mechanical Engineering	1.5	NRR, NRO, RES, NMSS
	Legal	Rulemaking	0.5	OGC
Licensing activities	Project/Program Management	Plant Licensing	0.75	NRR
	Technical	Electrical Engineering/Instrumentation and Control	2.0	NRR, NRO, RES, MSS
		Mechanical Engineering	2.0	NRR, NRO, RES, NMSS
	Legal	Plant Licensing	0.25	OGC
Inspection activities	Regional Inspection	Inspection	10.8	All Regions
	Project/Program Management	Inspection Program Management	0.5	NRR
	Technical	Electrical Engineering/Instrumentation and Control	0.2	NRR, NRO, RES, NMSS
		Mechanical Engineering	0.2	NRR, NRO, RES, NMSS
Total FTE			21.7	

Note:
1) Where appropriate and available, technical assistance dollars will be used to resolve this recommendation

Tier 2 - NTTF Recommendation 9.3
(Remaining Actions, Except ERDS Capability)

The Task Force recommends that the NRC require that facility emergency plans address prolonged SBO and multiunit events.

9.3 Order licensees to do the following until rulemaking is complete:

- Add guidance to the emergency plan that documents how to perform a multiunit dose assessment (including releases from spent fuel pools) using the licensee's site-specific dose assessment software and approach.
- Conduct periodic training and exercises for multiunit and prolonged SBO scenarios. Practice (simulate) the identification and acquisition of offsite resources, to the extent possible.
- Ensure that EP equipment and facilities are sufficient for dealing with multiunit and prolonged SBO scenarios.

Regulations and Guidance

1. 10 CFR 50.47, "Emergency Plans," includes the 16 planning standards of 10 CFR 50.47(b), and Appendix E, "Emergency Planning and Preparedness for Production and Utilization Facilities," to 10 CFR Part 50 describes information needed to demonstrate compliance with EP requirements.
2. NUREG-0654, "Criteria for Preparation and Evaluation of Radiological Emergency Response Plans and Preparedness in Support of Nuclear Power Plants," Revision 1, issued November 1980, describes guidance and an acceptable means for demonstrating compliance with the Commission's regulations.
3. SECY-11-0053, "Final Rule: Enhancement to Emergency Preparedness Regulations (10 CFR Part 50 and 10 CFR Part 52)," dated April 8, 2011, codifies hostile-action-based enhancements, among others.
4. Section IV of Appendix E to 10 CFR Part 50 codifies the requirements for the NRC's ERDS.
5. NUREG-0696, "Functional Criteria for Emergency Response Facilities," issued February 1981, describes the facilities and systems that licensees can use to improve emergency response to accidents, such as the technical support system, operational support center, and emergency offsite facility.

Staff Assessment and Basis for Prioritization

The NTTF report describes the relationship between Recommendation 9.3 and EP planning standards as follows: staffing, 10 CFR 50.47(b)(2) (identified in Tier 1 response); equipment and facilities, 10 CFR 50.47(b)(8); radiological assessment, 10 CFR 50.47(b)(9); training, 10 CFR 50.47(b)(15); exercises, 10 CFR 50.47(b)(14); offsite resources, 10 CFR

50.47(b)(3); and communications, 10 CFR 50.47(b)(6) (identified in Tier 1 response). The staff's guidance used to determine compliance with these planning standards did not envision multiunit or prolonged SBO events. The staff reviewed the remaining planning standards of 10 CFR 50.47(b) to determine if there were other areas that may be impacted by these scenarios and found that the scope of Recommendation 9.3 is complete in identifying the planning standard related area that should be upgraded to address SBO and multiunit events.

The staff will engage external stakeholders to inform the development of boundary conditions, implementation details, and acceptance criteria for licensees to perform acceptable analyses of each of these planning elements with respect to multiunit and SBO events. After stakeholder engagement, the staff will issue an order to require reanalysis and implementation of the results for each of the planning elements, as appropriate. The rulemaking envisioned in response to Recommendations 9.1 and 9.2 would make order requirements generically applicable.

The statements of consideration for the original ERDS Rule (56 FR 40178) specifically noted that ERDS is not a safety system; therefore, licensees have not been required to address the need to supply emergency power to the equipment and systems used to collect and transmit data to the NRC. In addition, as part of the ERDS modernization initiative, the staff selected a data transmission method (VPN, virtual private network) which utilizes licensees' non-safety related corporate computer networks and the internet to provide connectivity to the NRC's ERDS servers. Implementation of an ERDS capable of functioning during a prolonged SBO will likely require an extensive, if not complete, redesign of the licensees' current systems, as well as a reevaluation of the data transmission solution selected by the NRC.

ERDS is a system that provides for the transmission of data to assist NRC and the States in monitoring plant conditions during events at classifications of Alert and above. While ERDS is a current regulatory requirement, it is a supplement to other methods that exist in licensee, NRC and State incident response plans and procedures (e.g., NRC site teams, Emergency Notification System, and communication protocols between licensees and the States).

The ERDS modernization initiative currently underway substantially improves the reliability of the data transmission path during an accident. However, prolonged loss of power may present a challenge not only to data transmission, but also to the sources of ERDS data (the plant process computer, safety-related and non-safety-related instrument loops, etc.).

Given its supplementary nature and the need to consider this recommendation in a more deliberate, integrated manner, the staff recommends that the issuance of any new ERDS related requirements to licensees be deferred until a comprehensive set of requirements can be developed by the staff as part of the Tier 3 long term study of NTTF Recommendation 10.3.

Upon completion of the ERDS VPN transition, licensees will have the capability to transmit ERDS data to the NRC from all units simultaneously.

The staff has prioritized regulatory actions related to the portions of NTTF Recommendation 9.3 identified above in Tier 2.

Staff with critical skill sets necessary for the resolution of these portions of Recommendation 9.3 are currently involved in implementation of the recently issued EP Rule. These actions do not require long term study and can be initiated when sufficient resources become available.

Staff Recommendations

Once sufficient staff with critical skill sets are available, the staff recommends that the NRC undertake regulatory activities to:

1. Engage stakeholders to inform the development of acceptance criteria for the licensee examination of planning standard elements related to the recommendations,

and

2. Develop and issue an order to address those changes necessary in emergency plans to ensure adequate response to SBO and multiunit events specific to (1) adding guidance to the emergency plan that documents how to perform a multiunit dose assessment,
   - conduct periodic training and exercises for multiunit and prolonged SBO scenarios,
   - practice (simulate) the identification and acquisition of offsite resources, to the extent possible, and (4) ensure that EP equipment and facilities are sufficient for dealing with multiunit and prolonged SBO scenarios.

Unique Implementation Challenges

The staff is currently engaged in the implementation of the recently approved revision to the EP regulations. This is the most extensive revision since the EP regulations were promulgated in 1980 in response to the TMI accident.

The staff has committed to a significant outreach effort to help ensure consistent licensee implementation and in response to requests from offsite response organizations.

The development of technical information in support of Recommendation 9.3 will require significant effort from the staff and licensees and must be coordinated with the ongoing EP Rule implementation. The staff plans to initiate this action by mid-2012.

Schedule and Milestones

I. Develop and issue order – 6 months following initiation of action

   a) Interact with stakeholders to inform the development of the regulatory basis and acceptance criteria
   b) Issue order

II. Licensing activities - Schedule to be determined Licensee response

   a) Review of licensee emergency plans and issue staff safety evaluations

III. Inspection Activities – Schedule to be determined, dependent on order implementation

a) Develop Temporary Instruction
   b) Conduct inspections and document inspection results

IV. Issue letters to close out order – 1 month after last inspection

TIER 2 - NTTF RECOMMENDATION 9.3 (REMAINING ACTIONS, EXCEPT ERDS CAPABILITY)

Schedule

I. Develop and issue order – 6 months following initiation of action
II. Licensing activities – Schedule to be determined
III. Inspection activities – Schedule to be determined
IV. Issue letters to close out order – 1 month after last inspection

Resources

Activity	Resource Category	Specific Expertise Needed	Estimated FTE	Locations of Most Applicable Expertise within NRC
I. Develop and issue order	Project/Program Management	Plant Licensing	0.25	NRR
	Technical	Emergency Preparedness	2.0	NSIR
	Legal	Plant Licensing	0.25	OGC
Licensing activities	Project/Program Management	Plant Licensing	0.25	NRR
	Technical	Emergency Preparedness	1.0	NSIR
	Legal	Plant Licensing	0.25	OGC
Inspection activities	Regional Inspection	Inspection	4.2	All Regions
	Project/Program Management	Program Management	0.5	NRR
	Technical	Emergency Preparedness	0.1	NSIR
Issue letters to close out order	Project/Program Management	Plant Licensing	0.25	NRR
	Legal	Plant Licensing	0.25	OGC
Total FTE			9.3	

Note:
1) Where appropriate and available, technical assistance dollars will be used to resolve this recommendation.

INDEX

A

access, 6, 13, 65, 66, 145
accessibility, 99, 133
accident prevention, 7
actuation, 8
advancements, 26, 83
Advisory Committee for Reactor Safeguards (ACRS), viii, 87, 114
agencies, 52, 62, 108, 109
agency actions, 5
assessment, 5, 13, 23, 24, 26, 28, 52, 54, 55, 56, 57, 58, 61, 63, 64, 71, 73, 74, 76, 77, 89, 90, 91, 92, 95, 102, 103, 106, 107, 108, 112, 113, 115, 121, 129, 142, 147, 148, 149
atmosphere, 42, 43, 85
authorities, 52, 54, 55, 56, 66, 67
authority, 50, 55, 58, 66, 73
awareness, 16, 56

B

ban, 59
banks, 35, 45
barriers, 30, 31, 72, 84, 93, 94, 95, 116, 120, 121
base, 61, 65
batteries, 12, 36, 41, 46
benefits, 40, 62, 133
bounds, 22

C

cancer, 7
candidates, 24
categorization, 18
certification, 19, 22, 69, 70, 110
challenges, viii, 8, 17, 22, 25, 33, 36, 51, 54, 55, 56, 59, 61, 63, 87, 90, 105, 109, 111, 114, 122, 127, 130, 134, 136, 139, 146
citizens, 8
cladding, 42, 43
clarity, 9, 83
classification, 18
classroom, 49
closure, 32
coastal region, 30
Code of Federal Regulations, 2, 8, 89, 92, 107, 112, 114
collaboration, 79
combined effect, 25
combustion, 42
commercial, 6, 7, 25, 33
Commission direction, vii, 2, 5, 82, 89
communication, 10, 54, 55, 56, 76, 149
community, 58, 61, 109, 110
competition, 119, 124, 125, 128, 131
complement, 49
compliance, 8, 34, 36, 51, 63, 102, 141, 148
complications, 41
computer, 148, 149
configuration, 64
connectivity, 148
consensus, 47
consolidation, 56
construction, 8, 63, 69, 70, 83, 92, 114
consumers, 60
contaminated food, 59, 60
contamination, 1, 24
contingency, 56
cooling, 1, 6, 11, 12, 19, 20, 34, 36, 37, 38, 39, 40, 44, 46, 48, 59, 69, 71, 77, 84, 85, 96, 97, 99, 126, 129, 132, 135, 136, 145
cooperation, 67
coordination, 52, 54, 62, 67, 74, 76
coping strategies, 39, 47
cost, 17, 40, 67
covering, 44, 84
critical infrastructure, 61
culture, 63
current limit, 56

D

danger, 53
data collection, 53, 65
data set, 58, 74
deaths, 61
decay, 40, 47
degradation, 35, 38, 62, 71, 74, 96, 126
Department of Energy, 110
depth, 3, 4, 5, 6, 7, 8, 9, 10, 22, 23, 24, 25, 33, 37, 38, 46, 50, 63, 64, 67, 68, 71, 73, 82, 83, 86, 109, 113, 130, 145
destruction, 61
directors, 50, 55, 58, 71, 100, 138
disaster, 59
distribution, 34, 35, 36
dosage, 60
draft, 51, 93, 115, 116, 117, 122, 143
drainage, 93, 115

E

earthquakes, 25, 31, 35, 36, 61
education, 62
electricity, 7
emergency, vii, 2, 4, 6, 7, 8, 11, 12, 20, 23, 33, 34, 35, 36, 45, 47, 48, 49, 50, 52, 53, 54, 55, 56, 57, 58, 59, 61, 62, 68, 71, 72, 73, 74, 76, 77, 81, 82, 84, 85, 86, 89, 100, 101, 102, 107, 108, 109, 111, 112, 137, 138, 139, 141, 144, 147, 148, 149, 150
emergency communications, 53, 77
emergency planning, 7, 52, 59, 61, 77, 86, 102, 108
emergency preparedness, vii, 2, 4, 6, 8, 81, 82, 109, 111
emergency response, 4, 48, 49, 50, 52, 53, 54, 58, 59, 62, 68, 74, 84, 85, 100, 101, 102, 137, 139, 141, 148
enforcement, 63
engineering, 54
environment, vii, 2, 8, 19, 20, 25, 52, 65, 132, 136
Environmental Protection Agency, 60
EPA, 60
EPR, 66
equipment, 6, 8, 18, 26, 30, 31, 32, 33, 35, 36, 37, 38, 39, 40, 44, 46, 52, 53, 54, 55, 56, 57, 58, 59, 60, 62, 63, 70, 71, 72, 73, 74, 83, 84, 86, 93, 95, 96, 97, 98, 102, 103, 116, 121, 126, 129, 130, 141, 142, 145, 147, 148, 149
evacuation, 59, 60, 61
evolution, 22, 56
exclusion, 16
exercise, 19, 51, 101, 138
expertise, 93, 110, 115, 116
explosives, 34

exposure, 52, 55, 59, 60, 61, 62, 102

F

Federal Emergency Management Agency, vii, 6, 81, 88
Federal Register, 6
FEMA, 6, 52, 58, 59, 62, 74
filtration, 133
financial, 65
Finland, 21
fire fighting, 59
fire suppression, 31
fires, 2, 3, 4, 20, 22, 26, 27, 31, 32, 33, 35, 37, 43, 58, 68, 73, 77, 83, 98, 107, 113, 130
fission, 7, 8, 99, 132, 133
fitness, 69
flexibility, 52, 57, 106, 112, 116, 121, 126, 130, 133, 136, 139, 142
flooding, 4, 16, 17, 22, 26, 28, 30, 31, 32, 34, 35, 36, 37, 39, 68, 69, 71, 77, 83, 91, 92, 93, 94, 95, 107, 110, 113, 114, 116, 120, 121
floods, 4, 25, 26, 27, 29, 30, 31, 32, 33, 35, 38, 58, 61, 68, 73, 83, 92, 93, 94, 107, 113, 114, 116, 120
Food and Drug Administration, 60
force, 5, 60, 76, 77, 78, 79
France, 21, 66
Fukushima Dai-ichi Nuclear Power Plant, vii, 1, 2, 10, 11, 82
Fukushima Near-Term Task Force (NTTF), viii, 105
funding, 111

G

governments, 55
guidance, 3, 9, 19, 26, 27, 28, 29, 31, 32, 33, 34, 35, 36, 42, 48, 49, 51, 54, 55, 57, 58, 59, 60, 69, 70, 71, 73, 77, 91, 92, 93, 95, 96, 97, 99, 101, 102, 103, 114, 115, 116, 121, 127, 129, 132, 138, 139, 140, 141, 142, 145, 146, 147, 148, 149
guidelines, 2, 3, 4, 6, 8, 19, 25, 47, 48, 50, 72, 73, 77, 83, 89, 97, 100, 101, 107, 112, 116, 129, 137, 138, 139
Gulf of Mexico, 30

H

hazards, 25, 27, 28, 29, 30, 31, 34, 38, 58, 71, 83, 92, 93, 94, 95, 98, 107, 113, 114, 115, 116, 121, 130
health, vii, 1, 2, 7, 9, 24, 61, 62, 70, 82, 89
health effects, 1, 9, 24, 61
heat removal, 40, 43, 135, 145
height, 10, 12
high winds, 25, 26, 27, 29, 34, 35, 36, 37
historical data, 26
history, 22

Index

housing, 145
human, 54
Hurricane Katrina, 60
hurricanes, 26, 34, 35, 58, 60, 61
hydrogen, 4, 12, 36, 39, 41, 42, 43, 68, 73, 84, 85, 133
hydrogen gas, 12, 36, 41, 42, 43
hysteria, 62

I

identification, 57, 79, 147, 149
impact assessment, 3, 20
Impact Assessment, 21
improvements, vii, 2, 5, 20, 27, 29, 32, 40, 53, 67, 76, 77, 82, 89
independence, 6, 9, 62, 74
individuals, viii, 7, 65, 81
industry, viii, 2, 3, 6, 10, 19, 21, 22, 23, 34, 48, 49, 50, 63, 64, 69, 78, 81, 83, 88, 89, 100, 101, 103, 106, 108, 109, 110, 116, 138
information technology, 65
infrastructure, 10, 35, 45, 53, 54, 56, 58, 59, 62, 74
ingestion, 59, 60
initiation, 48, 54, 90, 127, 140, 143, 145, 146, 150
injuries, 61
inspections, 48, 49, 63, 64, 69, 90, 92, 95, 115, 117, 121, 122, 123, 127, 131, 134, 136, 140, 143, 146, 150
inspectors, 6, 49, 54, 63, 64, 73
integration, 49, 69, 89, 101, 107, 112, 138, 139
integrity, 26, 27, 31, 33, 35, 36, 38, 39, 41, 42, 45, 71, 84, 96, 126, 133
interface, 57, 76
International Atomic Energy Agency, 6, 121
iodine, 60
isolation, 11, 38, 41
issues, 2, 3, 9, 17, 20, 22, 23, 25, 26, 28, 29, 32, 38, 42, 65, 67, 69, 77, 82, 83, 86, 89, 90, 95, 101, 106, 107, 108, 109, 110, 112, 113, 116, 121, 130, 139

J

Japan, vii, 1, 2, 5, 6, 10, 13, 20, 25, 31, 33, 54, 66, 76, 77, 78, 88, 105, 109, 110

L

law enforcement, 59
lead, 8, 55
leadership, 67, 79
leakage, 34, 39, 41
light, vii, 2, 20, 24, 32, 55, 70, 82, 133
local authorities, 54
local community, 61, 62, 74

local government, 52, 55, 58, 60, 62

M

magnitude, 10, 31, 51, 82
man, 27
management, 3, 4, 6, 12, 46, 55, 58, 63, 64, 65, 66, 77, 83, 88, 89, 97, 100, 106, 107, 112, 129, 137
materials, 33, 34, 35, 44, 50, 52, 59, 60, 109
matter, 38, 60, 66
measurement, 60
media, 52, 62
medical, 59, 60, 62
melt, 61
meter, 37
methodology, 18, 93, 95, 101, 116, 121, 139, 142
migration, 43
mission, 65, 86
models, 28, 29, 30, 115, 117, 122, 123, 127, 131
modernization, 56, 58, 72, 89, 102, 103, 148, 149
modifications, 64, 83, 108, 113, 127, 146

N

National Response Framework, vii, 6, 81
natural disaster(s), 4, 38, 54, 55, 56, 58, 59, 60, 61, 62, 71, 74, 96, 126
natural hazards, 35
Near-Term Task Force, v, vii, viii, 1, 2, 79, 81, 82, 87, 91, 106, 112
neutral, 9, 25
nitrogen, 43
Nuclear Regulatory Commission (NRC), v, vii, viii, 2, 5, 7, 76, 77, 81, 87, 91, 110

O

Office of Management and Budget, 111, 127
officials, 61, 62
offsite emergency preparedness, vii, 6, 81
oil, 31
OMB, 127, 140, 146
openness, 9
operating range, 136
operating system, 45
operations, 48, 97, 111, 129
opportunities, 57
organs, 60
OSC, 54
outreach, 10, 62, 143, 150
overlap, 119, 124, 125, 128, 131
overlay, 55
oversight, 58, 63, 67, 69, 73, 109
oxygen, 42

P

Pacific, 30
pagers, 56
participants, 88
permission, iv, 50
permit, 41, 83, 92, 93, 115, 116
plants, vii, 2, 8, 11, 12, 17, 18, 22, 24, 26, 29, 30, 31, 32, 33, 34, 40, 47, 49, 53, 54, 55, 58, 61, 70, 73, 83, 85, 90, 92, 93, 95, 99, 115, 121, 132, 133
platform, 66
policy, vii, 2, 3, 5, 7, 9, 22, 25, 49, 70, 71, 78, 82, 110
policy issues, 78
pools, 12, 16, 33, 34, 35, 36, 44, 45, 46, 47, 55, 57, 72, 77, 85, 89, 144, 147
population, 7, 60, 61
post-Fukushima, viii, 6, 81
potassium, 59, 86, 109
power plants, vii, 2, 6, 9, 10, 17, 18, 19, 20, 27, 30, 31, 33, 38, 48, 50, 51, 82, 84
precipitation, 30, 37, 93, 115
predictability, 83
preparation, iv, 54, 109
preparedness, 5, 17, 55, 58, 61, 77, 82, 89, 107, 108, 112, 113
prevention, 19, 84, 85
principles, 9
probability, 34, 40, 51, 59
project, 55
protection, vii, 2, 3, 4, 5, 6, 7, 8, 9, 12, 17, 19, 20, 21, 22, 24, 25, 26, 27, 28, 29, 30, 31, 32, 33, 37, 38, 40, 43, 48, 50, 52, 54, 60, 63, 67, 68, 69, 70, 71, 72, 77, 82, 83, 85, 89, 90, 91, 93, 94, 95, 97, 98, 99, 109, 114, 115, 120, 121, 129, 130, 133
public affairs, 52
public awareness, 62
public education, 4, 62, 68, 108, 113
public health, 3, 9, 19, 20, 22, 38, 50, 59, 70, 82, 89, 90, 98, 99, 106, 109, 133
public interest, 10
publishing, 50, 100, 138
pumps, 12, 33, 37

Q

qualifications, 58, 73, 86
quality assurance, 18, 19, 39, 47, 69
quality standards, 21, 23
questioning, 18

R

radar, 29
radiation, 1, 4, 46, 50, 60, 61, 62, 68, 72, 74, 86, 108, 113, 133, 135, 136
radio, 55, 56, 60
radius, 59
reactions, 43
reading, 17
reality, 24, 56
recognition, vii, 2, 36
reconstruction, 56
recovery, 13, 58, 60, 61, 62, 74
redundancy, 7, 8, 33
regulations, vii, 2, 5, 9, 19, 20, 21, 22, 23, 24, 25, 26, 27, 28, 29, 32, 33, 37, 42, 44, 47, 49, 51, 52, 53, 54, 60, 63, 70, 73, 82, 91, 99, 102, 132, 141, 142, 148, 150
regulatory framework, 2, 3, 4, 17, 21, 22, 23, 24, 38, 50, 63, 67, 82, 83, 86, 106
regulatory oversight, 5, 64, 68, 86
regulatory requirements, 2, 3, 5, 8, 19, 21, 23, 24, 25, 47, 50, 70, 73, 76, 77, 83
regulatory system(s), vii, 2, 5, 21, 76, 77, 82
rejection, 20
relevance, 63
reliability, 33, 46, 136, 145, 149
relief, 54, 99, 132
repair, 54
RES, 118, 119, 123, 124, 125, 128, 131, 134, 135, 137, 140, 147
resilience, 1
resolution, 22, 32, 41, 67, 89, 93, 106, 107, 109, 112, 113, 115, 149
resources, 38, 39, 55, 57, 59, 61, 62, 63, 67, 71, 74, 88, 89, 91, 93, 96, 106, 107, 111, 113, 115, 117, 118, 119, 122, 124, 125, 126, 128, 131, 141, 143, 147, 148, 149
response, vii, viii, 2, 5, 6, 11, 12, 20, 38, 40, 42, 46, 47, 48, 49, 51, 52, 53, 54, 55, 56, 57, 59, 60, 61, 62, 64, 74, 76, 82, 85, 87, 95, 101, 102, 103, 105, 110, 121, 127, 136, 140, 141, 142, 143, 145, 146, 148, 149, 150
response capacity, 40
restoration, 35
restructuring, 24
risk(s), 3, 4, 7, 9, 17, 18, 19, 20, 23, 24, 25, 28, 29, 30, 32, 37, 38, 40, 44, 60, 63, 67, 70, 71, 73, 82, 83, 86, 93, 109, 110, 115, 116, 139, 145
risk assessment, 3, 7, 23, 24, 29, 110
robust design, 58
rods, 11
routes, 59
rules, 3, 19

S

saturation, 136
savings, 60, 67
scope, 10, 21, 23, 27, 32, 35, 39, 45, 50, 64, 73, 76, 133, 148
sea level, 37
security, 3, 9, 19, 20, 48, 53, 54, 97, 129
seismic data, 29, 30
Senate, 81
September 11, 3, 19, 20, 23, 44, 48, 51, 52, 63, 69
servers, 56, 149
shape, 59
shelter, 16
showing, 47
software, 55, 57, 147
solution, 53, 55, 56, 126, 149
specifications, 44, 47, 49, 50, 69, 72, 100, 138, 144
stability, 83
staff members, 65, 66, 79
staffing, 52, 54, 57, 71, 76, 86, 102, 103, 107, 112, 129, 142, 148
stakeholder engagement, viii, 87, 90, 105, 111, 114, 148
stakeholders, 6, 9, 56, 62, 63, 74, 78, 83, 88, 95, 96, 98, 100, 101, 103, 108, 109, 110, 116, 121, 127, 130, 133, 134, 136, 139, 142, 146, 148, 149, 150
standardization, 110
state(s), 3, 7, 9, 21, 22, 26, 29, 30, 32, 53, 58, 59, 61, 69, 77, 83, 93, 109, 115
storage, 31, 40, 44, 45, 97, 109, 111, 129, 135, 144, 145
structure, 20, 23, 43, 44, 48, 54, 58, 63, 70, 73, 77, 145
substitutes, 23
supervisor, 47
suppression, 13, 41, 43, 133

T

tanks, 31, 32, 37
teams, 54, 57, 61, 102, 103, 141, 142, 149
technical assistance, 118, 119, 124, 125, 128, 131, 135, 137, 141, 144, 147, 151
technical support, 48, 102, 141, 148
techniques, 2, 3, 20, 22, 28
technologies, 7
technology, 9, 25, 27, 53

telecommunications, 55
telephones, 55, 57, 102, 103, 141, 142
temperature, 43, 46, 72, 135, 136
tenure, 1
testing, 49
thyroid, 60
thyroid cancer, 60
thyroid gland, 60
tornadoes, 26, 29, 34, 35
training, 34, 38, 39, 47, 48, 49, 50, 53, 56, 57, 62, 64, 69, 71, 72, 73, 74, 86, 96, 100, 101, 108, 113, 126, 129, 130, 138, 139, 141, 147, 148, 149
transmission, 53, 56, 148, 149
transparency, 83
transport, 43
transportation, 36, 38, 39, 54, 71, 96, 126
transportation infrastructure, 36, 38, 71, 96, 126
treatment, 2, 3, 18, 22, 32, 49, 50

U

United, v, vii, 1, 2, 3, 20, 22, 28, 29, 30, 41, 51, 52, 58, 61, 63, 67, 81, 82, 84, 93, 111, 115
United States, v, vii, 1, 2, 3, 20, 22, 28, 29, 30, 41, 51, 52, 58, 61, 63, 67, 81, 82, 84, 93, 111, 115
updating, 28, 127
urban, 31
urban areas, 31

V

valve, 41
vehicles, 88, 91, 106, 112
ventilation, 33, 44
vision, 3, 17
vote, viii, 87, 89, 90, 99
vulnerability, 53

W

waste, 135, 145
water, 4, 12, 13, 14, 24, 31, 32, 34, 37, 39, 40, 42, 43, 44, 45, 46, 47, 59, 69, 72, 84, 85, 98, 109, 135, 136, 144, 145
Western Europe, 66
worldwide, 67

Z

zirconium, 43